ON-BOARD EMERGENCY HANDBOOK

TONY MEISEL

Author: Tony Meisel

Current printing (last digit)
10 9 8 7 6 5 4 3 2 1

First published in North America in 2006 by
International Marine/McGraw-Hill
PO Box 220
Camden, ME, 04843

A Marshall Edition
Conceived, edited, and designed by Marshall Editions
The Old Brewery
6 Blundell Street
London N7 9BH
UK
www.quarto.com

ISBN: 0-07-147467-6
Library of Congress Catalog Number available on request

Printed and bound in China by Midas Printing International Ltd.

Publisher: Richard Green
Commissioning Editor: Claudia Martin
Art Direction: Ivo Marloh
Editor: Johanna Geary
Design: Claire Van Rhyn
Illustrations: Robert Brandt
Indexer: Richard Bird
Production: Nikki Ingram

ON-BOARD EMERGENCY HANDBOOK

YOUR INDISPENSABLE GUIDE FOR HANDLING ANY CHALLENGE AT SEA

International Marine/McGraw-Hill
Camden, Maine

Contents

Introduction

When something goes wrong at sea, invariably it is a problem that you have never before experienced, the weather is fast deteriorating, and time is of the essence. You are not sure of the best course of action, and you certainly do not wish to be lectured at length about every possible solution. All your accumulated knowledge acquired through reading, study, and yacht club conversations suddenly seems too distant, too technical, and never quite appropriate to the situation.

The *On-Board Emergency Handbook* is designed for just such situations. Within these pages you will find direct responses to a wide assortment of waterborne difficulties. There may be other actions to take, more permanent repairs to be made, certainly more aesthetic resolutions. But the idea of this little book is to give you ready reference—an immediate answer to that desperate question: "What do I do now?"

Obviously, no book could cover every contingency. Every yacht and every sailor is different, and some ideas will work better for one than the other. There is no substitute for knowing your ship, its capabilities and your own; for preplanning and practice, both for yourself and your crew; or for calm, rational action when an emergency arises. Too many ships and sailors have been lost to panic, imprecise navigation, and hasty planning and fitting out. Think through everything: from gear stowage to passage routes, from emergency water to appropriate clothing, from ground tackle to life raft servicing.

The modern yacht is a collection of systems, some simple, some wildly complicated. But no matter how sophisticated your yacht may be, it is still subject to the vagaries of wind and wave. Setting out on a calm day, you may find yourself in a full gale within minutes. You have to be prepared for any contingency, because, no matter how strong your ship, how completely equipped it is, something will sooner or later break or malfunction.

Self-sufficiency is usually spoken of with nostalgia, but any yachtsperson worth their salt must have this quality in abundance. You must deal with the increasingly complex and sophisticated systems aboard the modern yacht, whether power or sail. Or, you must keep your ship as simple and basic as is humanly possible, not something most of us would wish to do. Nevertheless, if you are unable to use a screwdriver, you most probably should not be out on the water. A basic familiarity with hand tools and a proper tool chest are absolute musts. If the mast goes, will the cable cutters be at hand? Do you have a proper-sized wrench to disassemble the head? And do you have manuals for all the major systems and components? Read them now; don't wait until an emergency arises.

Too many yachtspeople, especially in the first few years of being on the water, assume that the courses they have taken, the lectures they attend, and the books they read will prepare them for any mishap. Unfortunately, as Pope noted, a little learning is a dangerous thing. Until you have found yourself in a gale, 30 miles at sea, with waves washing over the deck, the navigation lights out, forestay about to break, and your crew passed out below, you have no notion of what to do! But you must make decisions and act without hesitation to save the ship and crew. No amount of formal study will help. You are on your own. Every time you sail from your moorings, you are becoming a pioneer, an explorer. Like the proverbial Boy Scout, be prepared!

There are many degrees of emergencies. This book is not concerned with everyday advice unless it directly relates to a more serious problem. You will not, for example, be told how to anchor, but you may be given suggestions for anchoring off a lee shore when your engine dies and your sails have blown out. When you face an emergency you need sensible advice fast, and the *On-Board Emergency Handbook* will give you several possible suggestions for coping with any one situation, along with easy-to-follow illustrations, so that you can choose the response most appropriate for the particular set of circumstances in which you find yourself. The book can aid and advise only. It won't save you or your ship without your own skills and intelligence. Read it and keep it on board, ready to help when the unexpected occurs.

Tony Meisel
New Suffolk, New York

ABANDONING SHIP

When it becomes obvious that no amount of pumping, emergency repair, or assistance is capable of saving the ship, the only alternative is to abandon ship. This is not a decision to be taken lightly. A floating hull will offer protection from the elements, and will be a better target than a life raft for search and rescue. The decision must be made under traumatic conditions, but try to think it through before taking drastic action.

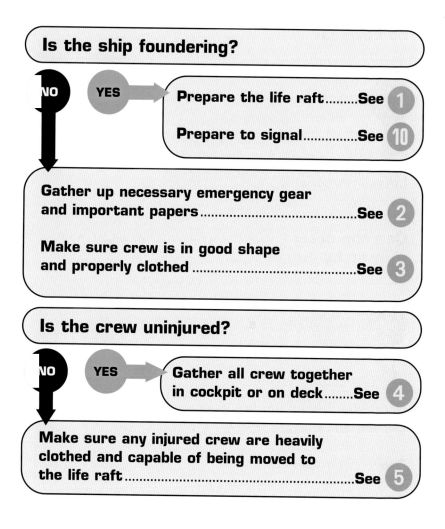

Is the ship foundering?

NO

YES → Prepare the life raft.........See **1**

Prepare to signal..............See **10**

Gather up necessary emergency gear and important papers...See **2**

Make sure crew is in good shape and properly clothed ....See **3**

Is the crew uninjured?

NO

YES → Gather all crew together in cockpit or on deck........See **4**

Make sure any injured crew are heavily clothed and capable of being moved to the life raft..See **5**

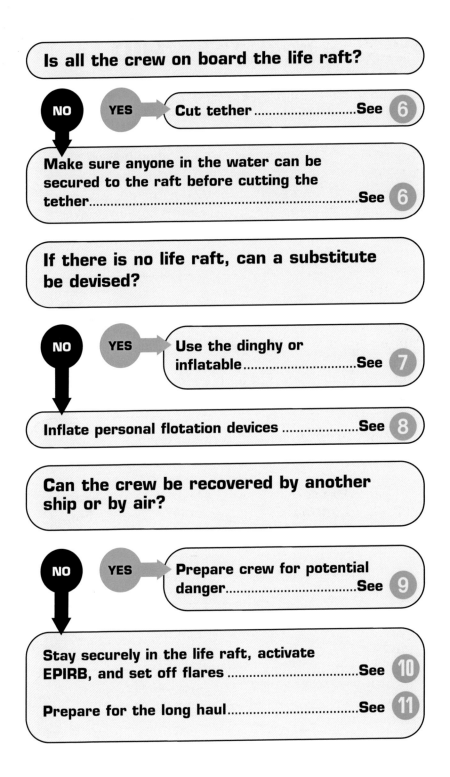

Is all the crew on board the life raft?

NO | YES ▸ Cut tether......................See ⑥

Make sure anyone in the water can be
secured to the raft before cutting the
tether...See ⑥

**If there is no life raft, can a substitute
be devised?**

NO | YES ▸ Use the dinghy or
inflatable.............................See ⑦

Inflate personal flotation devices ....See ⑧

**Can the crew be recovered by another
ship or by air?**

NO | YES ▸ Prepare crew for potential
danger...............................See ⑨

Stay securely in the life raft, activate
EPIRB, and set off flares ....See ⑩

Prepare for the long haul...............................See ⑪

Preparing the life raft.................... ①

If, and only if, the mother ship is in imminent danger of sinking, inflate the life raft on deck or by tossing it overboard to activate CO_2 cylinders (figure 1). Do not attempt inflation below or in the cockpit. Make sure the raft is tethered before inflating. In very heavy weather the raft may flip. Do not attempt to right it until necessary.

Fig. 1

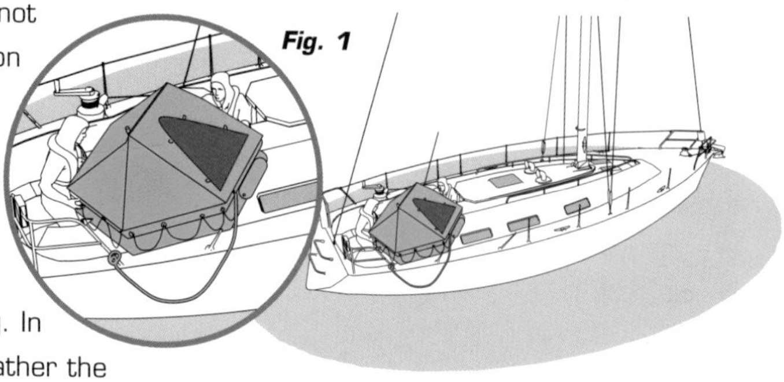

Gathering emergency supplies.......... ②

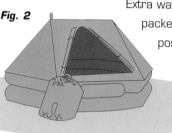

Fig. 2

Extra water, food, and other necessaries should be packed at hand in a duffle. Tie it to the raft if possible (figure 2). Ship's papers, passports, and other documents should be in a waterproof pouch. If at all possible, get extra flares, a radio emergency beacon, and a compass aboard, as well as a chart of the area. All this takes preplanning.

Keeping warm.................................. ③

Hypothermia is one of the surest ways to a quick death. Keep fully clothed, including a hat and boots. If you end up in the water, a partial wetsuit effect will be provided by water within the oilskins, and wet clothing, especially if wool or polypropylene, will have a high insulating effect. Move as little as possible in the water, only so much as is necessary to stay afloat. Attempting to swim, no matter how strong a swimmer you are, will result in heat loss on a massive scale, unconsciousness, and probable death. See also 8 opposite.

Gathering crew together...................... ④

Keep the crew gathered together. In gale or storm conditions, visibility, even on the deck of a small yacht, can be almost nil. Coupled with disorientation, confusion, and panic, conditions will require the crew to work together to save all.

Injured crew

If any member of the crew is injured and incapable of full movement, station another crew member with that person. Be prepared to help get the injured crew member into the life raft. This may not be easy, and brute strength may be necessary. See also Medical Emergencies p.141.

Boarding the life raft

Leave the raft tethered to the ship until everyone is aboard (figure 3). Too many people have been lost attempting to leap from ship to raft. Only when every member of the crew is aboard should you cut the tether. Take care not to cut the raft.

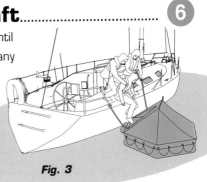

Fig. 3

Substitute life rafts

Fig. 4

If the life raft is not functioning or if there is none, use a dingy (figure 4). It should be heavily fendered to avoid damage from the mother ship and fitted out with a strong, sufficiently sized sea anchor to hold it bow to wind. A permanent flotation and an enclosed form of protection to avoid boarding seas and exposure will be necessary (figure 5). When boarding, coordinate your stepping aboard with the rhythm of the two boats to avoid descending rapidly into thin air to break limbs upon your sudden entry. Cut the tether from the yacht only when all crew is aboard.

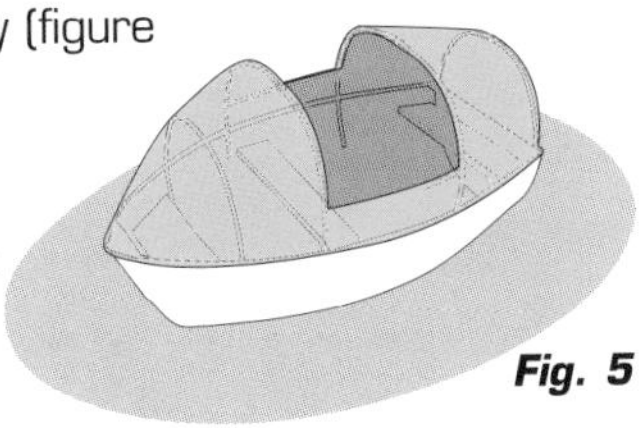

Fig. 5

Other flotation devices

If no life raft or dinghy exists, put on your life jacket and enter the water from the windward side of the boat. From any other point the boat can drift down, or back down, or slip to windward, endangering anyone in the water. Keep all clothes on (see 3 above), and assume a fetal position to conserve body heat (figure 6). A light, whistle, and knife should be attached to the life vest. Stay calm.

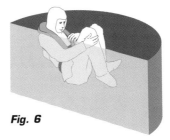

Fig. 6

Ship and helicopter rescue .... ⑨

Pick-up by ship or helicopter is a dangerous maneuver. Inevitably the ship will be larger than your vessel, and the chances of collision and dismasting are great. Try to be hoisted aboard, rather than climbing a ladder. Leave the yacht from bow or stern and coincide moving up with the crest of a wave. In heavy weather you will probably be safer in the lee of the larger ship, but move fast. Helicopter rescues demand even more thought. Clear the cockpit and release any rigging located there, even if the mast goes over forward. Do NOT fasten the helicopter line to any part of your vessel; this could damage the line or bring down the helicopter. The harness, attached to the helicopter by a steel cable, may cause a shock when wet. Ground it against the ship before using it, if possible.

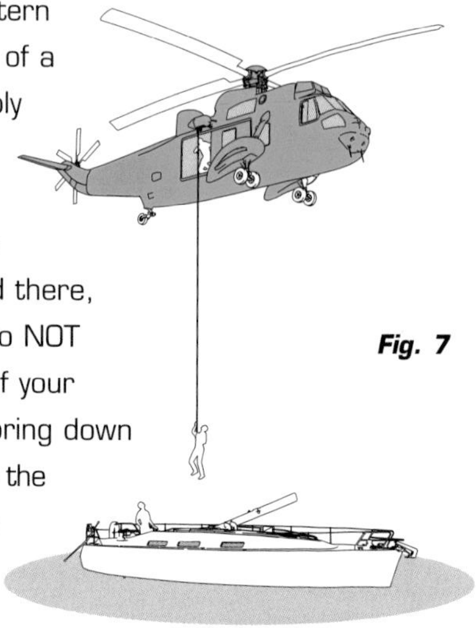

Fig. 7

Grab the harness lowered and help each crew member into it (figure 7). Signal via hand-held VHF or hand signals when prepared to leave. It may be safer to be picked up from the dinghy or life raft towed astern, but you will be a smaller target, and have a less stable platform for the pick-up.

Signaling .... ⑩

When disaster strikes, attempt to make radio contact by sending a MAYDAY with the condition of ship and crew and your position. If there is no response, activate the EPIRB so that search vessels and aircraft can home in on your position (see Signals p.172). Do not set off flares until a ship or plane is visible. See also "Flares and smoke signals" p.173.

Survival .... ⑪

If you have abandoned ship, and no immediate rescue is in sight, the only requirement is to survive. The life raft should be as dry as possible, the doors closed and secured, and any water ballast or drogues activated. Keep all crewmembers warm, and have fresh water to drink—sparingly. An emergency, waterproof bag, containing extra flares, a flashlight and batteries, personal papers, charts, high-energy food supplements, tinned water, a first aid kit, and light but warm clothing, should be prepared for such rare but possible occasions. Extra water and/or a hand-operated desalinator packed with the survival gear can ensure against dehydration.

AGROUND

Sooner or later, everyone runs aground. If it's a soft bottom in calm conditions, you can await a rising tide, or attempt to kedge off. However, in rough conditions or a rocky bottom, grounding can endanger both ship and crew.

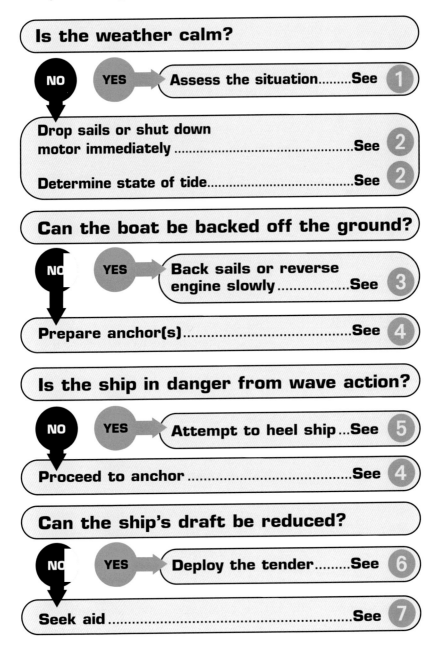

Is the weather calm?

NO / YES → Assess the situation.........See ①

Drop sails or shut down
motor immediately ....See ②

Determine state of tide...............................See ②

Can the boat be backed off the ground?

NO / YES → Back sails or reverse
engine slowly ....See ③

Prepare anchor(s)..See ④

Is the ship in danger from wave action?

NO / YES → Attempt to heel ship...See ⑤

Proceed to anchor ....See ④

Can the ship's draft be reduced?

NO / YES → Deploy the tender.........See ⑥

Seek aid ....See ⑦

Calm weather

In calm weather, and with a soft bottom, your best
option is to lay out an anchor and wait for the tide
to rise. Twin-keel yachts and motorboats will
have far fewer problems in these conditions.
Deep-keel yachts will naturally fall on the
beam, so as the water recedes (if the
yacht is without drying-out legs,
figure 1) try to cushion the hull with
fenders, seat cushions, or other
soft objects, perhaps stuffed in a
sail bag. Sand and mud can
contain hard objects that
cause damage as the
hull bobs on a
rising tide.

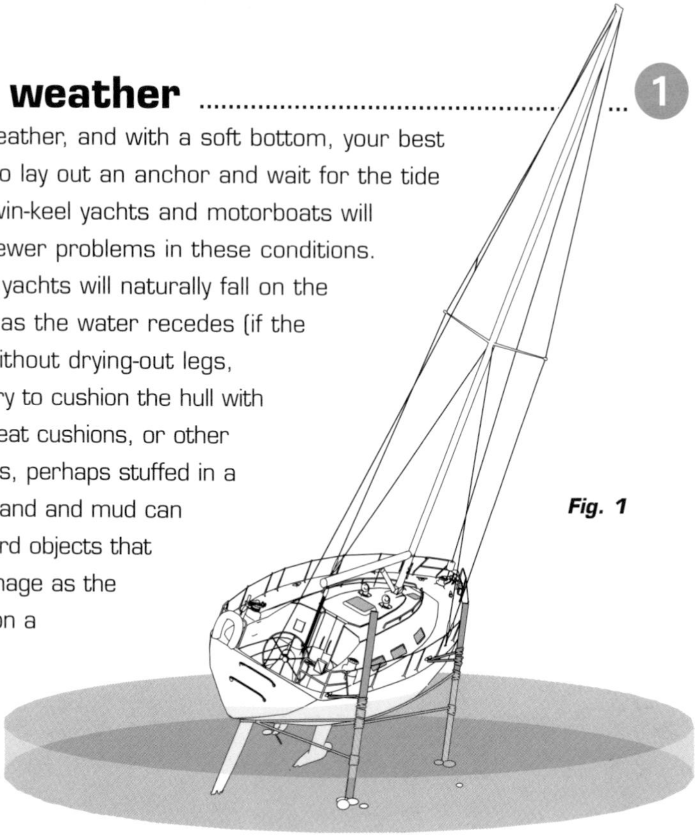

Fig. 1

Rough weather

If the seas are in a confused state or running with any turbulence,
chances are the boat will pound on the bottom. Without detailed
knowledge of bottom composition, this can be exceedingly dangerous.
If you cannot power off, shut down the engine, drop sails, and deploy
an anchor. In a rising tide, you may be able to kedge or power off, but
in a falling tide, the hull and/or keel has a good chance of sustaining
serious damage.

Backing off

If you are able to, try backing the sails (figure 2). Drop the main, and
try to back the jib. There is less chance of an accidental gybe. Onshore
winds can vary in strength. In a gale the engine will probably not be
sufficiently powerful to pull you off the ground. You will have to set a
kedge anchor. Do it carefully in heavy conditions. Try to shelter the
tender in the lee of the boat to prevent violent movement and possible
swamping. Have the anchor and anchor cable coiled in the tender, ready

for release (figure 3). Also, it is a good idea to tether the tender to the mother ship to prevent being blown away. If you plan to kedge and power at the same time, be wary of fouling the propeller with the kedge warp. Either keep it taut or use a floating line.

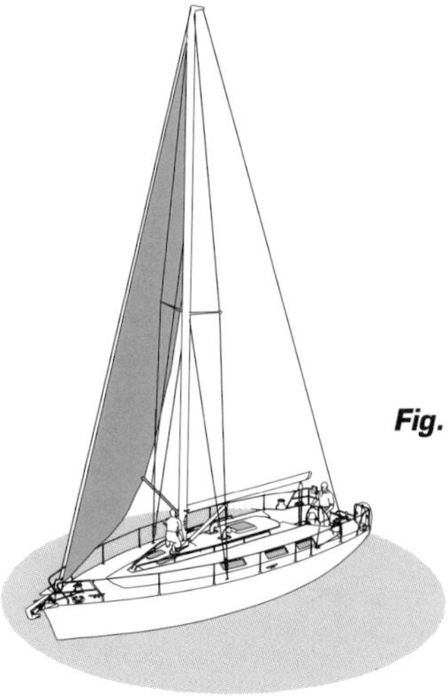

Fig. 2

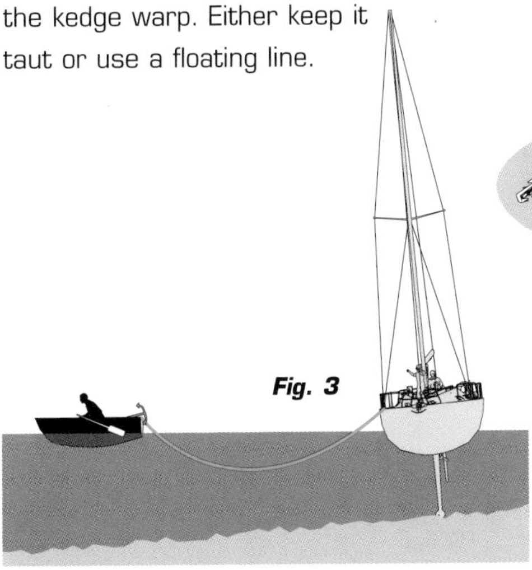

Fig. 3

Preparing to anchor 4

Fig. 4

If the tide is falling rapidly, best prepare to dry out as comfortably as possible. With fast ebb and heavy seas you may have to prepare to abandon ship, especially if the boat is on rocks. If the tide is rising and you are on a lee shore, get the kedge out as fast as possible or you may be swept further ashore. Wing keels can cause problems, since the boat may not pivot on the keel and thus tip over (figure 4). Legs are the best solution.

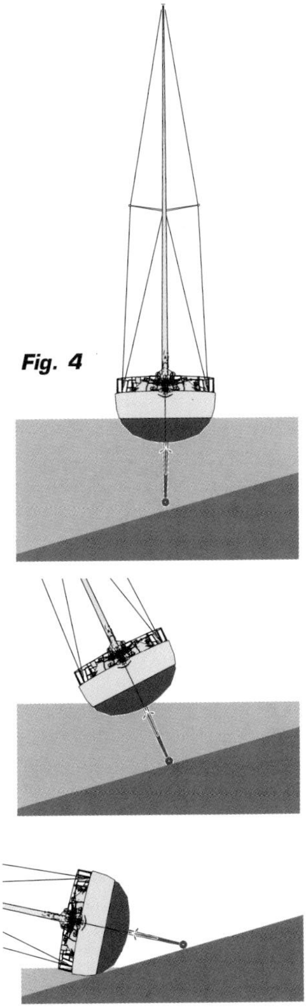

Heeling the yacht 5

Much depends on the profile and configuration of the boat's keel. If a long, sloping keel, you will have less trouble backing off. If a fin keel, you may be able to spin the boat about and reach or run off into deeper water. Twin-keel boats should not be heeled, as you will only increase the draft (figure 5). In calm conditions, prepare to sit out the tide. In heavy going, you will have to kedge or power off. Heeling a single-keeled boat can be accomplished in several ways: move the crew to the shallow water deck; swing crew or loaded dinghy off the boom end (figure 6). In a very small boat, you may be able to use the main halyard taken ashore for leverage. (Beware: masthead fittings cannot take much abuse. Do not try this maneuver in a heavy-displacement vessel.)

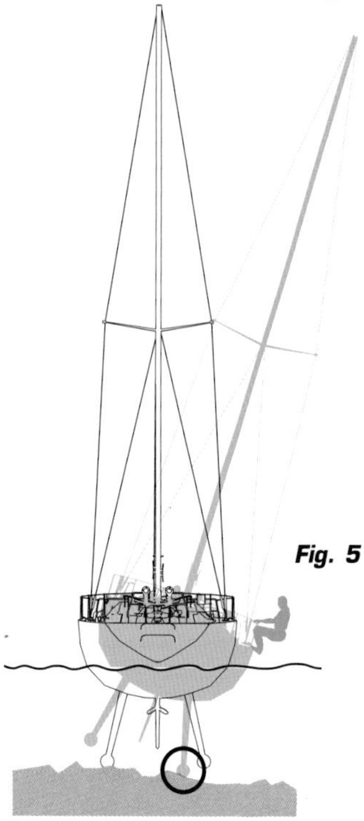

Fig. 5

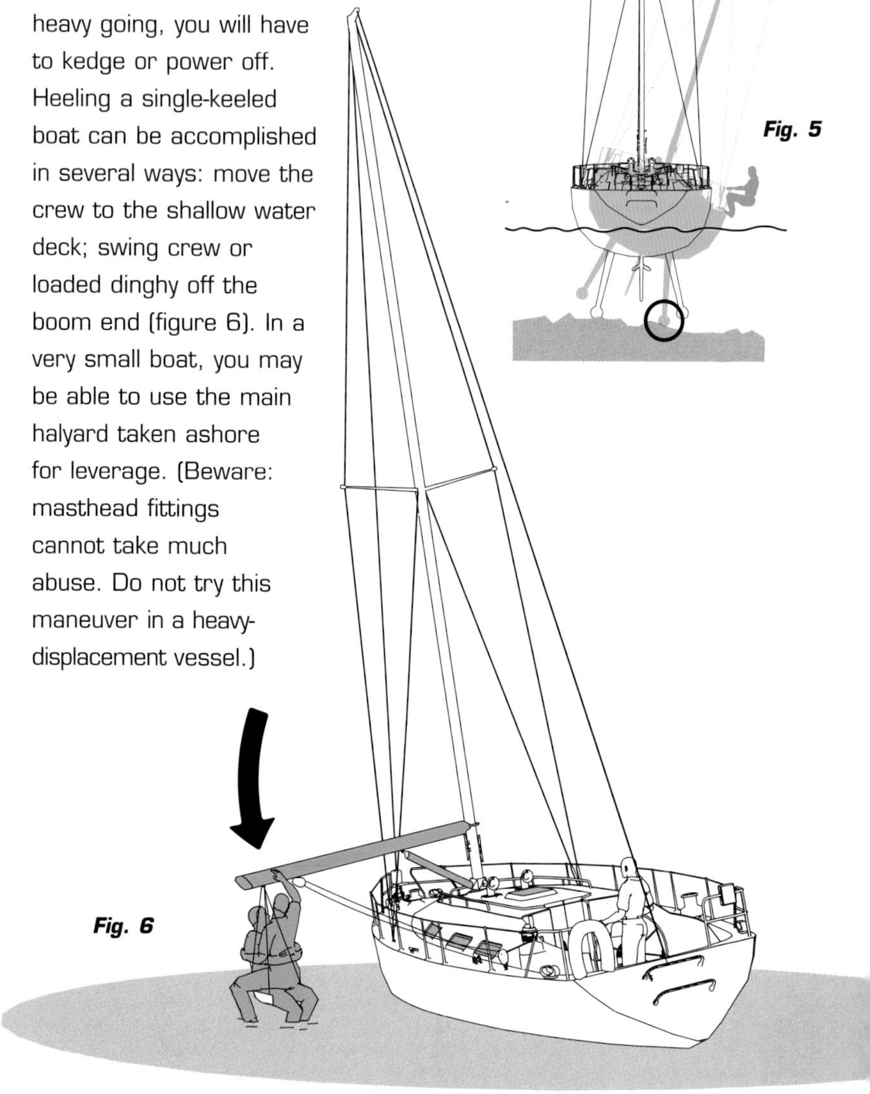

Fig. 6

The tender as warehouse 6

You may be able to reduce the draft by lightening the ship. Remove heavy gear to the dinghy and possibly drain the water tanks. In a light-displacement boat, this could decrease the draft by the inch or two needed to free the keel.

Outside assistance 7

Hauling off can be done with the bow anchor while the crew heels the boat. It may also be accomplished by an aiding vessel. If another ship can help, first make sure that questions of salvage are resolved (see Salvage p.168). Then, depending on your position, pass your line to the assisting vessel. Make the line secure first to the foredeck bollard or stern cleats with a bridle, or secure it around the mast or cabin house (figure 7). Instruct the other vessel to slowly pull you seaward without any surge of acceleration. This is most important. A quick application of throttle could result in damaged decks or dismasting. When you are free and able to maneuver, request your line freed. For such tows, polypropylene cordage, because it floats, is best employed, lessening the chances of fouled propellers and rudders.

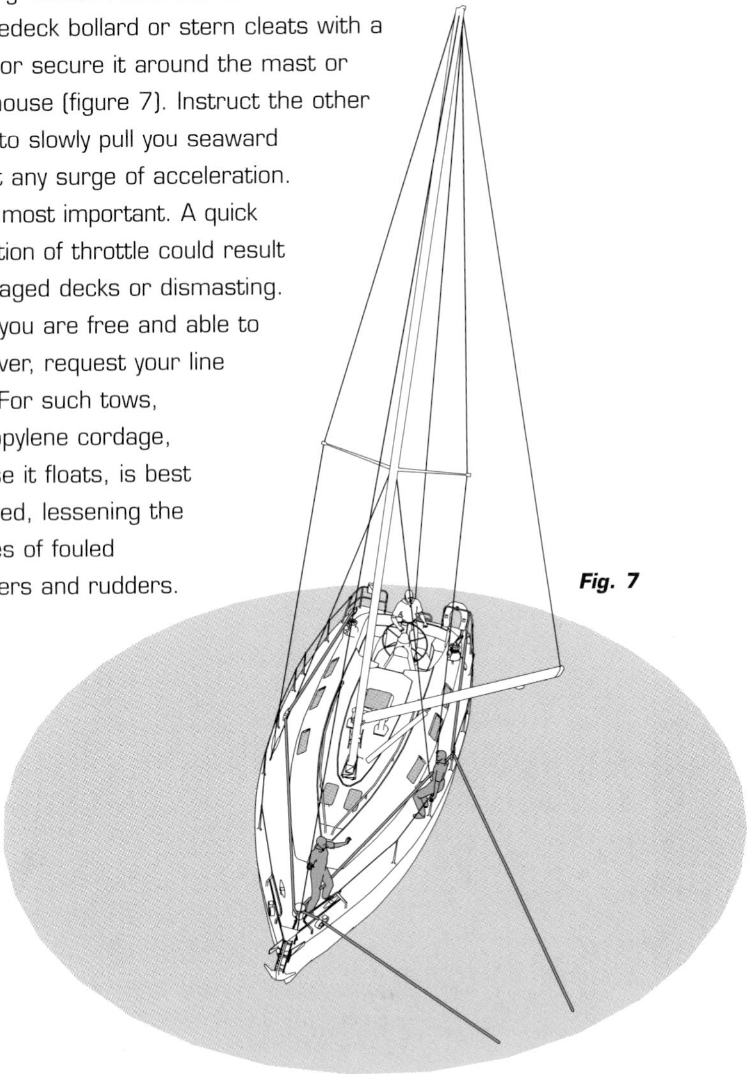

Fig. 7

ANCHORING

With the proliferation of marinas, more crowded anchorages, and fewer free anchorages, yachtsmen are anchoring less and less. However, there are times when anchoring technique can make the difference between security and devastation. When engines fail or sails foul, dropping the anchor may save you from damage or loss of life. When in proximity to land, always have your main anchor at the ready—and learn how to use it.

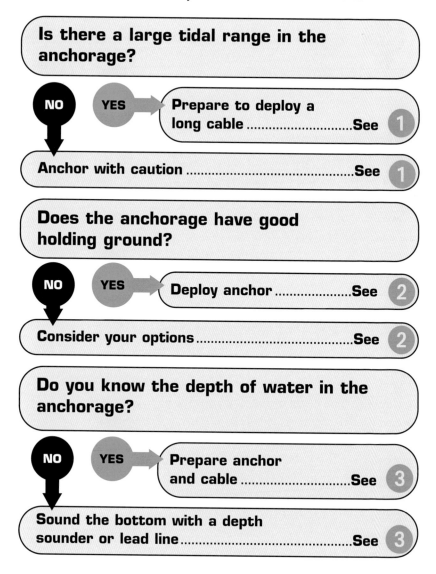

Is there a large tidal range in the anchorage?

NO

YES → Prepare to deploy a long cable ....See **1**

Anchor with caution ....See **1**

Does the anchorage have good holding ground?

NO

YES → Deploy anchor ....See **2**

Consider your options...See **2**

Do you know the depth of water in the anchorage?

NO

YES → Prepare anchor and cable ....See **3**

Sound the bottom with a depth sounder or lead line...See **3**

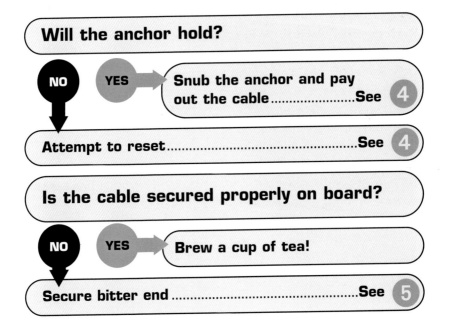

Will the anchor hold?

NO / YES → Snub the anchor and pay out the cable.......................See ④

Attempt to reset...See ④

Is the cable secured properly on board?

NO / YES → Brew a cup of tea!

Secure bitter end ....See ⑤

Tidal ranges.. ①

Knowing the state of the tide and the rate of inflow and outflow is vital. In areas of small tidal range, such as the Mediterranean or the Chesapeake, this is not quite so important, but make sure you have allowed for lower-than-normal spring tides when assessing the position the boat will take when anchored. Allow for swinging room and for reversal of position when the tide ebbs. In areas of vast tidal range, with swift inrushing tides, such as Brittany or the Bay of Fundy—where ranges can be upward of 30 feet (9 meters)—you will have to anchor far out with very long cables. In such conditions, two anchors should probably be set, especially when tides boil in at as much as 10 knots.

Holding ground .... ②

Bottom composition can be determined by a depth sounder, chart reference or hand lead armed with tallow or grease. The bottom will determine the type and size of anchor you set. Mud, soft sand, and mixed bottoms indicate a Danforth-type or plow anchor. Hard sand, as is found in the Aegean and Caribbean, will hold with either but may demand hand setting. Weed will foil a Danforth with ease, and sometimes a plow. Rocky bottoms will be best served with a good old-fashioned fisherman (Herreshoff preferred if you can find one) or a Bruce anchor. These two will usually dig past weed the best. If the bottom is mixed—small pebbles or shale, or weed and shale—use a fisherman; the goal will be to get underneath the top layer as quickly as possible. Coral accepts fishermen and plows best, though the shank of a plow can be badly bent by coral and chain cable is almost a necessity to avoid chafe. Remember that in many areas around the world, anchoring in coral is illegal. Coral is a living organism, and is vital to the biological survival of numerous species. Be forewarned. Too often anchors are tossed, dropped, or slung over the bows. By carefully and slowly lowering it you will be able to ascertain the rate of drift, and will avoid permanently damaging the hull, deck, or yourself.

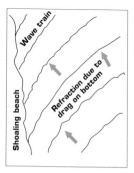

1. Refracted waves begin to drag in shallow water, altering direction as they approach the shore.

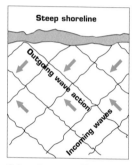

2. Incoming waves will reflect off a steep shoreline at an angle equal to that of their forward motion. Where they intersect they create a nasty chop.

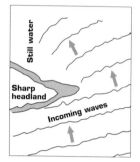

3. Sharp headlands will stall the force of incoming waves and provide protection behind.

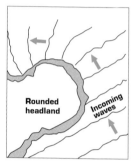

4. Rounded headlands will promote wave action around their entire perimeter. Not a good place to anchor.

Determining scope....................................... ③

Scope depends upon depth at high water, holding ground, and whether you use chain or rope cable. Rope cables should have at least 15 feet (5 meters) of chain between the end of the rope and the anchor to prevent chafe and increase holding power (figure 1). All-chain cable permits shorter scope (as little as 3:1), but can snub more easily than rope. Rope, having great elasticity (nylon), will act as a better shock absorber, especially when in surging conditions. However, rope must be heavily padded—either with patent chafe gear, rags, or leather—

Fig. 1

15 feet minimum

to avoid catastrophe at the stem-head, roller, or chocks. The holding ground will make a difference: the better the bottom, the shorter the scope. Mud and soft sand will usually hold best, assuming you deploy the appropriate anchor. In any case, be prepared to set rope cable with a minimum of 6:1 scope and chain with a minimum of 4:1 scope. Under deteriorating weather and sea conditions, scope needs to be increased and the possibility of a second or even third anchor being set must be considered.

Setting the anchor 4

Making sure the anchor is properly set is the most important single step you can take when anchoring. Either back the sails, throw the engine in reverse or hand snub it when the appropriate amount of scope has been payed out. Be sure the cable is attached to a strong point below decks and is secured to the Samson post, cleat, or anchor winch (figure 2). Even with chain cable, a nylon snubber is a good idea—especially as cables

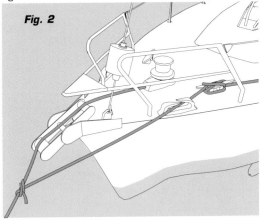

Fig. 2

can sometimes be distorted or even snap at the stemhead fitting or roller—rigged from a second cleat inboard to the cable several feet outboard of the stem. Not only can this save you an anchor and cable, but will act as a shock absorber in heavy surge situations.

Securing the cable on board 5

Not only should the inboard end of the cable be securely fastened to the ship, but the cable must be bowsed down in a proper stemhead fitting. In a roller, the cheeks must be high enough to prevent the cable from jumping out; a retaining pin should be fitted, and all metal should be filed down so that no sharp edges are evident at any point at which the cable might touch the roller or cheeks. Chain can be fatigued by friction against metal. If your roller lacks a retaining pin, or if you must pass the cable through a chock, use a short length of light stuff to tie down the rope or chain, either around the fitting or in some way to close off the openings and make for a rope loop.

ANCHORING: Special

There are a number of situations that call for more than the usual dropping and snubbing of the anchor. Fouling, sudden wind shifts, currents, and tides all affect how you anchor and the techniques you use.

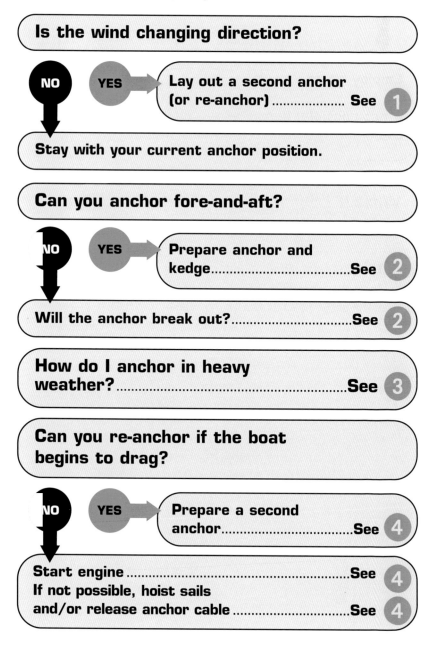

Is the wind changing direction?

NO

YES → Lay out a second anchor (or re-anchor).................. See **1**

Stay with your current anchor position.

Can you anchor fore-and-aft?

NO

YES → Prepare anchor and kedge..............................See **2**

Will the anchor break out?...............................See **2**

How do I anchor in heavy weather?..See **3**

Can you re-anchor if the boat begins to drag?

NO

YES → Prepare a second anchor..............................See **4**

Start engine ....See **4**
If not possible, hoist sails and/or release anchor cable ....See **4**

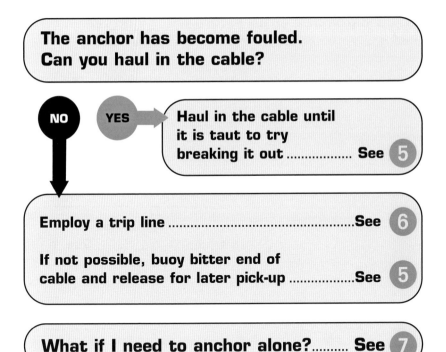

The anchor has become fouled. Can you haul in the cable?

NO

YES → Haul in the cable until it is taut to try breaking it out .... See **5**

Employ a trip line .... See **6**

If not possible, buoy bitter end of cable and release for later pick-up .... See **5**

What if I need to anchor alone? .... See **7**

Wind changes **1**

When the wind shows signs of veering, be prepared to lay out a second anchor. The second anchor can be the kedge and can be equipped with chain and rope cable. Lower it off the bows in the direction from which the wind is veering. Pay out cable as the boat begins to swing until more or less equal strain is taken by both anchors and the boat becomes the fulcrum of an easy-swinging pendulum, so to speak (figure 1). When the appropriate scope is achieved, snub the anchor and make fast to a separate cleat. Try to minimize the strain on the cleat, windlass, or Samson post holding the main anchor.

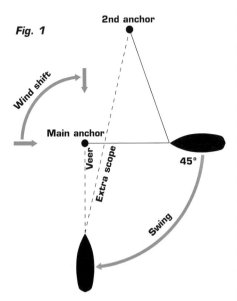

Fig. 1

2nd anchor

Wind shift

Main anchor

Veer

Extra scope

45°

Swing

Fore-and-aft anchoring 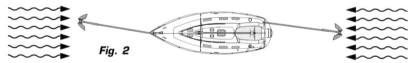 .... ②

In a river where the tidal stream runs strong and will reverse or where there is little or no room to swing, anchoring fore-and-aft is a sensible and safe solution (figure 2). Anchor in the normal way, letting out double the amount of cable needed for the situation—a good reason to carry at least

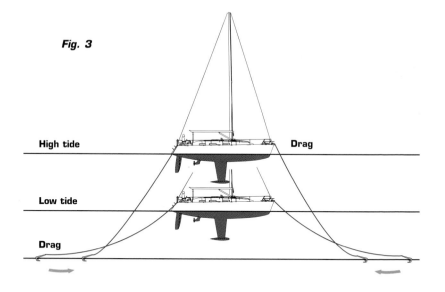

Fig. 2

250 to 300 feet (75 to 100 meters) of cable—and set the hook. Then drop a stern anchor and motor or winch the ship forward, paying out an amount of cable to get the ship in the required position. Station crew in the bows to take in the excess cable at the same time you are moving forward to avoid fouling the propeller or wrapping a rope cable around the keel, skeg, or rudder. Be sure to allow a small amount of slack—at high water—in both cables, but not so much as to make for uncomfortable movement (figure 3). When the tide ebbs, adjust the cables to avoid drifting into a channel, again depending on the force of the current.

Fig. 3

High tide   Drag

Low tide

Drag

Heavy-weather anchoring .... ③

Anchoring in heavy weather or off a lee shore is always a fearful and difficult experience. However, there are times when no other alternative presents itself. Two basic methods are available for effective holding power. First, drop one anchor in the normal manner, paying out double the length of cable needed. Then lay a second—much as fore-

and-aft technique—bringing up on the first cable (figure 4). If the two anchors are dropped, one to windward and one to leeward, the chances of holding in a wind shift are greatly increased, especially important if anchoring not far offshore in an open roadstead.

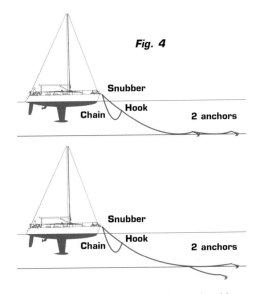

Fig. 4

Snubber

Hook

Chain

2 anchors

Snubber

Hook

Chain

2 anchors

Lay out extra cable so that both lines will not foul the underbody of the boat. A second possibility is to use two anchors in line. That is, attach the kedge with chain to the main anchor ring with a shackle. Lower the kedge first, then the main anchor while making sternway (figure 5). Or, drop the main anchor first with the kedge attached at

least the depth of the water distance aft on the cable, certainly no less than 22 to 25 feet (7 to 8 meters) distance. Remember, in any storm situation the strains on deck attachment points will be extreme. Make sure that chain cable can be released instantly if you must drop the anchor and run. Buoy the chain before releasing it.

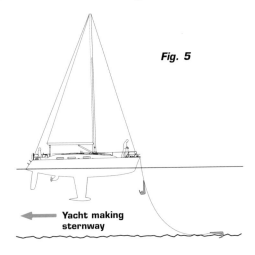

Fig. 5

Yacht making sternway

Dragging 4

Dragging can be much more than a nuisance. On a lee shore it can be deadly. If your boat begins to drag—something you can tell from reference to landmarks—start the engine immediately. Then pay out more cable. If this doesn't work, motor up, taking in cable, and reset the anchor. If the bottom is suspect, try running a rider weight down the anchor cable (figure 6, over the page). This can be a patent device or a ball of chain. Just make sure that whatever weight you use is reasonably heavy, say equal to the weight of the kedge. If this doesn't work effectively, set a second anchor at an angle of 25 to 35 degrees. If the engine fails or will not start, set a foresail and tack up to the anchor. This can be tricky, as when you go to haul in the anchor, the crew may be flogged by the sail. A roller-furling sail makes it easier. Be cautious in setting the mainsail for this maneuver. There is no guarantee you can remain in stays while the anchor is being raised.

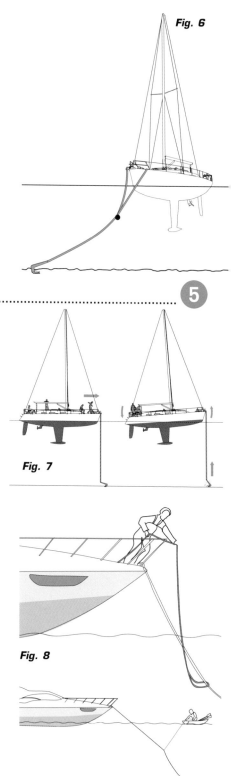

Fig. 6

Fouled anchor ⑤

There are times when the anchor becomes fouled, either on seabed refuse, underwater cables, or with another anchor. First, try hauling in the cable until it is vertical and taut and move crew weight aft to try breaking it out or supply appropriate leverage via a windlass (figure 7). If this doesn't work, try sailing or motoring out, pulling in the opposite direction from which the anchor was originally set. If this is ineffective, try running a loop of line or chain down over the anchor cable, carry it out in the dinghy, and then haul from the opposite direction (figure 8). Or you can use a grapnel from the anchored dinghy to try to pick up the main anchor, or any obstructing cable. Members of the crew must be stationed at the bow of the mother ship and at the wheel to cover any possibility of backward drift. If the anchor and

Fig. 7

Fig. 8

cable are fouled by another boat's ground tackle, attempt to raise both anchor and cable, securing it by a line to the boat as you lift the pair higher and higher. Then try to free the anchor by hand from the dinghy (tethered to the mother ship). You can also buoy the bitter end of the anchor cable and pick it up later, if all else fails.

Setting a trip line............................ 6

When the chance exists that you will be in a crowded anchorage or expect

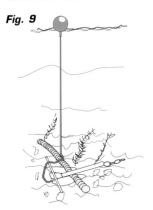

Fig. 9

that you shall have to depart an anchorage with greater dispatch than you had perhaps originally planned, it is a good idea to set up a buoyed trip line. Shackle a length of chain to the crown of the anchor, then a ⅓-inch (8mm) line from the chain to a small buoy or plastic bottle (figure 9). This will tend to keep other boats away; and give you a ready-set method for breaking a fouled anchor free.

Single-handed anchoring 7

If you single-hand, setting an anchor can be a frantic experience. First, lower and secure the mainsail. You will find it much easier to handle the boat under just foresail and without the danger of swinging booms and backing sails. Pass the rode or cable outside of all stanchions and lines aft to the cockpit, making sure the cable is secured, with the necessary scope, to the foredeck (figure 10). You can release both anchor and jib sheets together, calmly move forward, and snub anchor and lower the jib one after the other. Release latches to drop the anchor from a roller chock are not to be recommended. They have a tendency to stick or you may release the anchor and accidentally overshoot the rode, creating a large tangled mass about the underwater appendages of your boat.

Fig. 10

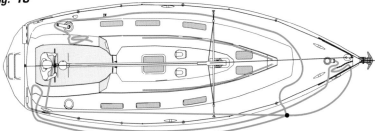

BOOM BREAKS

Sailing in heavy weather puts enormous strain on the spars. The strain of a sudden gybe or the mainsheet getting jerked suddenly can cause the boom to distort, bend, or break. If you cope well with the breakage, you can save the mainsail, keep your crew safe, and continue your passage with reasonable speed.

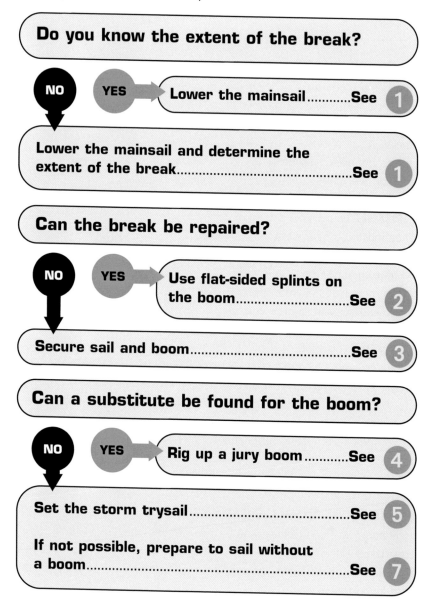

Do you know the extent of the break?

NO YES → Lower the mainsail...........See ①

Lower the mainsail and determine the extent of the break.................................See ①

Can the break be repaired?

NO YES → Use flat-sided splints on the boom.............................See ②

Secure sail and boom.................................See ③

Can a substitute be found for the boom?

NO YES → Rig up a jury boom...........See ④

Set the storm trysail.................................See ⑤

If not possible, prepare to sail without a boom.................................See ⑦

Is there a substitute for a fractured gooseneck or mast fitting?

 **NO**

 YES ➡ Lash inboard end of the jury boom to mast using reefing hooks......................See **6**

Lash the jury rig to the mast cleats..............See **6**

Extent of the break.................................. **1**

Depending on the type of boom, a break can occur anywhere, but the most likely spots are at the gooseneck (where constant strain can cause metal fatigue) or at attachment points for the mainsheet blocks. A crack in the metal can be temporarily fixed with lashing or waterproof epoxy, but be sure to take all strain off the spar by lowering the mainsail immediately.

Repairs.. **2**

Since most booms are round or oval in cross section, you will have to scrounge for any strong, flat pieces of wood or metal, and suitable lengths of strong, stretch-resistant rope. Wood—such as floorboards, fiddles, and bunk

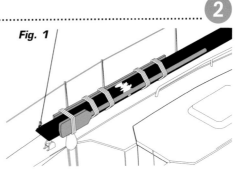
Fig. 1

boards—is preferable, since it can be easily cut to size. Lower the boom into the cockpit and secure it. To equalize strains, use several splints around the boom—a single splint will not hold. Lash the splints to either side of the boom, extending a couple of feet beyond the break to either side (figure 1). Lashings should be tightly wound and as even as is possible in a seaway.

Securing the sail and boom.................. **3**

If the boom is beyond repair, and before even thinking of a solution, lower the mainsail if you have not done so already. Get the boom off the mast and lash both boom and sail securely to the rail. Keep the cockpit clear for further repairs.

Jury booms 4

Lash a spinnaker pole, boat hook, or such to the gooseneck, with the mainsail reefed (figure 2). The stress on the clew will be great and you stand a good chance of ripping the clew fitting out if you do not spread the strains along the foot by tying off reef points.

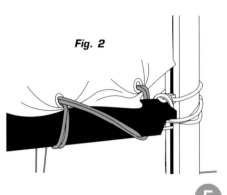

Fig. 2

Storm trysails 5

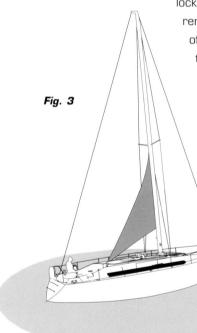

Fig. 3

When all else fails, a storm trysail is the best solution since it is designed to be used without a boom. Too often, they are stuffed in a locker and ignored, but trysails are remarkably efficient sails. You should, of course, have practiced setting the trysail in calm weather, and have it in readiness and good repair with its sheets attached. Unless you have installed a second track on the mast for the trysail, you must remove the main entirely. Hoist the trysail with sheets—tied with bowlines—led to the quarters (figure 3). Mooring cleats may be the best anchor points for the sheets. In a really bad blow, turning blocks may jam or rip from the deck.

Attaching jury boom to mast 6

Lashing a boom to the mast without benefit of the gooseneck is a dangerous and difficult job. Immediately drop the main and tie down the boom to prevent damage to boat and crew. Lash the inboard end of the jury boom to the mast using reefing hooks or any projection (figure 4).

Use several heavy lashings tied off independently of one another. Apply as much chafe protection as possible, especially to the inboard end of the boom. If no other mast hardware presents itself, use mast cleats, making sure the jury boom is tied equally to cleats on both sides of the mast.

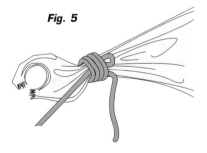

Fig. 4

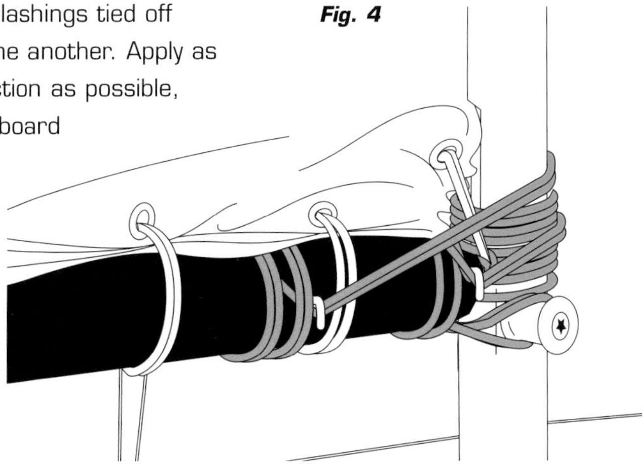

Sailing without a boom .... ⑦

If all else fails and you must sail without a boom, reinforce the clew and lead separate sheets to both quarters, then forward to winches by way of the spinnaker turning blocks; or in desperation, bend sheets to clew fitting, lash around the clew corner, and lead as above. Boomless jury-rigged mains are no laughing matter. You may destroy the sail without proper

Fig. 5

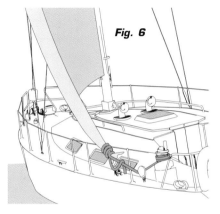

Fig. 6

reinforcement (figure 5). Sail shape will be distorted, and the forces on the clew will be extreme. Leads can be either to turning blocks or snatch blocks on the rail (figure 6). Remember that the forces are doubled and the snatch blocks and their deck attachment points must be massively robust.

CHAFE

Chafe is the enemy of all yachtsmen. Most commonly, chafe occurs on sails where they touch spreaders, where lines pass through a block, and on mooring lines and anchor cables where they pass through fairleads. There are a number of ways to lessen chafe, some elegant and many less so.

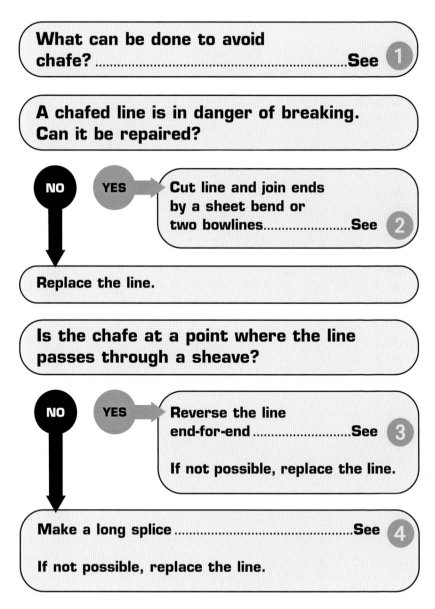

What can be done to avoid chafe? ....**See** 1

A chafed line is in danger of breaking. Can it be repaired?

NO **YES** → **Cut line and join ends by a sheet bend or two bowlines** ....**See** 2

Replace the line.

Is the chafe at a point where the line passes through a sheave?

NO **YES** → **Reverse the line end-for-end** ....**See** 3

If not possible, replace the line.

Make a long splice ....**See** 4

If not possible, replace the line.

Avoiding chafe

1

Padding—whether by plastic tubing or hose, rags, leather, a sacrificial rope whipping, or baggywrinkle—is as old a practice as the sailor has. Where sail chafe is involved, the best recourse is to have the sail recut or reinforced. Baggywrinkle is ugly, soils the sails, and creates a surprising amount of windage. It is better to use shroud rollers or spreader tips (figure 1). No matter what method is chosen, the padding must be secured, either with tape or whipping.

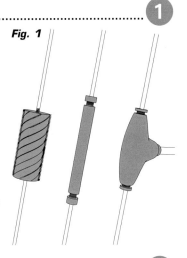

Fig. 1

Joining lines

2

A sheet bend is the quickest way to take care of serious chafe, though it must be remembered that knots will never be as strong as the original or as a splice. Using two bowlines will have the advantage of your being able to undo the knots no matter how heavy the strain on the lines (figure 2).

Fig. 2

End-to-end line

The easiest thing to do is to end-for-end the line, although, depending on the application, this can cause further chafe and weakening of the line. However, with modern fiber rope this is rarely a problem, and top-quality polyester rope will last as long as twenty years with proper care. Get rid of the original cause of the chafing: unfair leads, rough edges (especially on metal fitting, the application of a fine-toothed file will achieve wonders), and so on.

Splicing

4

The most secure method of repairing a chafed line, short of replacing the line altogether, is to cut and splice it (figure 3). A short splice will be stronger, but will not be able to pass through a block sheave; a long splice will be close to the original diameter of the line and will pass, providing the sheave is large enough in the first place.

Fig. 3

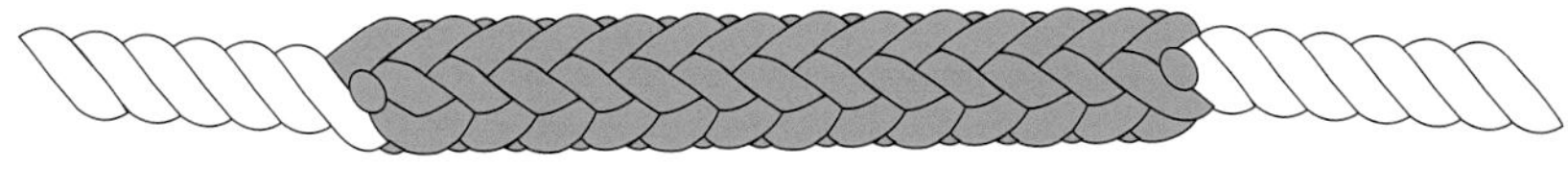

COLLISION

Colliding with another ship, a dock, or any large and relatively immobile object, is something to be feared without reservation. Most collisions occur due to inattention on the part of the helmsman, whether in crossing traffic separation lanes, excess speed, loss of steerage, or loss of power. Keeping a constant lookout, especially in heavily traveled waters, is a must. Following a GPS course is no excuse for lack of attention. You must take bearings of any moving ships in sight, and be prepared to take evasive action. Rules of the road are not always followed by large ships, and a good rule of thumb is to keep your distance. Most commercial ships will be traveling at as much as four times your speed through the water, and they can have a disconcerting—not to say dangerous—habit of suddenly looming over you. Not all ships keep a proper radar watch, despite COLREGS. Be prepared.

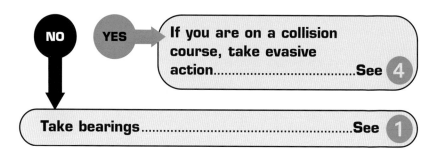

Have you taken a series of bearings of any moving ships in sight?

NO

YES → If you are on a collision course, take evasive action.....................See **4**

Take bearings...See **1**

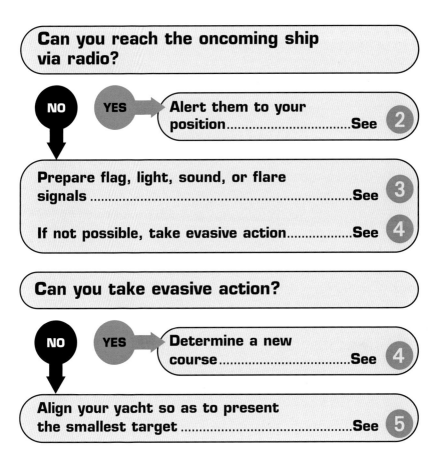

Can you reach the oncoming ship via radio?

NO

YES ▶ Alert them to your position...................See ②

Prepare flag, light, sound, or flare signals ....See ③

If not possible, take evasive action.................See ④

Can you take evasive action?

NO

YES ▶ Determine a new course.................................See ④

Align your yacht so as to present the smallest target ....See ⑤

Taking bearings.. ①

If bearings remain constant, chances are you are on a collision course. Taking bearings at night can be especially difficult. Try to keep one set of the approaching ship's range lights in line.

Radio contact.. ②

The first action is to attempt to raise the ship on VHF. Not all large ships monitor VHF as they should in congested waters. If you cannot make contact on ship-to-ship or emergency channels, try other means of signaling (see "Signaling" p.36).

Signaling.. ③

Chances are that a large ship will not spot you until after you have spotted her. You will probably have to take evasive action, but you should attempt to signal first. Five or more short blasts of a horn will be taken as a warning. At night, make either five short flashes of a strong light, or the Morse code "U" (2 short and 1 long flashes). Also, a flashlight shone against the sails or a white flare will indicate your presence. You can also activate a masthead strobe light if you have one, ring the ship's bell, or set off a flare. However, remember that a flare will be assumed to signal a ship in distress, and may invite closer inspection from the oncoming ship, jeopardizing your position further.

Warning signals

One blast: I am altering course to starboard.

Two blasts: I am altering course to port.

Three blasts: I am going astern.

Five blasts: Watch out! or I do not comprehend your intentions or actions.

Evasive action.. ④

Evasive action does not mean sailing until you see the whites of their eyes! Make all maneuvers positively. Course changes should be large, and the new course should be held. At any distance, your intentions must be visible from the bridge of the oncoming ship. Do not constantly change course: you will only confuse the oncoming ship. Always try to pass astern of the approaching vessel. Despite all the rules of the road, you should not hold to etiquette. Forget everything you ever learned about sail over power. You should be the one to avoid the other vessel.

Especially with large ships at sea, the watch will often be short-handed or they will not be manning the radar, particularly with flag-of-convenience registry vessels. Right of way is only relevant if the other vessel responds in kind; otherwise, assume she is going to make mincemeat of you and act accordingly. If there is a chance of a head-on collision, both vessels SHOULD alter their courses to starboard (figure 1). If the other does not, take immediate evasive action, by the fastest means possible, full speed ahead.

Fig. 1

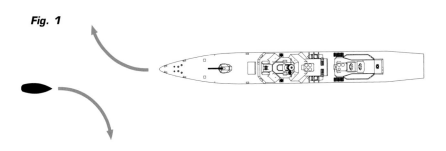

Collision 5

If a collision is unavoidable, try to present the smallest area of your ship as is possible to the oncoming vessel. This will, hopefully, lessen the impact and the resultant damage. If you are struck, the other vessel—if a large tanker, say—may not even know she has hit you. Set off distress flares as fast as possible (figure 2). Sound horns, bells, sirens—anything to attract attention. Have the crew stand by to abandon ship. See Abandoning Ship p.8.

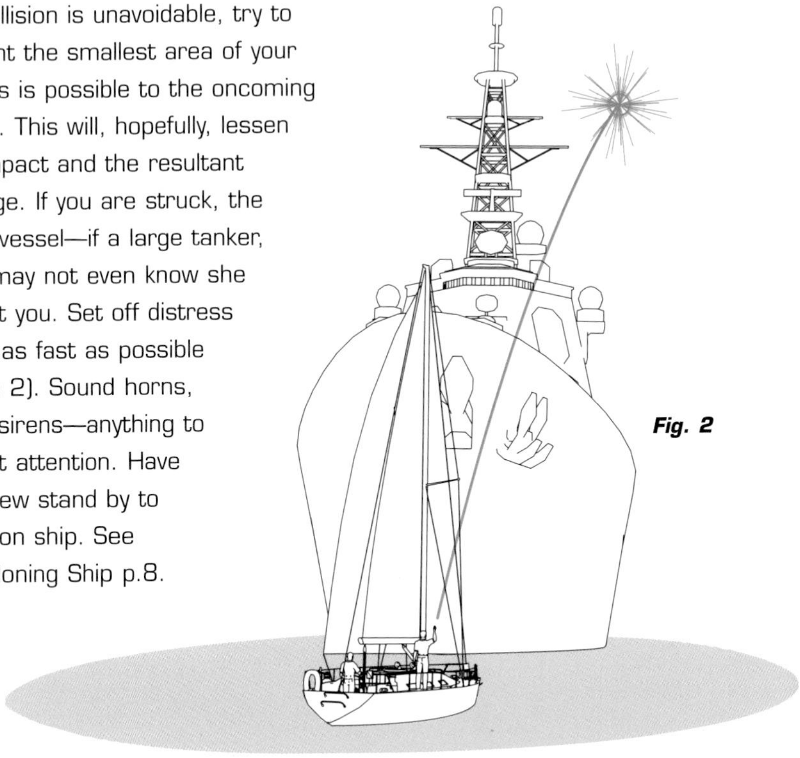

Fig. 2

DINGHIES AND TENDERS

Although a dinghy or tender is an absolute necessity for anything more than a day sail, it is often thought of as something of a nuisance and a drag on the yacht underway. But your tender is not only a lifeline to shore, it is a potential life raft, grocery cart, and leisure-time amusement. Whether a hard dinghy or an inflatable, certain procedures must be followed to maintain your safety and prevent injury or drowning.

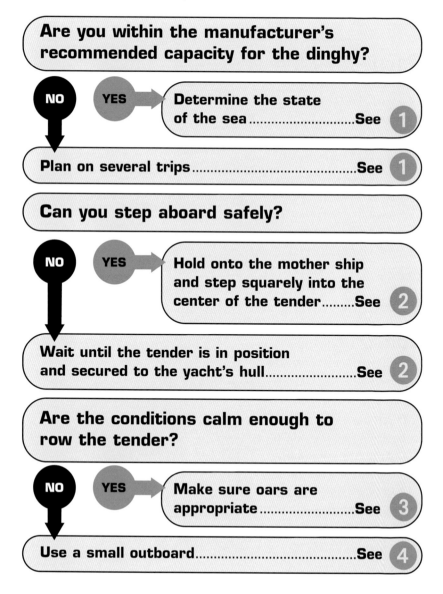

Are you within the manufacturer's recommended capacity for the dinghy?

NO

YES → Determine the state of the sea .... See **1**

Plan on several trips .... See **1**

Can you step aboard safely?

NO

YES → Hold onto the mother ship and step squarely into the center of the tender .... See **2**

Wait until the tender is in position and secured to the yacht's hull .... See **2**

Are the conditions calm enough to row the tender?

NO

YES → Make sure oars are appropriate .... See **3**

Use a small outboard .... See **4**

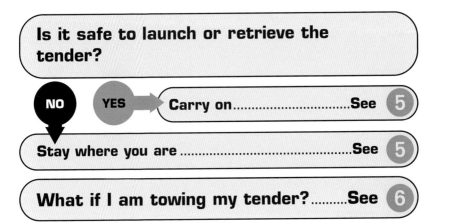

Is it safe to launch or retrieve the tender?

NO   **YES** ➤ Carry on...............................See ⑤

Stay where you are ....See ⑤

What if I am towing my tender?..........See ⑥

Capacity.. ①

More deaths are probably caused by swamped and capsized dinghies than by anything else on the water. The average tender is perhaps 8 to 10 feet (3 to 4 meters) in length and cannot really hold more than three people in anything but a dead calm. In truly rough water, no more than two should attempt a journey. As well as

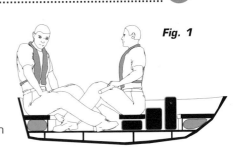

Fig. 1

not overloading with people, you must be careful to avoid masses of gear, especially in the ends of the boat. Try to keep the boat carefully trimmed and balanced, both athwartships and fore-and-aft (figure 1). Do not overload! If more than the allotted capacity is likely, make another trip.

Boarding.. ②

The novice will inevitably step on the gunwale when trying to board. This can lead to lacerations or a dunking. In most hard tenders, you can step directly into the center portion of the floorboards (figure 2).

However, if the dock or float is particularly high, you may have to alight on the center thwart and descend quickly. The idea is to sit down as quickly as possible, while the next crewmember comes aboard. Never board a dinghy with your hands full. Either load first, or

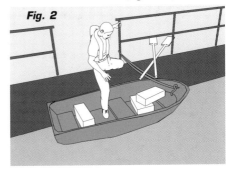

Fig. 2

enter and have someone else hand the cargo to you once you are seated. Make sure the tender is alongside and tied fore-and-aft to the yacht. A sudden wave could swing the stern out and leave you dangling in the water or, worse, hit by the tender when it swings back. Boarding from a stern platform is easier, as the step will be on much the same level as the tender. Inflatables without keels will often be skittish, so it is necessary to keep them as close to the boarding platform as possible. With a hard dinghy, make sure the gunwales are fendered.

Oars .... ③

Most dinghy oars are far too heavy and ill-balanced. Ideally, they should fit into the tender, be made of spruce, and shaped to be comfortable to use and efficient at propelling the boat. Far too few people ever bother to learn to row properly. A fairly sound rule of thumb is: the beamier the boat, the shorter the strokes; and the heavier the seas, the shorter the strokes. However, load, windage, sea state, and wetted surface all play a part in the best (most effective and least tiring) way to row. Practice. And be sure that you have oarlocks, leathers, and a rowing position—with foot brace—that can stand up to the job. Trial and error will find the way.

Motors .... ④

Inflatable tenders are virtually impossible to row except in calm conditions. You will probably need a small outboard. You are not going waterskiing, so keep the horsepower reasonable. The motor will have to be retrieved from the deck and clamped on to the inflatable in the water. Weight is something to consider, and a large motor will be impossible to safely wrest from the deck. Make sure the motor is both firmly screwed to the motor board and secured with a cable or chain.

Launching and retrieving .... ⑤

Getting the tender into the water and back on board is the first concern of the cruising sailor. It must always be tethered to the mother ship. Too often a perfect launch is followed by a perfect drift into the distance. Obviously, the method of launching is dependent upon the ship, but usually some sort of hoist and tackle

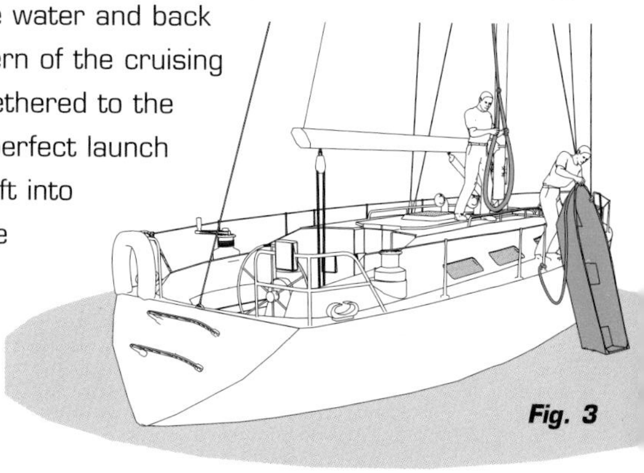

Fig. 3

arrangement will be necessary to accomplish the job with minimum fuss and danger (figure 3). Always try to have an extra hand to assist. Probably the greatest danger—other than overloading—is in landing or launching through surf. This is never a deed to be undertaken lightly. With oar power, the difficulty will be to restrain the dinghy enough or propel it fast enough. With an outboard, the problems are stalling, cavitation, and general unreliability if swamped. The key danger is always swamping or capsizing. If the surf is running, you would be well advised to stay on the ship or beach. Otherwise, you will need a large enough boat and crew to power through. Do not underestimate the power of breaking seas. They can crack your boat into pieces and kill you and your crew.

Towing .... ⑥

Some yachtsmen wish to use a hard tender but have no room on deck to stow it. Others wish to tow the inflatable. The techniques applicable to either are different. In towing a hard tender, the painter or tow line must be long enough to keep the tender from riding up the stern of the yacht. Equally, a bridle needs to be rigged so that the tender does not yaw, cutting down your speed and potentially allowing the tender to broach and fill (figure 4). An inflatable, on the other hand, needs to be carried tight to the yacht, sometimes with the bows carried over the stern. Being lightweight, inflatables can easily flip in the wind or actually go flying. This will surely cause the painter to snap, resulting in a lost tender. Remove any and all movable objects—oars, motors, bailers, tanks, etc.—from the tender before starting to tow. Even tied down, any of these can be lost.

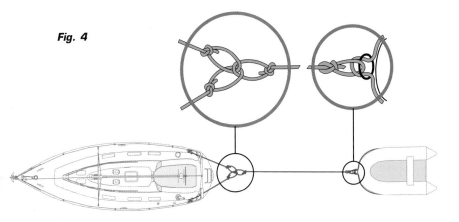

Fig. 4

DISMASTING

If the mast breaks at or near the base, it will go overboard, presenting a serious threat to the boat, especially in heavy weather. A long shaft of metal banging against the side of the hull can easily smash a hole in the boat. In calm seas, the crew may be able to hoist the mast back on board. It's a different story in rough seas, and the mast will either have to be abandoned or towed in the water, the motion of the boat making it difficult and dangerous to retrieve. If the forestay parts while beating, the mast can fracture and fall aft into the cockpit, causing possible injury to the crew. If the mast breaks at the spreaders, it must be untangled and a jury rig set. No matter what, immediate action will be necessary. Move fast to avoid damage to the ship, but not so fast as to endanger the crew. Think out your actions first and instruct the crew clearly on what must be done.

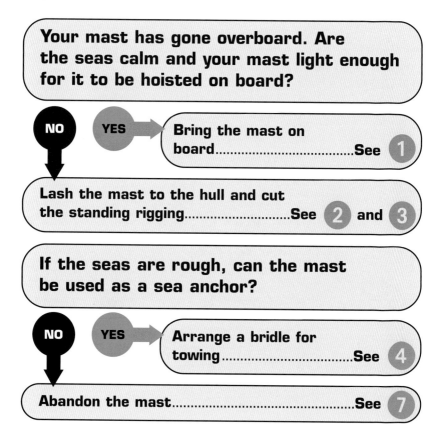

Your mast has gone overboard. Are the seas calm and your mast light enough for it to be hoisted on board?

NO **YES** → Bring the mast on board.............................See **1**

Lash the mast to the hull and cut the standing rigging.............................See **2** and **3**

If the seas are rough, can the mast be used as a sea anchor?

NO **YES** → Arrange a bridle for towing.............................See **4**

Abandon the mast.............................See **7**

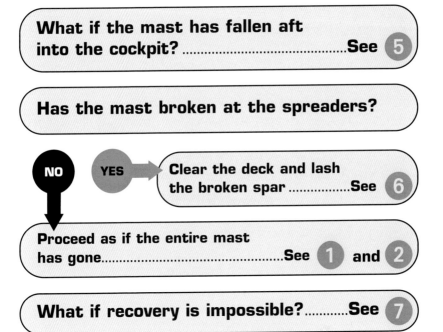

What if the mast has fallen aft into the cockpit? ....See **5**

Has the mast broken at the spreaders?

NO

YES ➤ Clear the deck and lash the broken spar ....See **6**

Proceed as if the entire mast has gone..................................See **1** and **2**

What if recovery is impossible? ....See **7**

Bringing the mast onboard **1**

A mast that has gone overboard presents a serious threat to the continuing integrity of the hull, especially in heavy weather. In calm seas, you and the crew may be able to hoist the mast back on board (figure 1). If the mast is sizeable and therefore heavy, a better procedure will be to lash it to the hull. Hoisting will necessitate securing the spar on at least three points along its length, and rigging tackles fore, aft, and

Fig. 1

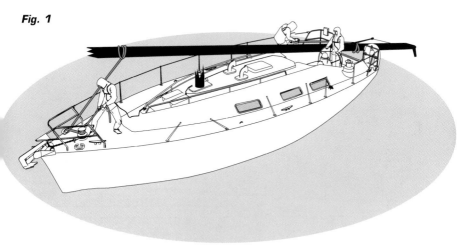

amidships—using winches in the cockpit, perhaps the vang to the mast step and the anchor windlass with appropriate jury-rigged fairleads. Station crew at each location and be sure that the hull is appropriately fendered; in this instance, every fender aboard should be secured to the rail on the hoisting side. Chances are that the lifelines and stanchions went by the board when the mast went over, so safety harnesses are an absolute must.

Lashing the mast to the hull 2

If the mast is sizeable and heavy or the seas are high, do not attempt to hoist it onboard. It should be lashed alongside the hull, as far above the waterline as possible to prevent the mast from crashing into the hull (figure 2). Metal masts, unless foam-filled, will sink fairly quickly. It is imperative to move with speed and caution. As above, it is likely that lifelines and stanchions surrounding the deck went overboard or were badly damaged. Safety harnesses must be worn by all crew. To pull it out of the water, the mast should be secured at three points along its length—using tackles fore, aft, and amidships. To secure the mast well, make use of the cockpit winches as well as the windlass to aid in tightening the lines. Be aware that a wildly bucking boat in this situation will soon cause unprotected rope or line to wear through and break. Therefore,

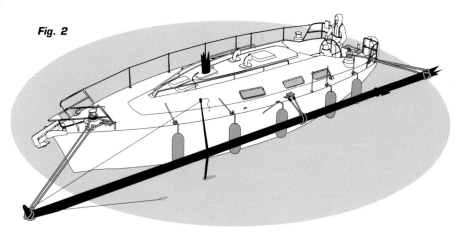

Fig. 2

ensure that the lines are protected from chafing and abrasion by wrapping them with rags or split rubber hose where they rub against hardware or the edge of the deck. Station crew at each line location in case something breaks or gets tangled, and be sure to protect the hull by padding it with every fender on board. Since the mast will add considerable weight to the side to which it is lashed, it may also be necessary, especially in a light-displacement vessel, to move heavy items below deck to the opposite side of the boat for balance.

Cutting away standing rigging .... ③

If you decide to lash the mast to the side of the yacht, a large part of the rigging will have to be cut away. This can be accomplished by breaking off the turnbuckles or rigging screws; however, they may have been bent out of shape by the shock, and be difficult, if not impossible, to remove. If this is the case, cut the rigging wires, either with cable cutters, a cold chisel and hammer against a steel block, or a hacksaw. Cutting steel wire is not an easy task. In fact, a bi-metal hacksaw in a stiff frame is probably the best option since one hand is kept free to hold onto a rail for balance. Note that the rod rigging will be difficult to part from the mast. The lower shrouds (the wires running from below the spreaders to the deck) on the side of the vessel on which the mast went over should remain attached for added security. Remember, however, that if weather conditions should worsen, you may have to abandon the mast completely and, in doing so, any remaining attachments will need to be cut away quickly.

Using the mast as a sea anchor .... ④

The mast may be left trailing from bow or stern to act as a sea anchor (figure 3, over the page). In truly monstrous seas, this might be the best way to retain some steerage and control. The mast must be attached to the boat in such a way as to withstand the enormous strain imposed on the deck hardware. Through-bolted cleats can sometimes be torn from the deck under these conditions. It's best, therefore, to run the securing lines around the winches first, then around the cleats to distribute the tremendous force on the line. Also, this way, you can adjust the tension on the lines without danger of injury (the winches hold the mast while you adjust the lines on the cleats). All this must be accompanied by a constant watch in case the trailing mast is flung onto the ship by breaking seas. If this should happen, secure the mast with ropes rather than rigging wire, because should you need to cut the mast loose, you can then hack the ropes with an axe. These ropes must be at least five times the length of the boat and the strongest on board. The force placed upon them is measured in multiples of tons.

Fig. 3

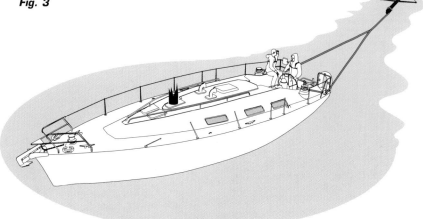

Mast in the cockpit 5

Should the mast fall into the cockpit, chances are that a crewmember in the cockpit may be injured, the wheel or tiller may be broken, and/or the cabin house may be crushed. An injured crewmember should be moved below into the cabin and placed on a berth. Make sure he or she is immobilized in a safe place where there is no risk of being thrown out. If possible, leave someone with the injured person while the remainder of the crew works the deck. The cockpit will be a jumble of metal, wire, and wood. Clear this overboard as soon as possible. Assess the damage and make emergency repairs. If the steering mechanism is broken see Jury Rigs: Rudders p.104 and Steering Gear p.175.

Break at the spreaders 6

Breaks at the spreaders are more common than might be supposed. Because of the many fittings and terminals at this point, the mast can

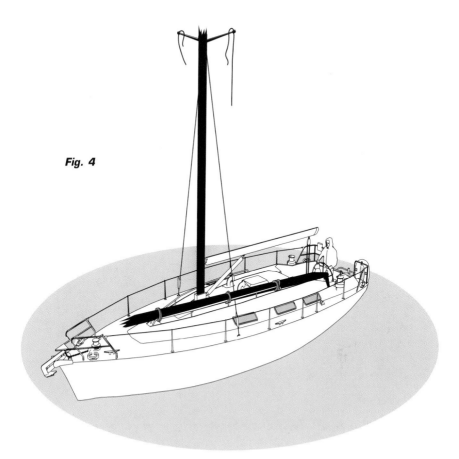

Fig. 4

be weakened. If the mast should fracture and the section above the spreaders should come tumbling down, lash it to the deck (figure 4) and proceed to Jury Rigs: Masts p.99. If the mast is left dangling, use a rope to lash the upper part to the portion left standing. It's best not to cut down the top since maneuvering it to the deck can be a tricky and dangerous job.

Abandoning the mast................................. 7

If there is no hope of recovering the mast or all attempts have failed and the boat is threatened, it becomes necessary to cut away the mast. Move quickly and use any available means to detach the mast. See "Cutting away standing rigging" p.45.

DIVING

There are times when the anchor may be fouled or the propeller, rudder, or keel may become fouled by seaweed, errant ropes, plastic sheeting, or other flotsam. There is no other solution but to send someone over the side to clear the obstruction. Diving is always a dangerous undertaking, and all possible precautions should be observed.

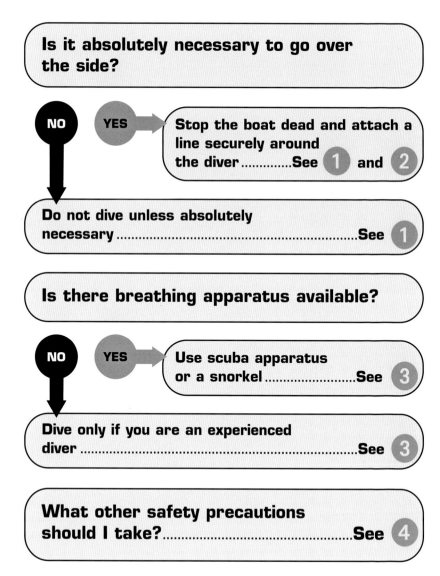

Is it absolutely necessary to go over the side?

NO **YES** → **Stop the boat dead and attach a line securely around the diver**............**See** **1** and **2**

Do not dive unless absolutely necessary..**See** **1**

Is there breathing apparatus available?

NO **YES** → **Use scuba apparatus or a snorkel**........................**See** **3**

Dive only if you are an experienced diver..**See** **3**

What other safety precautions should I take?.................................**See** **4**

Going over the side 1

The most usual reason for having to dive is either to unfoul the anchor or to clear the propeller. In either case, the boat must be stopped dead in the water. If under power, shut the engines down. If under sail, drop all sails or heave to. If possible, anchor the boat. If the anchor is fouled, see Anchoring: Special, "Fouled anchor" p.26. Attempting to dive when the boat is in motion is foolhardy in the extreme. Any additional movement will make any underwater task extraordinarily difficult for the diver.

Tethering 2

Since few people can remain underwater without artificial breathing apparatus for more than 45 seconds to one minute, especially when exerting themselves, a safety line is a must (figure 1). Additionally, should the boat drift or move away from the diver, no other means exists to retrieve the person in the water. The person on deck should have prearranged signals with the diver: for example, one jerk on the line, pull up; two jerks, help. Only dive without a line if you are an experienced diver and the boat is at anchor. As long as the boat is anchored, you can use the anchor cable to pull yourself back to the yacht. Beware of unknown currents. The best time to dive is always at slack water.

Fig. 1

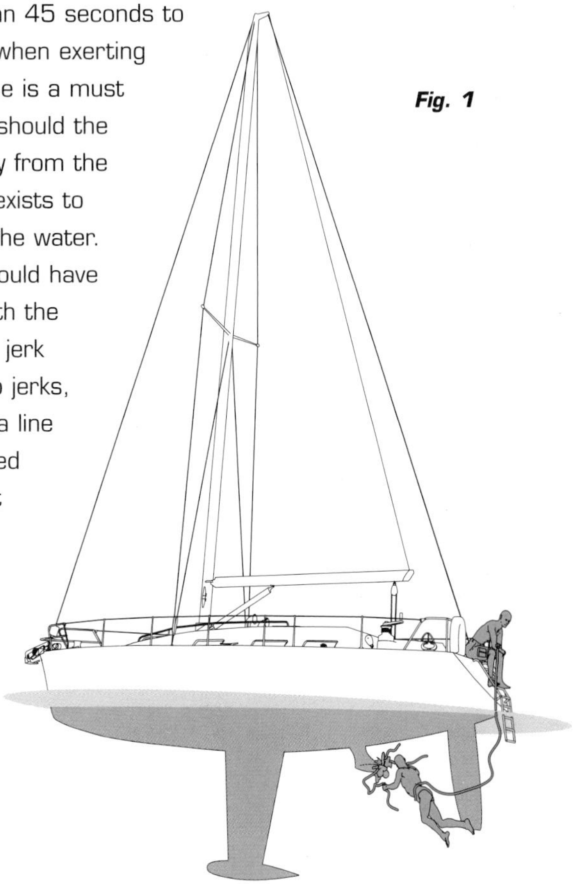

Breathing apparatus... ③

Diving without breathing apparatus is only for the experienced. Even a snorkel can help. If you are a certified diver, with diving equipment aboard, you will know what to do. Otherwise, do not attempt to stay under for as long as you can hold your breath. Allow a safety margin. You may need to repeatedly dive to clear any obstruction. Reserve your strength.

Spotter .... ④

A line without a tender is useless. The person on deck will often sight danger before the diver, such as a shark approaching or a squall coming. You may not be able to regain the deck by yourself if fatigued. The spotter can lend a hand. Always have a boarding ladder secured before the diver goes in. He or she will know where it is and there will be no fumbling when it is needed. Make it as long as possible and weight the bottom rung (figure 2).

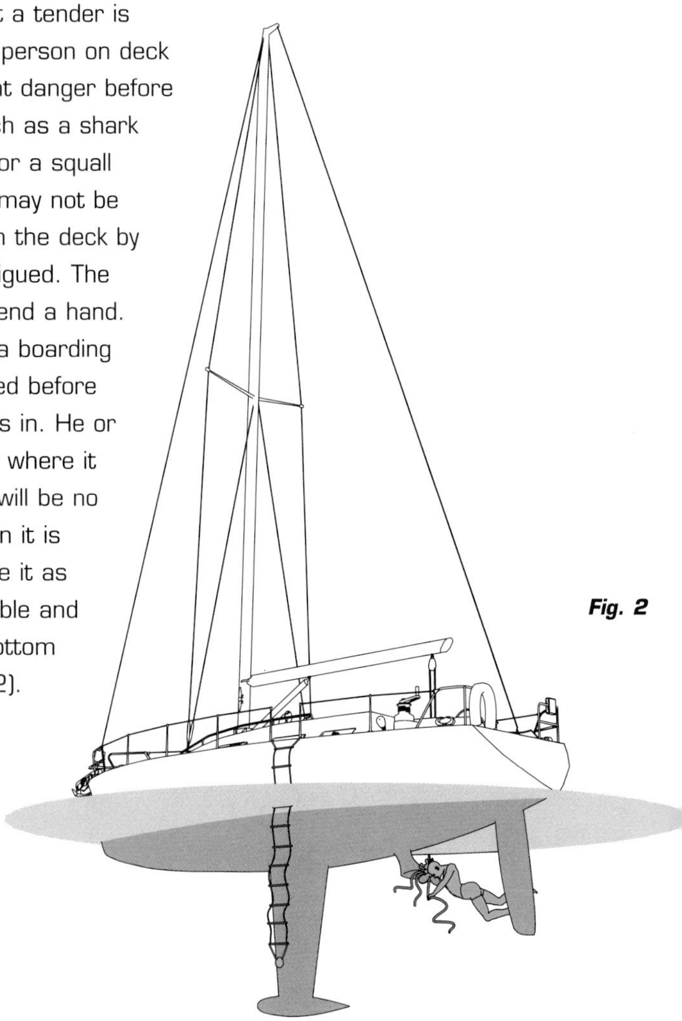

Fig. 2

DOCKING

Approaching a dock or pontoon can easily cause apprehension. After all, you are moving one heavy object toward another. Depending on wind, wave action, tide, and current, the procedure can be simple or fraught with danger. Always have a second option available should your approach be thwarted. In a gale or storm, you may be better off picking up a mooring or anchoring.

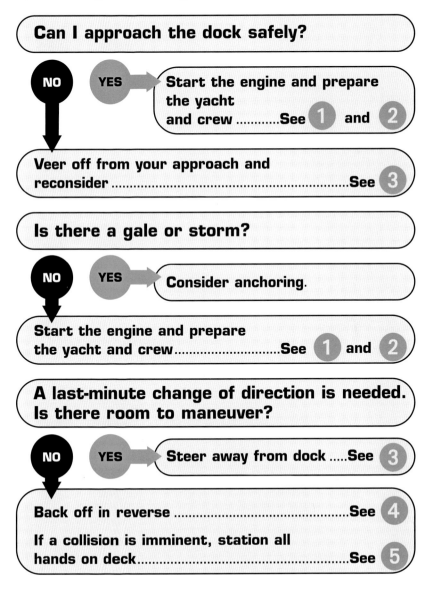

Can I approach the dock safely?

NO   YES → Start the engine and prepare the yacht and crew ....See **1** and **2**

Veer off from your approach and reconsider ....See **3**

Is there a gale or storm?

NO   YES → Consider anchoring.

Start the engine and prepare the yacht and crew...............................See **1** and **2**

A last-minute change of direction is needed. Is there room to maneuver?

NO   YES → Steer away from dock .....See **3**

Back off in reverse ....See **4**

If a collision is imminent, station all hands on deck...See **5**

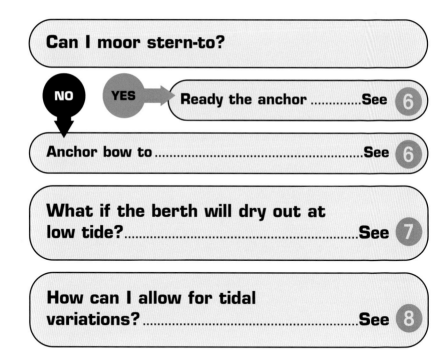

Can I moor stern-to?

NO   YES ➡ **Ready the anchor** .... See ⑥

Anchor bow to .... See ⑥

What if the berth will dry out at low tide? .... See ⑦

How can I allow for tidal variations? .... See ⑧

Approach .... ①

Approaching any dock, quay, or pontoon is made more difficult by the tight quarters, proximity of other vessels, and the tricks tidal streams can play amongst pilings and walls. Make due allowance for windage, drift, and lost control at low speeds. Know how your ship

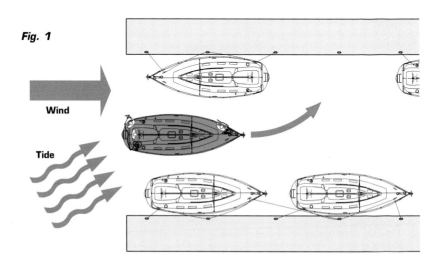

Fig. 1

Wind

Tide

handles. Attempt to approach to windward, with the engine at slow forward. With wind and tide behind you (figure 1), you will have to either play with bursts of reverse on the throttle or have a crew member stationed to drop a stern anchor to slow down the ship and allow for some control. The same maneuver can be practiced with current abeam, though it is always preferable to approach against a current.

Preparation............. ②

Cleat all lines and pass through chocks, then outboard and over any rails or lifelines. Secure all fenders overboard. If approaching a concrete or stone pier, use fender-boards. Quite often the pier will be quite high; a crew member should be stationed so they can scale the wall (hopefully by ladder) with both bow and stern lines in hand (figure 2). The same is true if sailing alone or with one crew. Spring lines can be rigged after bow and stern

Fig. 2

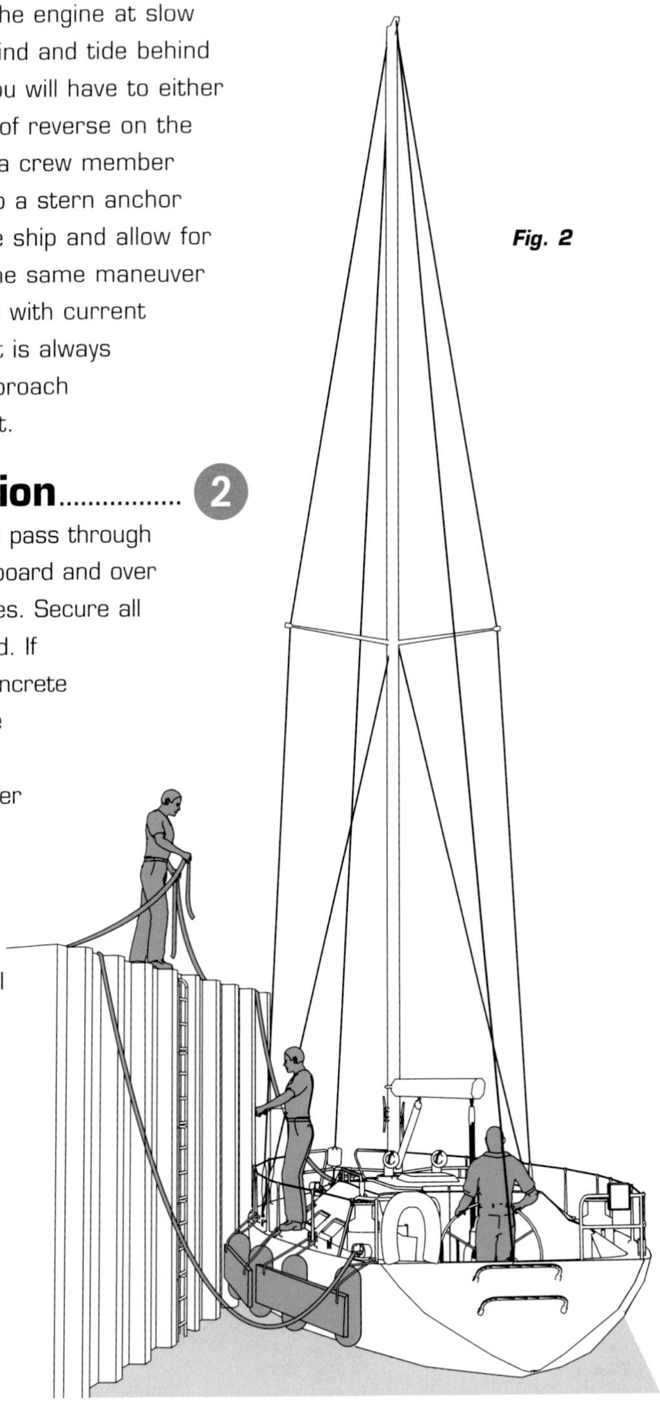

are secured. Should the ship be tied up on the windward side of the dock, a kedge can be run out to hold it off, either from a spring cleat amidships or with two warps leading from the kedge to both bow and stern cleats (figure 3).

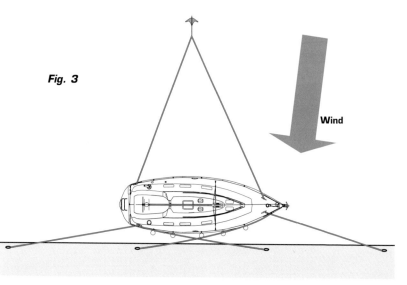

Fig. 3

Wind

Changing approach .... ③

You could suddenly have to alter your intended approach or goal, either due to the unexpected appearance of a smaller, hitherto unseen boat, or to directions from the dock master. Lines, fenders, etc., will have to be quickly switched. If you have enough time, it pays to back off and re-approach after these chores have been completed. If not, and the area is crowded on first approach, it is a good idea to rig lines and fenders on both sides of the yacht. In places like St. Peter Port, Newport, or Annapolis, at the height of the season, docking is always at a premium. Plan accordingly.

Backing off .... ④

In tight quarters, your only option may be to back off from the dock in reverse. Depending on the underwater configuration and the handling characteristics of your yacht, this can be a tricky maneuver. Throwing an engine into reverse quickly can cause the boat to buck and swerve, and you must be prepared to correct the helm instantly. In a twin-screw motor yacht, these considerations are easier to cope with, but you must still know how to apply power to both engines to achieve your goal. If you have approached the dock slowly, you can back off slowly. Monitor your speed through the water carefully, and try not to apply power suddenly.

Collision 5

With little room to maneuver, and the possibility of colliding with another yacht or the dock itself, station crew to port and starboard, to fend off as much as possible. Make sure the yacht is fendered port and starboard. Most collisions are caused when approaching too fast, and striking another yacht on its quarter or the dock head-on. The only solution is a combination of the crew fending off and the application of judicious reverse power. Any sudden moves on the part of the helmsman can cause further damage and grievous injury to the crew. Do not panic.

Mediterranean mooring 6

In most of the Mediterranean, tying up stern-to is the norm. This is accomplished by letting out the best bower about 100 feet (30 meters) plus the length of the ship from the quay and backing toward the dock. Unfortunately, with adverse conditions this can be at best a tricky maneuver. Better to drop the hook from the stern and go in bow first (figure 4). Most boats have greater control in forward, as well as greater stopping power. In addition, should you desire such things, your privacy will be that much more. If you wish you can end-for-end the bow and anchor lines—providing there is room port and starboard—and turn the ship around. If boats are wedged in on both sides, extend the line to the quay and haul well clear of your neighbors before attempting to make the turn.

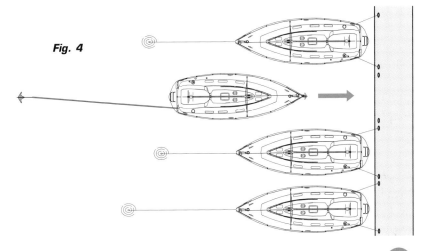

Fig. 4

Drying out 7

Should the berth be one that dries out at low tide, attempt to heel the boat slightly inward toward the quay. A line passed about the mast at spreader height and led ashore usually will do the trick. Be careful that the rigging does not come in contact with the dock, and that the spreaders will not be damaged. A block attached to a halyard and also held around the mast with a strop or loose loop of rope can be hoisted aloft to just below the spreaders after a line from the dock has been led through it and back to the dock or to a cleat on deck (figure 5). In addition, a heavy anchor can be placed on the dockside deck of the vessel. If the yacht's keel does not have much length at its base, do not attempt to dry out—either the hull will pitch forward, the keel will sink into the mud, or the keel will turn and the ends of the hull may be damaged.

Fig. 5

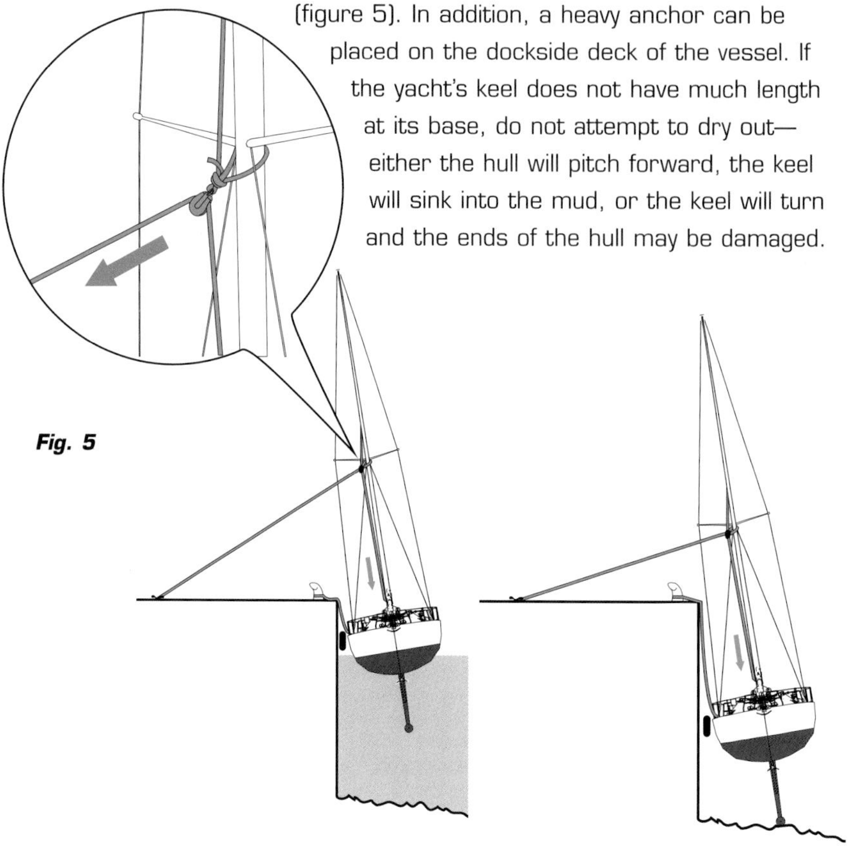

Tidal variations ....(8)

Be sure that enough slack is kept in the docking lines to allow for the rise and fall of the tide. A good idea is to lead the lines to the dock pilings or cleats in a bight and then back again to the deck cleats (figure 6). In this manner, you will be able to make adjustments without leaving the deck. Be sure to allow enough slack to accommodate the largest tidal range you may encounter.

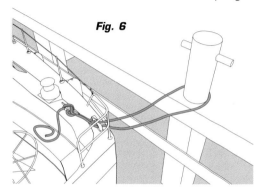

Fig. 6

ELECTRICS

Modern yachts have an ever increasing number of electrical devices onboard. There are a number of ways to power these—batteries, solar panels, generators—but eventually the majority work off the batteries. Keeping batteries charged has become a primary task of the boat owner. The days of hand-cranked engines are virtually passed, so make sure your belts, alternator, and batteries are in peak condition and operating efficiently. Otherwise you may find yourself with no lights or an engine that just won't start.

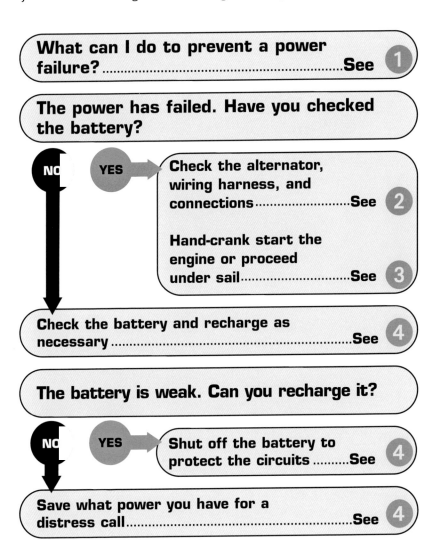

What can I do to prevent a power failure? ....**See** ①

The power has failed. Have you checked the battery?

NO **YES** → **Check the alternator, wiring harness, and connections** ....**See** ②

Hand-crank start the engine or proceed under sail ....**See** ③

Check the battery and recharge as necessary ....**See** ④

The battery is weak. Can you recharge it?

NO **YES** → **Shut off the battery to protect the circuits** ....**See** ④

Save what power you have for a distress call ....**See** ④

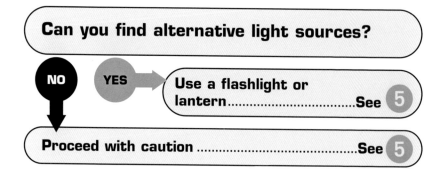

Can you find alternative light sources?

NO　　**YES** ➤ Use a flashlight or lantern..........................See 5

Proceed with caution ....See 5

Power failure..1

It is a sorry fact of life afloat that sooner or later salt air and moisture will have a detrimental effect on your boat's electrical system. You can guard against run-of-the-mill failure by checking all connections, wiring, fuses, junction boxes, circuit breakers, battery installations, etc., at the commencement of every season and at least twice during the course of the season. Battery terminals must be cleaned and, after reconnecting, coated with a thin layer of grease (waterproof). Check all wire clips to see that no breaks have occurred in the insulation. Any wires running low in the ship, especially in the bilges, should be rerouted away from any possible water contamination. Overhaul the alternator and generator. Replace all fuses and lamp bulbs as a matter of course. See that all connections and connecting clips are free from corrosion and coated after cleaning and reassembly. Top up batteries and secure. Make sure they are properly vented. Check engine-wiring harnesses and make sure all wires are securely clipped and away from any excessive heat sources.

Checking connections...............................2

Assuming you have done all the above and the power fails, what do you do? First check the battery. It may be dry. A connection may be vibrated or torn loose. The alternator may not be functioning. A fuse may be blown, or a cable may have shorted out.

Engine failure...3

If the engine has no hand-crank starting capability, and a second battery is available, jump or reconnect the cables (figure 1). If you cannot restart the engine, signal for help or proceed under sail. See Signals p.172.

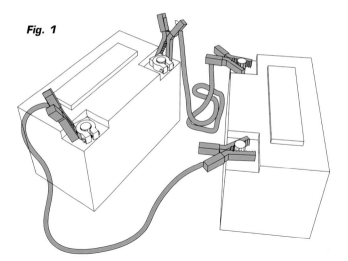

Fig. 1

Charging batteries .... ④

When charging batteries, it's always a good idea to isolate other circuitry when possible. A sudden surge can fry delicate electronic equipment. Isolate the batteries. If you cannot charge the battery, something is wrong either in the circuitry or with the alternator. Unless you are experienced in these matters, it is best to call for help. Any use of electrical devices will quickly drain the battery, so save what power you have to radio a distress call.

Alternative lights .... ⑤

If the lights have failed and the situation is beyond repair, you are in danger at dusk or at night. Use a kerosene/paraffin lantern hung in the rigging instead of navigation lights (figure 2). At worst you will be thought a fisherman! Or use an electric/battery anchor light. If a ship approaches, use flares to show your position.

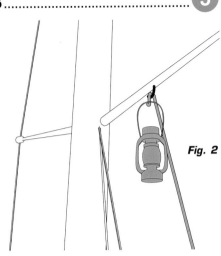

Fig. 2

ELECTRONICS

Virtually every boat on the water today, other than day sailers and rowing boats, is equipped with various electronic instruments, including depth sounders, logs, plotters, GPS, and radios. Although modern sailing instruments are vastly more sophisticated and reliable than they were even a decade ago, they are all subject to the same problems: corrosion, short circuits, water damage, and lack of effective back-ups. This section is intended to remind you, above all else, not to rely only on electronic navigation!

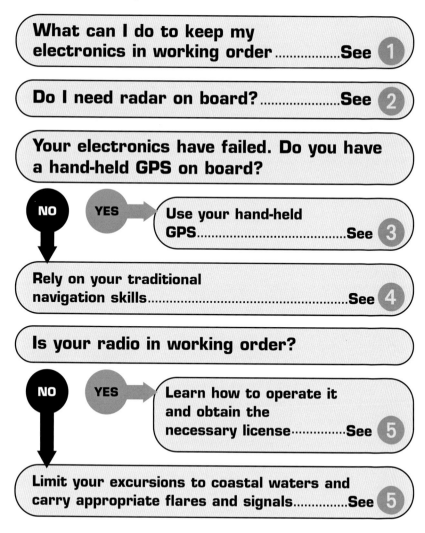

What can I do to keep my electronics in working order ....**See** ①

Do I need radar on board? ....**See** ②

Your electronics have failed. Do you have a hand-held GPS on board?

NO   **YES**   **Use your hand-held GPS** ....**See** ③

Rely on your traditional navigation skills ....**See** ④

Is your radio in working order?

NO   **YES**   **Learn how to operate it and obtain the necessary license** ....**See** ⑤

Limit your excursions to coastal waters and carry appropriate flares and signals ....**See** ⑤

Electronics maintenance

Keeping your electronics working is a matter of prime importance. Salt water will eventually ruin anything it comes into contact with. Make sure all cockpit instruments are properly sealed and bedded. Coat all connections with petroleum jelly. Have your instruments calibrated at the beginning of each season. Keep any software, especially charts, up to date. Remember that computers, unless specifically packaged for marine use, are delicate devices. Handle them with care.

Radar

Radar (figure 1) is increasingly carried on boats, even on boats of under 39 feet (12 meters). On sailing yachts, it can be an encumbrance, but in fog or at night, radar can be invaluable, not only in spotting other ships, but in pinpointing your position in relation to a coast. Depending on the range set and the sensitivity of the set, even rocks and breakers can be detected.

Fig. 1

GPS and old-fashioned navigation

GPS has become the main means of navigation offshore. Without doubt, it is the most accurate and precise method of finding out exactly where you are, usually within a few meters. Nevertheless, it is a good idea to keep a spare on board. A dropped GPS will very likely break. Always carry a hand-held GPS on board in case your electronics fail (figure 2, over the page). It should always be run in parallel with your main GPS. Of course, the old skills of navigation should always be kept in reserve. Plotting a course on a paper chart, reading tide tables and tidal stream charts, working out distance off, reading the water for depth changes and wind shifts, dead reckoning, taking sun sights and working them out—all these, and more, used to be mandatory for the mariner. This book is no place to teach you how to navigate, but this is as good a place as any to forewarn you that sooner or later you will have to fall back on these ancient skills. Do not go offshore without a thorough grounding in traditional navigational skills.

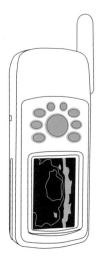

Fig. 2

Traditional navigation skills...................... 4

Anyone who goes on the water must be able to navigate without instruments, no ifs, ands, or buts! The traditional skills that every sailor should have include: plotting a passage, dead reckoning, taking bearings, sounding by hand with a leadline, estimating wind speed and speed through the water, estimating tides and current, and (if heading offshore) taking sights with a sextant. No amount of electronic gear will help when the battery dies or the systems short out.

Radio 5

Almost all boats will be equipped with VHF radio. Be sure you know how to operate it in emergencies, and make sure you carry the appropriate license. Certain types of atmospheric interference can decrease the range of VHF. Aerial installation is critical and should be carried out by a reputable electronics technician. See Radio p.156. As back-up, carry the recommended flares and signaling devices on board. See Signals p.172.

ENGINE FAILURE: Diesel

The modern diesel engine is a remarkably durable piece of machinery. However, like everything mechanical, it can be subject to breakdown, usually at the most difficult moments. Most often the cause is dirty fuel. The one filter that came with the engine is not enough to prevent matter, moisture, or debris from entering the injectors and wrecking havoc. Secondary filters should be installed and maintained regularly. If the engine stops, overheats, runs unevenly, or the oil pressure drops—always stop the engine.

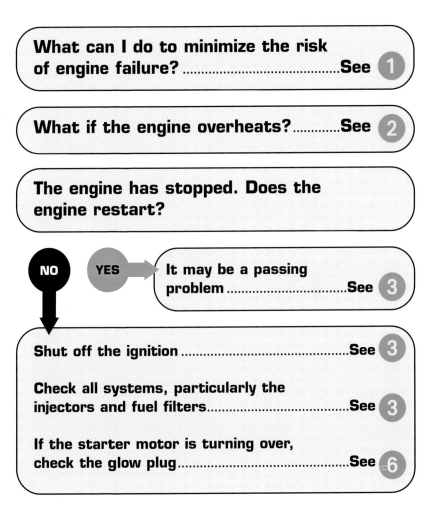

What can I do to minimize the risk of engine failure? ....**See** **1**

What if the engine overheats? ....**See** **2**

The engine has stopped. Does the engine restart?

NO   **YES** ➤ **It may be a passing problem** ....**See** **3**

Shut off the ignition ....**See** **3**

Check all systems, particularly the injectors and fuel filters................................**See** **3**

If the starter motor is turning over, check the glow plug...**See** **6**

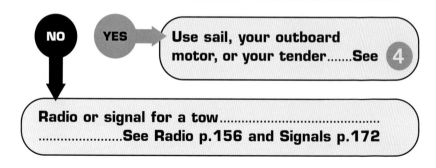

The engine cannot be restarted. Is there any alternative means of power?

NO **YES** → Use sail, your outboard motor, or your tender.......See **4**

Radio or signal for a tow..
.........................See Radio p.156 and Signals p.172

What if the oil pressure drops?..........See **5**

What if the engine is running unevenly? ....See **6**

Engine care.. **1**

A full spare kit as well as the manufacturer's manual should be aboard for anything more than a day sail. Read the manual before setting out on a cruise. Make sure you have the necessary tools on board. If anything seems wrong—high temperature, rough running, frequent stoppages, oil-pressure fluctuations—stop the engine immediately. Failure to do so may cause major damage. Remember that anything that moves needs maintenance. As much as you might hate the engine, it is part of the yacht and needs the same care as the brightwork and winches.

Engine overheating.. **2**

Overheating is the most common problem with diesels and is most often the result of a torn or failed water-cooling pump impeller. Switch off the ignition. First, check the water inlet for debris and blockage (figure 1). Also check the belt to the water pump and make sure the propeller is not fouled. This is the place to warn you: Always carry a spare impeller on board. Changing it is a ten-minute job at most, but for want of a spare, you may be disabled until you can signal for a tow (in a powerboat) or the breeze picks up.

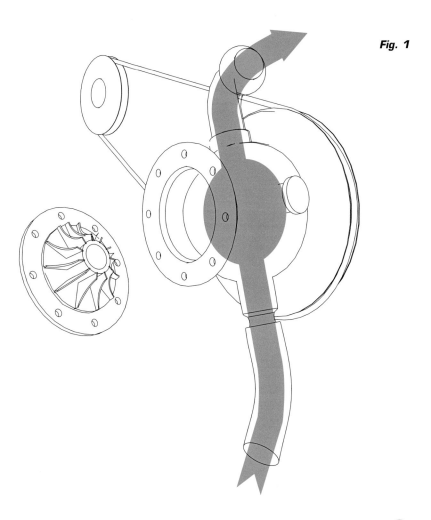

Fig. 1

Engine stoppage .... ③

If the engine stops on its own accord, switch off the ignition. Check the fuel system (figure 2, over the page). Filters must be free of dirt and water. They should be filled with oil. The possibility exists that the tanks are empty. The filters may be only partly filled if this is the case.

However, partial filter filling may also be due to a fuel line blockage. If the engine won't restart, you will have to bleed both filters and possibly injectors. Consult your owner's manual.

Fig. 2

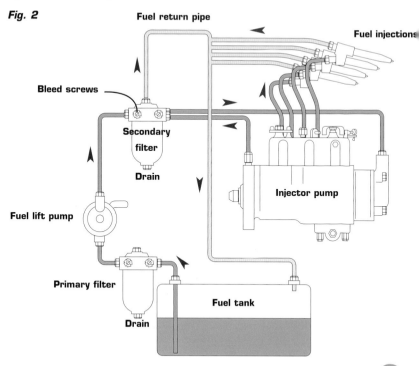

Alternative power 4

Besides sailing, one of the most obvious solutions to actually getting somewhere is to make provision for mounting your outboard on or over the stern of the boat. Even the smallest outboard motor can push a boat through the water in calm conditions. Another possibility is to push the boat forward using the tender, lashed to the stern quarter.

Oil pressure 5

Oil pressure dropping can indicate a major problem. Switch off the ignition. Check the oil level and top up. If water has mixed with the oil, the head gasket may have ruptured. Do not run the engine above very low rpms (no higher than 1500 rpm in most modern marine diesels).

Engine troubleshooting 6

If the engine will not start but the starter motor is turning over, the glow plug may need replacement. Uneven running may be due to a clogged or broken injector. If possible, replace it; if not, run the engine very, very slowly. Check the owner's manual for specific advice.

ENGINE FAILURE:
Gasoline/Petrol

Although few modern yachts carry gas/petrol engines as primary propulsion, many smaller powerboats do. And most boats will carry an outboard for the tender. Gasoline/petrol is far more volatile than diesel fuel, and fire and/or explosion must be prevented, through proper ventilation, secure fuel lines, and spark suppression.

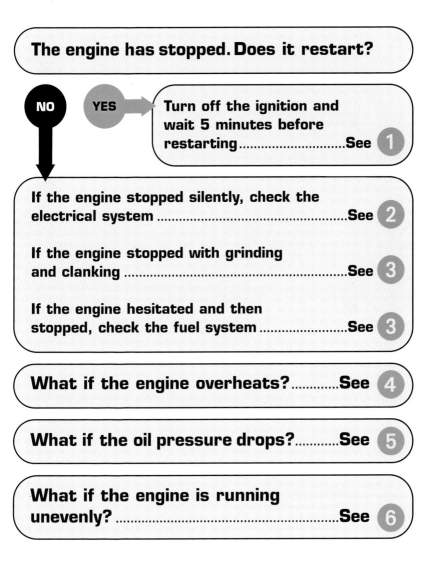

The engine has stopped. Does it restart?

NO

YES → **Turn off the ignition and wait 5 minutes before restarting**................**See** **1**

If the engine stopped silently, check the electrical system................................**See** **2**

If the engine stopped with grinding and clanking................................**See** **3**

If the engine hesitated and then stopped, check the fuel system................**See** **3**

What if the engine overheats?............**See** **4**

What if the oil pressure drops?............**See** **5**

What if the engine is running unevenly?..............................**See** **6**

Restarting and venting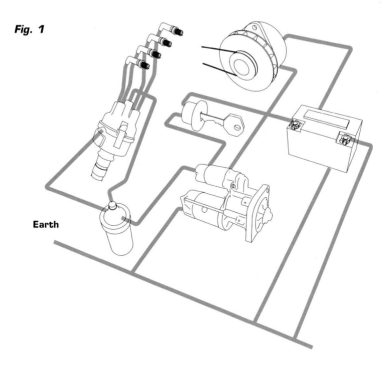

If the engine stops, wait at least 5 minutes before restarting to allow any fuel fumes to disperse. All boats with an inboard gasoline/petrol engine need to have proper fresh-air ducting to their engine compartments. Under most national marine safety regulations, a blower/extractor system should also be installed.

Engine electrical systems

If no noise occurred when the engine stopped, an electrical fault is probable. Check the electrical system (figure 1). The battery may be dead, especially if the starter motor will not turn over. A connection between the battery ignition switch and starter motor circuit may be defective. Check the spark plugs and distributor head. Often, only the plugs will have to be replaced: always carry spares.

Fig. 1

Earth

Engine faults ...... ③

If the engine stops with grinding and clanking noises, serious damage is probably at hand. If it hesitates and stops, the fault is most likely with the fuel system. Check the instruction manual. The fuel tank may be empty. If not, there is probably a blockage in the line, or the fuel pump may have malfunctioned. Blow out the fuel line. If there is still no result, dismantle or replace the pump (check its instruction manual) (figure 2).

Fig. 2

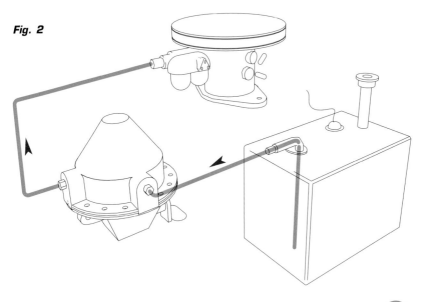

Overheating ...... ④

If the temperature rises, turn off the engine immediately. Overheating can be caused by a blocked water inlet, a broken pump, low oil level, or a fouled propeller. Most likely, it will be a failed impeller in the water pump. Install a spare.

Oil pressure ...... ⑤

If the oil-pressure drops, stop the engine and check the oil level. Refill as necessary. Do not run the engine unless absolutely necessary.

Uneven running ...... ⑥

Uneven running is probably due to a fouled plug or bad timing. Replace the sparkplug. Also check the fuel filter for debris. If unevenness persists, have a mechanic check it out.

FIRE: Engine

An engine fire is—short of sinking—the most frightening emergency possible in a yacht. Electrical short circuiting, explosions, and sparking can all cause a major blaze. Since the engine(s) are almost always located toward the stern of the boat, it is imperative that fire extinguishers be kept both at the companionway and in a cockpit locker. Modern engine installations may have a self-activating extinguishing system in the engine compartment. Make sure that the engine is shut down as fast as is possible.

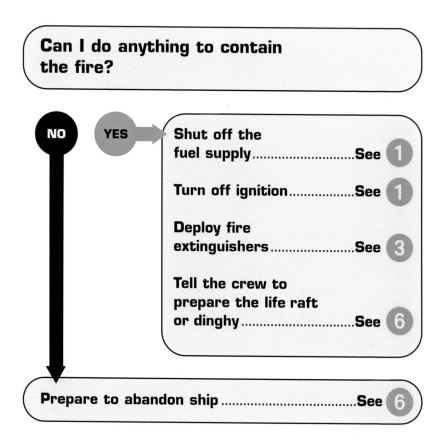

Can I do anything to contain the fire?

NO

YES

Shut off the
fuel supply .... See 1

Turn off ignition .... See 1

Deploy fire
extinguishers .... See 3

Tell the crew to
prepare the life raft
or dinghy .... See 6

Prepare to abandon ship .... See 6

Do you have an automatic extinguishing system?

NO

YES →

Keep it maintained ....See **2**

If you have a Halon unit, shut off exhaust systems..............................See **4**

Stand by with a hand-operated unit ....See **3**

Have manual fire extinguishers at the ready...See **3**

Stand clear and aim carefully ....See **5**

Starving the engine **1**

It is vital to stop both fuel supply and ignition as soon as possible. This is especially true of gasoline/petrol engines, as an explosion can occur both within the engine and back to the fuel tanks which, since they are usually located beneath or alongside the cockpit, can cause serious injury or death.

Automatic extinguishing systems **2**

Please, please inspect and, if necessary, replace all engine room extinguisher valves at least twice each season. Since engine spaces are usually the most ignored places aboard—at least on sailing vessels— they are subject to all the ills of bad boat husbandry: oil accumulation, severe damp, grit, and old rags. Valves cannot only be corroded, they can be blocked by grease and debris. Likewise, all wiring for all systems should be kept clear of the bilges; should not be run near or over working or hot parts of the engine; should be secured carefully; and should have all terminal fittings lightly coated with waterproof grease.

If any of these precautions is ignored, it is very likely that the system will fail when you most need it. In case of fire, do not rely absolutely on your automatic system: stand by with an appropriate hand-operated unit.

Manual fire extinguishers...................3

Keep extinguishers both at the companionway and in a cockpit locker. Using hand-operated extinguishers is not difficult, but does demand calm and intelligence. Different types of fires (ordinary combustibles, type A; flammable liquids, type B; electrical fires, type C) require different types of extinguishers. Water extinguishers can be used for type A fires, CO_2 for types A and B, and dry powder for all three. You should carry several types of extinguisher and everyone on board should be acquainted with their operation. Fire one off in practice, with crew present. Hold them steady and point them directly at the source of the flame (figure 1).

Fig. 1

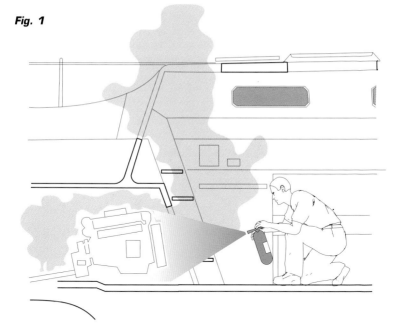

Halon extinguishing units...................4

The new production of halon is banned in the United States and Europe, but some older boats are equipped with Halon extinguishing units. When using one, close the exhaust valve (even before shutting off the ignition), as Halon can be sucked out through the engine before it can work effectively.

Firefighting

Engines are, of course, rarely out in the open—they are covered by hatches, companion steps, or casings. If you are in the cockpit when the fire commences, get below before you open the engine compartment. Cockpit engine hatches should not be opened, as the flames shooting out will be sure to burn someone.

Escape

If the fire gets out of control while you are below, DO NOT ATTEMPT TO ESCAPE THROUGH THE COMPANIONWAY. Use the forward hatch, and prepare to abandon ship (figure 2). In the event of any fire, have the crew prepare the life raft or dinghy to stand by. Unless you are aboard a steel or aluminum boat, the chances of a runaway blaze not causing the boat to founder are minimal. Fiberglass, unless laid-up with fire-retardant resins, will soon turn into an inferno. If you cannot contain the fire, don't fight in vain. GET OFF THE BOAT.

Fig. 2

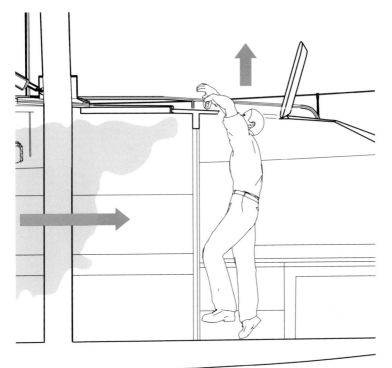

FIRE: Stove

Although not nearly as horrifying as an engine fire, stove flare-ups and fires can still cause serious damage to a boat. Alcohol (meths) and kerosene (paraffin) are intrinsically safer fuels than gas, but most yachts are fitted with gas stoves. Most common is LPG (liquid petroleum gas), held in a separate tank in a self-draining locker. In some areas natural gas can be found. Being lighter than air, it poses less danger, but it will mean fitting your stove with new burners.

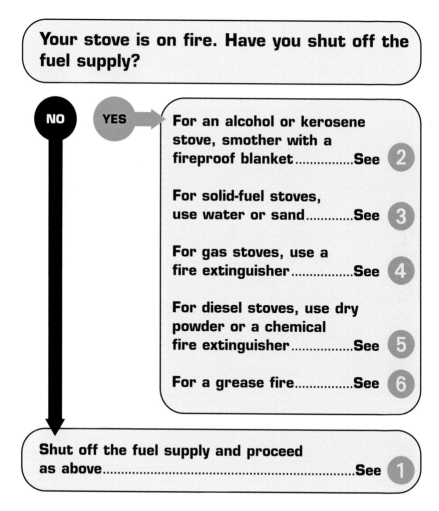

Your stove is on fire. Have you shut off the fuel supply?

NO   YES

For an alcohol or kerosene stove, smother with a fireproof blanket..............See **2**

For solid-fuel stoves, use water or sand............See **3**

For gas stoves, use a fire extinguisher................See **4**

For diesel stoves, use dry powder or a chemical fire extinguisher................See **5**

For a grease fire................See **6**

Shut off the fuel supply and proceed as above...See **1**

**Your gas or diesel stove is on fire.
Do you have a suitable fire extinguisher?**

NO

YES ➤ **Follow procedures outlined
in Fire: Engine p.72.**

Smother the flames with a
fireproof blanket..See **2**

How can I safeguard against gas
explosions?..See **4**

What can I do to prevent other
stove fires?..See **6**

Shut off valves..**1**

Both stove and tank valves must be closed. If the stove valve cannot
be reached due to flames, shut off the tank valve. Some modern installations
have remote-control valves, either mechanical or electrical. These can
be wired to simultaneously cut the fuel supply at both valve locations.

Alcohol (meths) and kerosene
(paraffin) stoves..**2**

Use a fiberglass or other flame-
retardant treated blanket to
smother the flames (figure 1).
The blanket must be kept close
at hand. Alcohol stoves, though
rarely used except in the USA,
have a low flash point and can be
extinguished with water (figure 2,
over the page). However, the
splashing water can also carry
flaming alcohol with it, possibly
igniting curtains, upholstery, or
even the container of spirits used
for preheating the burners.

Fig. 1

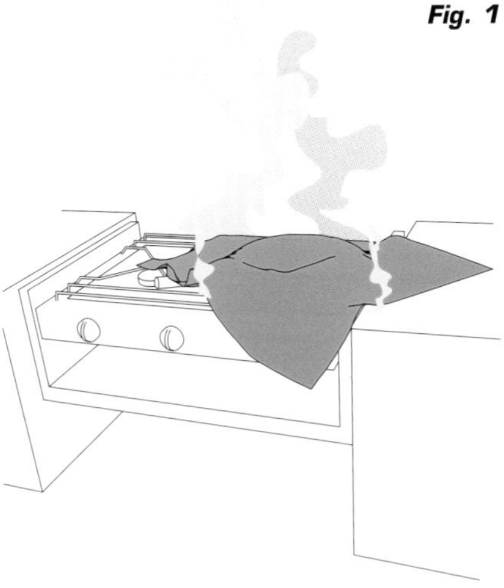

Fig. 2

Wood and coal stoves ....

Wood and coal fires can of course be put out with water. However, it is handy to keep a container or bag of sand nearby (figure 3). It will be safer than using water—no steam—and usually easier to clean up afterwards. This applies to both heating and cooking stoves.

Fig. 3

Gas stoves 4

Propane and other gas fires are the most dangerous. Flames can travel through these fuel lines much faster than with other fuels. A fail-safe device must be fitted to the stove, and every precaution must be made to keep all equipment in prime operating condition. Explosion is the greatest risk. If a flare-up occurs, immediately shut off the gas and resort to a fire extinguisher (figure 4). Use the utmost caution when lighting a gas stove. Constantly check the system for gas leaks using soapy water on the valves and connection points of the hoses. Make sure the connectors are secure and the hoses are undamaged at least once a season. With the exception of CNG (compressed natural gas) this entire class of fuels is heavier than air, and can be ignited by the simple act of striking a wrench against the engine block.

Fig. 4

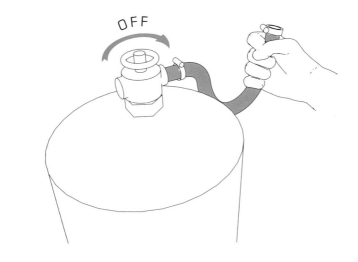

Diesel stoves 5

Use dry powder or a chemical fire extinguisher. These should be kept to hand.

Grease fires 6

Keep the stove clean! A grease fire can cause just as much damage as any other. Either smother a grease fire or use a fire extinguisher.

FOG

We rely almost totally on our eyes when on the water. Fog puts an end to that, resulting in insecurity, confusion, and fear. Fog also distorts our hearing, making it difficult to judge direction and distance of oncoming ships. GPS and radar have helped immeasurably in coping with fog, but basic seamanship must not be forgotten.

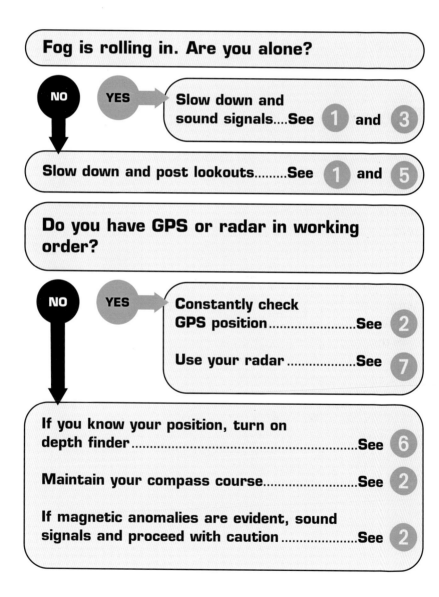

Fog is rolling in. Are you alone?

NO / YES → Slow down and sound signals....See **1** and **3**

Slow down and post lookouts........See **1** and **5**

Do you have GPS or radar in working order?

NO / YES → Constantly check GPS position.....................See **2**

Use your radar.................See **7**

If you know your position, turn on depth finder...See **6**

Maintain your compass course.......................See **2**

If magnetic anomalies are evident, sound signals and proceed with caution...................See **2**

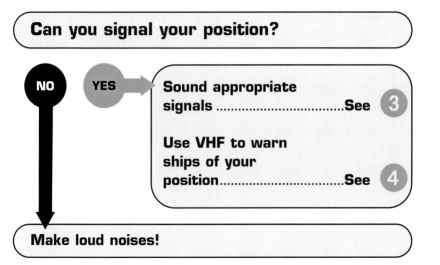

Can you signal your position?

NO → **Make loud noises!**

YES → Sound appropriate signals ....See ③

Use VHF to warn ships of your position ....See ④

Reducing speed .... ①

Fog is usually accompanied by little or no wind. However, there are times and places where dense fog will coexist with strong breezes. In such situations, decrease throttle if under power or reduce sail more than you would normally. In dense fogs, visibility may be down to less than 300 feet (100 meters), and anything other than dead slow ahead poses a real threat to the vessel and crew.

Navigation .... ②

Human senses become less than reliable in foggy conditions: sounds are distorted, shapes appear and disappear, ships creep in and out of banks that suddenly close in. GPS and radar can help determine your position, but if they fail for any reason, the most reliable navigational tool in such situations is the traditional ship's compass. Of course, you have made sure it is corrected and compensated before setting out. Trust it! No matter what your senses indicate, the compass is a safer bet. It is not subject to psychological pressures, it doesn't drink, and it won't fall overboard. If magnetic anomalies are evident, proceed with utmost caution at dead slow ahead.

Signals 3

Sound signals international rules

One blast: I am turning to starboard.

Two blasts: I am turning to port.

Three blasts: I am going astern.

Five blasts: Beware! I am in doubt concerning your intentions.

Short, long, short blasts: Warning! Danger of collision.

The signals above are to be sounded on a horn or whistle. The ringing of a bell signifies a vessel aground or at anchor. If attempting to home in on an audible signal, remember that fog can distort apparent sound direction. Proceed with utmost caution.

VHF radio 4

Knowing how to use your VHF radio is an absolute necessity. Post a crew member at the VHF and relay your position at regular intervals. If you hear breakers or what sounds like a large ship approaching, request coast guard aid, or send a MAYDAY. See Radio p.156.

Lookouts ....

Always post the person with the best eyesight in the bows (figure 1). They will be able to give some warning of impending danger. Prearrange signals with the helmsman.

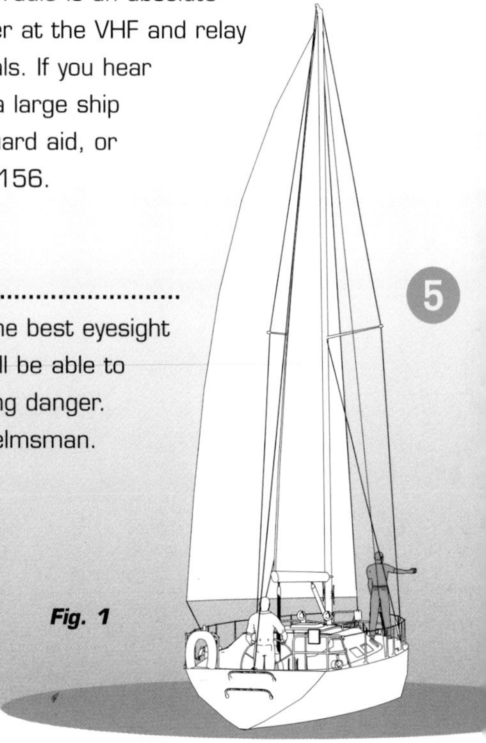

Fig. 1

Contour navigation

6

Contour navigation—following a sounding line on the chart—can be most useful in fog conditions (figure 2). You must know your position, and must have an accurate, calibrated depth finder aboard, as well as an adjusted compass with deviation table. You then proceed to take soundings in a continuous run in the charted direction. Any deviation from the charted sounding line will become immediately apparent from the soundings. One person should man the chart and depth sounder and call out bearings, course, and soundings to the helmsman.

Fig. 2

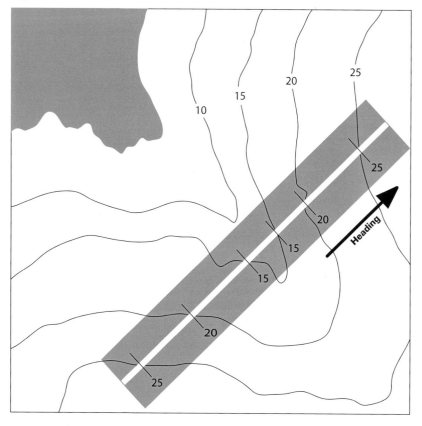

Radar

7

Radar is not often found aboard small yachts, but recent developments are putting it in the range of affordability, and scanner size and power requirements are decreasing. Radar, depending on range, it can show you exactly what is ahead of you in most, if not all, conditions. See Radar p.153.

Rounding a headland in fog

You find yourself in fog with a headland to round and must calculate an accurate DR approach. Figure 3 shows A as your DR plot. Give yourself a large area of uncertainty, say 8 percent instead of 5 percent of distance sailed, then take the two worst points on the circle: A1 the most easterly and A2 the most southerly. A, B, C would be your normal fine weather course, but if sailed from A1 or A2 would run you ashore. Figure 4 shows a course 265°, 8 miles (13 km); 223°, 7.5 miles (12 km); 180° onward if sailed from A1 or A2 would take you clear of the headland.

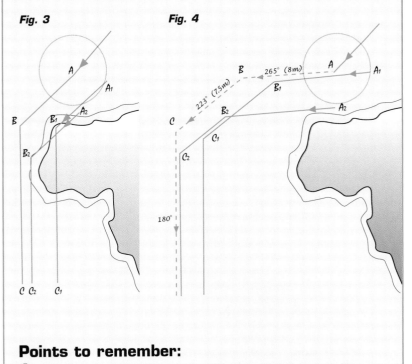

Fig. 3

Fig. 4

Points to remember:

1. This course must be corrected for tidal direction prevailing at the time.

2. Your area of uncertainty is growing continually and if the fog does not lift you should keep off after rounding the headland.

3. At all times you will be plotting radio bearings, listening for fog signals, and using your depth sounder. DO NOT CUT INSIDE your safe course unless you are certain it is safe to do so.

HEAVY WEATHER:
Prepare

Deteriorating weather conditions are never to be taken lightly. How you and your boat are prepared for heavy weather can make the difference between safe arrival in port and disaster. There is nothing man can build that nature can't destroy. Take time before setting out on any voyage to assess your boat and its capabilities in survival conditions.

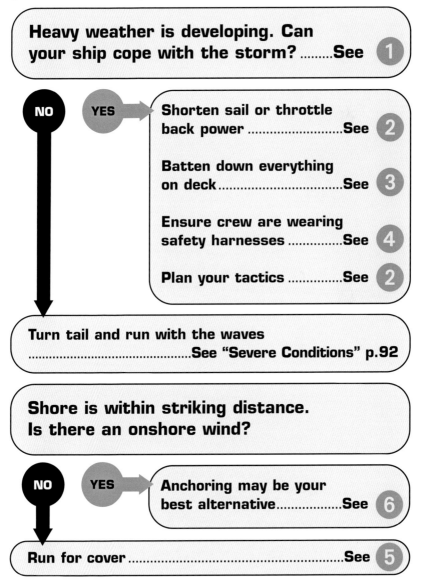

Heavy weather is developing. Can your ship cope with the storm? ....See **1**

NO

YES → **Shorten sail or throttle back power** ....See **2**

Batten down everything on deck ....See **3**

Ensure crew are wearing safety harnesses ....See **4**

Plan your tactics ....See **2**

Turn tail and run with the waves ....See "Severe Conditions" p.92

Shore is within striking distance. Is there an onshore wind?

NO

YES → **Anchoring may be your best alternative** ....See **6**

Run for cover ....See **5**

Deteriorating weather 1

When the weather deteriorates to a point where handling the ship under reduced sail or power becomes difficult, when the size of the seas endangers the integrity of the ship, or when progress in a safe direction becomes near impossible, you are in danger. These three criteria are not the only ones, but they can serve as a good guide to the next set of maneuvers. All are dependent on weather fronts, winds, and depressions. The size and displacement of your vessel will have some bearing upon meeting the above criteria. Obviously a ketch of 45 feet (15 meters) LOA will be able to cope with large seas with greater assurance and safety than a power vessel of 30 feet (10 meters) LOA. Any sound vessel, however, can undertake precautionary maneuvers to allow more or less equitable coping with bad conditions.

Tactics 2

When the wind pipes up, the first thing to do is to reduce sail. However, balance is equally important, especially when reaching or beating to windward. The larger vessel will be able to hold a course longer in a rising wind than a small boat, due to displacement, sail-carrying ability, and a larger crew (figure 1). A powerboat, without the ballast or lateral plane of a sailing yacht, will have different problems to cope with. The key is to keep green water from coming aboard. Running in a powerboat demands keeping speed at one with the wave length, plowing to windward invariably demands throttling back, while progress in beam seas is very much a function of the dynamic stability of the hull. When the weather is truly nasty, an appropriate reduction of speed is invariably the best seamanlike judgment.

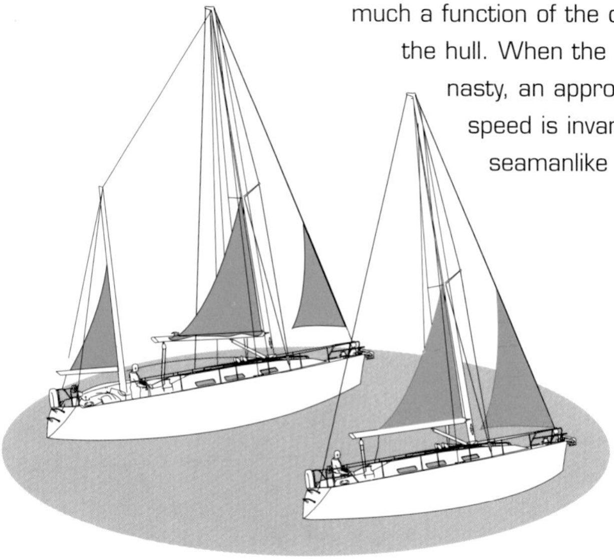

Fig. 1

Battening down

Everything on deck and below must be secured in heavy weather. Sails, anchors, lines, and life raft must be attached to the boat in a manner that precludes loss overboard (figure 2). Anchors should be given double lashings with heavy line: a loose object of such shape and weight can easily hole a hull given the opportunity. Below decks, batteries have to be tied down, locker doors made strong and secure—no friction or magnetic catches—books fiddled or lashed in place, stove gimbals closed, etc. Even floorboards should be able to be fastened, perhaps with button catches. In a knockdown, you will have a mess below, but any heavy object or glass or sharp implement can cause major injuries or even death. Try to avoid the worst. At the beginning of the season, it's even a good idea to tighten the engine bed fastenings. There have been cases of engines tearing loose from their mountings and causing boats to founder. Be sure to secure all hatches, ventilators, hatch boards, and sea cocks.

Fig. 2

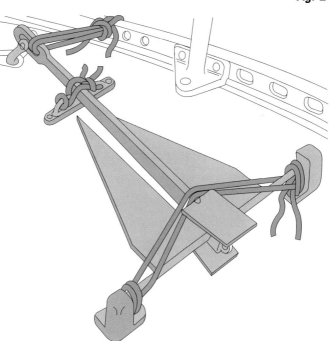

Safety harnesses 4

Safety harnesses are *de rigueur* at night and in anything over a Force 5 (figure 3). They ought to be to government standard and constructed with two lanyards with proofed hooks/snaps. The deck attachment points must be through-bolted (figure 4). Lacking such, or in emergencies, crew can lash themselves to binnacle or tracks.

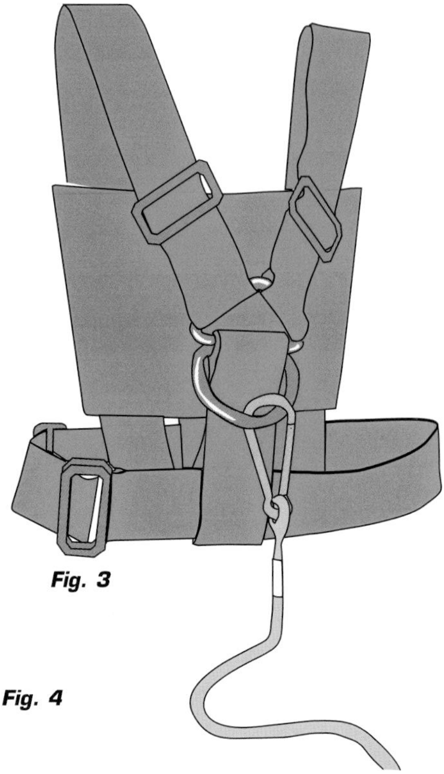

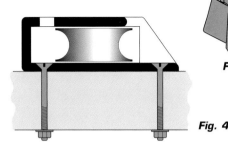

Fig. 3

Fig. 4

Safe havens 5

If you are within striking distance of a safe harbor, it may be wise to run for cover. However, in any onshore wind, entering harbor may be extremely hazardous, especially if a bar must be crossed. Unless you have local knowledge, you are better off riding out the storm at sea.

Anchoring 6

How you will actually handle the boat in heavy weather depends to a great extent on the size of the ship, the capacity of the crew, the size of the seas, and strength of the wind. Proximity to land plays a major role in deciding tactics. In a storm, with a lee shore in sight, the inability to beat to windward and an inexperienced crew, anchoring—providing the proper ground tackle is aboard—may be the only alternative. But every situation demands informed judgment—see Heavy Weather: Tactics p.87.

HEAVY WEATHER:
Tactics

In heavy weather conditions, preparation and alertness are vital. Although it is hard to keep calm when faced with a Force 10 storm, your survival depends on it. When an unexpected storm arises, it is essential that you are aware of the dangers and match your maneuvers to the sailing conditions.

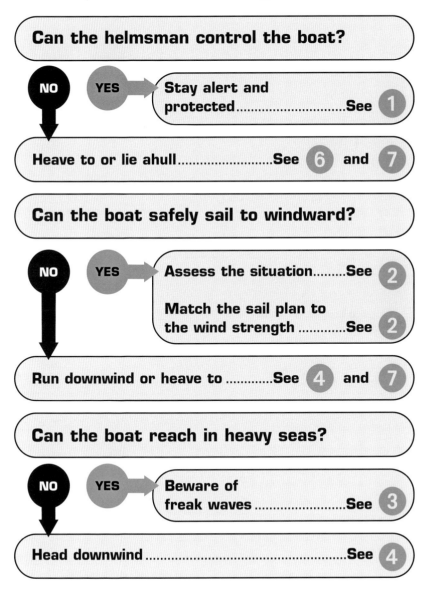

Can the helmsman control the boat?

NO   YES → Stay alert and protected..............................See **1**

Heave to or lie ahull.........................See **6** and **7**

Can the boat safely sail to windward?

NO   YES → Assess the situation.........See **2**

Match the sail plan to the wind strength ....See **2**

Run downwind or heave to ....See **4** and **7**

Can the boat reach in heavy seas?

NO   YES → Beware of freak waves ....See **3**

Head downwind ....See **4**

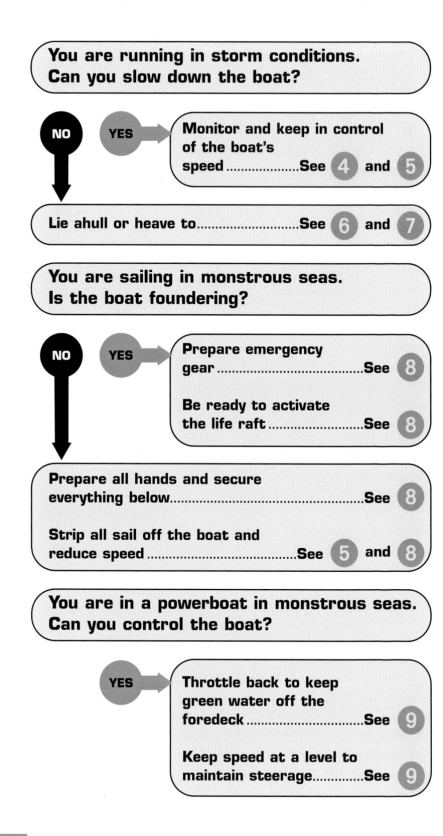

You are running in storm conditions.
Can you slow down the boat?

NO   **YES** → Monitor and keep in control of the boat's speed .... See **4** and **5**

Lie ahull or heave to .... See **6** and **7**

You are sailing in monstrous seas.
Is the boat foundering?

NO   **YES** → Prepare emergency gear .... See **8**

Be ready to activate the life raft .... See **8**

Prepare all hands and secure everything below .... See **8**

Strip all sail off the boat and reduce speed .... See **5** and **8**

You are in a powerboat in monstrous seas.
Can you control the boat?

YES → Throttle back to keep green water off the foredeck .... See **9**

Keep speed at a level to maintain steerage .... See **9**

NO

Send a MAYDAY
if floating............................See Signals p.172 and 9

Prepare to abandon ship
if sinking ....See Abandoning Ship p.8 and 9

The helmsman 1

The key person as the weather deteriorates is the helmsman. He (or she) needs to be fresh, alert, and sensitive. He must keep a watch to windward for approaching waves, and must be alert to the need for sudden maneuvers. Keep him as protected, warm, and dry as possible. When changing the guard, allow the relief to acclimatize himself to the course, conditions, and feel of the helm before switching. A less experienced hand may require that sail be reduced to give greater control. This is a decision the skipper must make, giving due regard to approaching fronts, the need to reach port, etc.

Sailing to windward 2

Sailing to windward demands not only a good eye. The necessity of pacing the boat to the height of the waves is vital. The helm should luff slightly as he comes down the face of a wave, slowing the boat and allowing the bows to rise to the oncoming crest (figure 1). Otherwise there is a good chance of burying the bows and causing loss and damage to the deck gear and crew. The boat should have minimum steerage when approaching the crest of the next wave, as the speed generated surfing down the back of the wave will usually be sufficient to ascend the next one. The maneuver is one of weaving, and increasing and decreasing speed offwind and upwind so as to keep the boat moving with a reasonable motion and as little threat to ship and crew as possible.

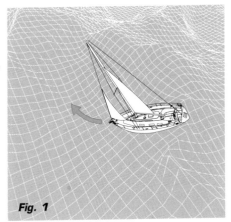

Fig. 1

Wind on the beam .... (3)

In really heavy weather, sailing in a beam sea can be courting disaster. Cresting waves can fill cockpits, cause knockdowns, or stove in a deckhouse. In less momentous seas, a tendency to broach or a difficulty in steering will probably be experienced. Either shorten sail or head off with the wind on the quarter (figure 2).

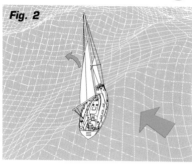
Fig. 2

Running .... (4)

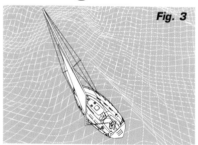
Fig. 3

Running can be an exhilarating experience. However, when seas build to a point where steering becomes difficult, extreme care will be needed at the helm to avoid a broach. In gale or storm conditions, don't play racer and try to carry spinnakers. Rather, reduce sail to a point where the boat is moving at optimum speed (figure 3), neither in danger of surfing so fast as to be falling off the wave tops nor so slow as to lose steerage way. In mid-ocean monster storms, you will almost always need to slow the boat down (see "Reducing speed" below).

Reducing speed .... (5)

To reduce speed in severe conditions, several methods are available. Trailing warps from the stern does work (figure 4). However, they must be many and attached so as to distribute the strains around the ship. Occasionally, anchors can be trailed from the stern on warps or bundles of chain (figure 5). However, be sure to rig tripping devices or you may never get the items aboard again. Ideally, you will let the warps out as needed. This does assume, however, that several hundred meters

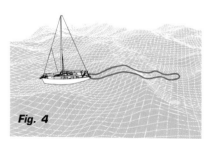
Fig. 4

Fig. 5

of heavy line are aboard. Another possibility is to stream a Galerider (figure 6) or Jordan series drogue. These webbing baskets (Galerider) or fabric cones (Jordan) are attached along a length of line and slow the vessel with minimal strain.

Fig. 6

Lying ahull 6

Fig. 7

When you can no longer sail under reduced canvas and/or exhaustion sets in you may try lying ahull, when all sail is stowed, tiller is lashed, and the ship left to look after herself (figure 7). This can be a perfectly sound tactic, providing the sea room exists for leeward drift and some forward motion due to the area presented by rigging, spars, and hull and tophamper. Some experiences have suggested that a shallow-hulled craft will be safer at this maneuver than a deep-draft one, as the deep keel can cause a tripping effect in certain sized seas, possibly causing a knockdown or rollover. It is also a good tactic for the single-hander in a small boat.

Heaving to 7

Heaving to is a simple way to slow a boat down. The only maneuver is to tack, leaving the headsail as is (figure 8). Ease the main and lash the helm to leeward (rudder to windward). By adjusting the mainsheet and helm, the boat will forereach slowly—depending on tophamper, sail area, keel depth, etc. The headsail should be brought in tightly before heaving to. In heavier conditions the main might well be dropped and secured. Leeway will be made, so do not attempt to heave to off a lee shore except for a short time and with little sail and a deep-draft hull. Make adjustments to allow for as little leeway as possible, perhaps by trimming the main to allow stronger forereaching. Chafe is a problem when hove to; the practice is better with a working jib or storm jib than with a genoa or lapper. Chafe protection around the sheet where it crosses the shrouds will not go amiss. The old saw about heaving to on the starboard tack is irrelevant. Most

Fig. 8

commercial shipping will not alter course even if they see you.

Caution: Many modern sailing hulls cannot be made to heave to effectively. Their underwater profile is so slight that they will head off downwind or be knocked down no matter what tactics you may attempt.

Severe conditions.. 8

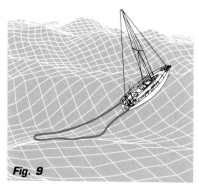

Fig. 9

In survival conditions—Force 10 (or Force 9 in a smaller yacht) and upward—the strength of the wind and the severity and height of the seas, will mean that the only possible point of sail will be running. Rid the deck of all impediments that may be carried away or hamper whatever work on deck is possible. Trailing warps or deploying a Galerider or Jordan drogue are the best tactics (figure 9). Warps should be streamed one at a time until the speed of the ship is lowered so that control is possible and following seas present the least threat. High concentration at the helm is necessary and watches may be only one hour or less. If the lines trailed are in a bight and long enough to coincide with the seas aft, the bight may well serve to inhibit crests and smooth the attacking demons. In any storm or ultimate seas, stay with the boat unless it is truly foundering. Life rafts are too easily flipped, drift away, or cannot be entered with any degree of safety. Even with improvements—ballast pockets, drogues, heavy tether lines—chances are that you will be safer in the mother ship so long as she remains tight. In any case, be prepared!

Powerboats 9

Powerboats have both advantages and disadvantages over sailing yachts in bad weather. Due to their speed, they can often outrun a storm front. However, they have far less maneuverability at slow speeds than a sailboat, especially with their high bridges and smaller, if any, keels. If seas are so high that solid water starts to come over the bows, the boat should be turned downwind, and speed kept at a level that is in rhythm with the waves. This is not easy, as the wide beam and flat sterns of many powerboats cause the ship to yaw in heavy going. The ship must not be allowed to come beam on to the seas—rollover or capsize is a real possibility. If you are unable to control the boat and she remains floating, stay with the ship and send a MAYDAY. Otherwise, prepare to abandon ship. See Abandoning Ship p.8.

Beaufort Scale

Force	Speed in Knots	Description	Specifications
0	0–1	Calm	Sea like a mirror.
1	1–3	Light Air	Ripples with the appearance of scales are formed, but without foam crests.
2	4–6	Light Breeze	Small wavelets, still short, but more pronounced. Crests have glassy appearance, do not break.
3	7–10	Gentle Breeze	Large wavelets. Crests begin to break. Foam of glassy appearance. Perhaps scattered white horses.
4	11–16	Moderate Breeze	Small waves, becoming larger; fairly frequent white horses.
5	17–21	Fresh Breeze	Moderate waves, taking a more pronounced long form; many white horses are formed. Chance of spray.
6	22–27	Strong Breeze	Large waves begin to form; the white foam crests are more extensive everywhere. Probably some spray.
7	28–33	Near Gale	Sea heaps up and white foam from breaking waves begins to be blown in streaks along the direction of the wind.
8	34–40	Gale	Moderately high waves of greater length; edges of crests begin to break into spindrift. The foam is blown in well-marked streaks along the direction of the wind.
9	41–47	Severe Gale	High waves. Dense streaks of foam along the direction of the wind. Crests of waves begin to topple, tumble, and roll over. Spray may affect visibility.
10	48–55	Storm	Very high waves with long over-hanging crests. The resulting foam, in great patches, is blown in dense white streaks along the direction of the wind. On the whole, the surface of the sea takes on a white appearance. The "tumbling" of the sea becomes heavy and shock-like. Visibility affected.
11	56–63	Violent Storm	Exceptionally high waves (small and medium-size ships might be for a time lost to view behind the waves). The sea is completely covered with long white patches of foam lying along the direction of the wind. Everywhere the edges of the wave crests are blown into froth. Visibility affected.
12	64–71	Hurricane	The air is filled with foam and spray. Sea completely white with driving spray; visibility very seriously affected.

HOLING

The random scattering of rocks around out coasts is one of the pesky little facts of geology. Coupled with the almost endless supply of flotsam and jetsam lurking at, or just below, the surface of our waters, the chances of hitting a submerged object is increasing at an alarming rate. If you do manage to run over or hit a rock, floating log, or container, you may well damage the hull. You must act *fast*! Any ingress of water is a potential death sentence for your boat.

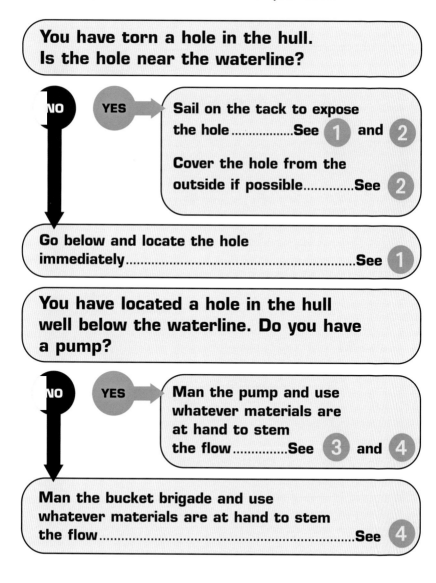

You have torn a hole in the hull. Is the hole near the waterline?

NO

YES → Sail on the tack to expose the hole.................See **1** and **2**

Cover the hole from the outside if possible.............See **2**

Go below and locate the hole immediately...See **1**

You have located a hole in the hull well below the waterline. Do you have a pump?

NO

YES → Man the pump and use whatever materials are at hand to stem the flow...............See **3** and **4**

Man the bucket brigade and use whatever materials are at hand to stem the flow..See **4**

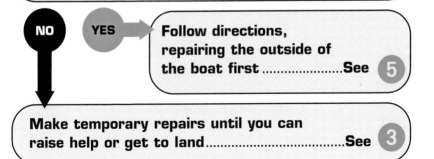

You have slowed a leak and need to make repairs. Do you have underwater-hardening epoxy paste?

NO

YES → Follow directions, repairing the outside of the boat first ....**See** 5

Make temporary repairs until you can raise help or get to land.......................................**See** 3

Assessing the damage 1

If you strike an object, immediately go below and check for damage. If the hull has been holed near the waterline, sail on the tack to keep the hole above water. More than likely, the hole will be hidden behind bunks or lockers or beneath immoveable floorboards. There is only one solution: TEAR THE FURNITURE OUT! It hurts, but failure to do so will likely result in foundering. Using a pry bar, axe, or large wrench, remove the offending woodwork (or glasswork).

Changing tack 2

Any ingress of water caused by holing near the waterline can be staunched by changing tack, thus exposing the hole. This may even allow you to cover the break from the outside. In the process, shorten sail to the minimum needed to keep the yacht heeled over.

Stemming the flow 3

Use either an umbrella patch or cushions stuffed into or against the hole to stop the major flow (figure 1, over the page). Another possibility is to use a plumber's helper over the hole, preferably from the outside. If the hole is well below the waterline, the inflow of water will be close to twice as fast as higher up, and may be much harder to reach. The storm jib, with lines at each corner, can be passed around the hull from the outside to form a patch. Reduce the speed of the vessel to allow the sail to stay in position. Weight one corner to allow it to sink below the water with chain or odd fitments shackled together.

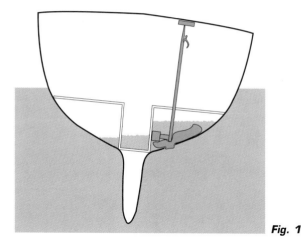

Fig. 1

Pumping 4

No matter how hard and fast you work, a lot of water will enter the
ship. The average manual bilge pump—25 gallons per minute—will be
next to useless when up against a flow of over 200 gallons per minute,
which is what you can expect from a hole about 4 inches in diameter.
Only a high-capacity engine-driven pump can handle a flow like that, and
then only if the engine has not been flooded. A bucket brigade can be of
help, but the key is speed in locating the hole and speed and efficiency
in stemming the flow.

Permanent repairs 5

Once the flow is stopped, or slowed to a leak, more permanent repairs
can be effected. Perhaps the best material, in anything but a wooden
boat, is underwater-hardening epoxy paste. Follow directions, but do try
to apply on the outside first with some sort of temporary board or
backing held in place. Then apply to the interior. Remember to spread
the paste well past the area of the hole to allow for good surface
adhesion. In a wooden ship, boards and caulking can be used to first
seal the opening from within, with further repairs made from the
outside as conditions allow.

ICING

Not many of us venture out on the water in winter, but for those who do, winter gales pose more threats than summer storms. Icing is a particularly insidious danger as it will increase weight and lessen stability, creating the conditions for a knockdown or capsize.

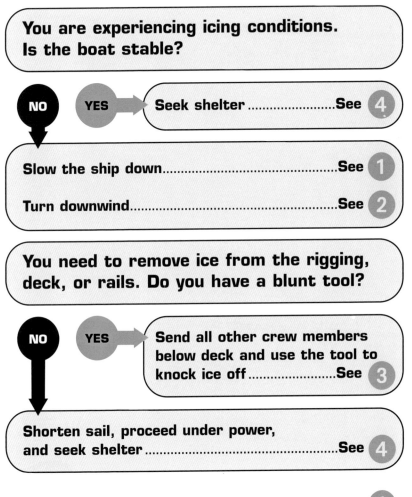

You are experiencing icing conditions. Is the boat stable?

NO / YES → Seek shelter ....See **4**

Slow the ship down................................See **1**

Turn downwind...See **2**

You need to remove ice from the rigging, deck, or rails. Do you have a blunt tool?

NO / YES → Send all other crew members below deck and use the tool to knock ice off ....See **3**

Shorten sail, proceed under power, and seek shelter ....See **4**

Slowing down **1**

Ice will increase the topside weight, reducing stability and the righting moment of any ship. Slowing the vessel will permit gentler motion and more time to remedy the condition.

Running downwind... 2

Since a sailing vessel is generally more stable when running, there will be less chance of capsize and an easier motion to work aloft. Keep up only enough sail to reduce rolling.

Ice removal.. 3

The only way to remove ice from the rigging, deck, or rails is to hack it off with a mallet or the dull side of a small axe (figure 1). Other than the deck man handling the bosun's chair, no one else should be on deck, as falling ice can inflict serious injury.

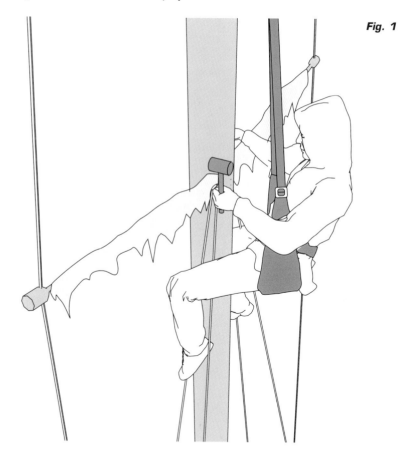

Fig. 1

Seeking shelter... 4

If conditions permit, keep up only a patch of sail to reduce rolling and proceed under power until the ice has been removed. Under any icing conditions, seek refuge as soon as possible. Not only is the ship in danger, but the crew can suffer from hypothermia and frostbite.

JURY RIGS: Masts

There are times—rare, to be sure—when the mast will be damaged or lost, fuel supply is low or nonexistent, and you must improvise to keep the ship moving. How you create a viable rig depends, of course, on your original sail plan, the length of the remaining spars, and the skills of you and the crew.

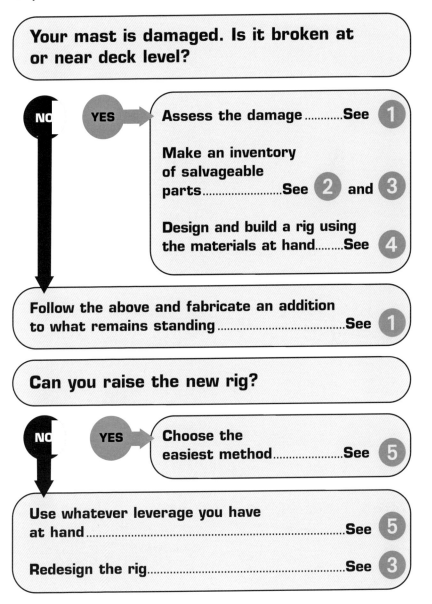

Your mast is damaged. Is it broken at or near deck level?

NO

YES

Assess the damage ....See **1**

Make an inventory of salvageable parts ....See **2** and **3**

Design and build a rig using the materials at hand ....See **4**

Follow the above and fabricate an addition to what remains standing ....See **1**

Can you raise the new rig?

NO

YES

Choose the easiest method ....See **5**

Use whatever leverage you have at hand ....See **5**

Redesign the rig ....See **3**

Do the sails fit the new rig?

NO

YES → Proceed using the best and safest means of propulsion.............................See **6**

Try different sail combinations or re-cut the sails...See **6**

Assessing the damage.............................. **1**

Depending upon the damage inflicted to the mast (see Dismasting p.42), a jury rig may be an addition to what remains standing, or it may be an entire make-do structure. If the mast has broken above the spreaders, the storm trysail may work as a mainsail with only a forestay and backstay pieced together from spare wire and wire rope clips, also known as bulldog clamps (figure 1). If only the mizzen remains, a forestay can be fashioned—albeit at a very low angle—and a jib can be modified to be set flying from said stay (figure 2). As long as the remaining bit of mast has retained the lower shrouds, a low-efficiency sailing rig is not only possible, but relatively simple to fabricate.

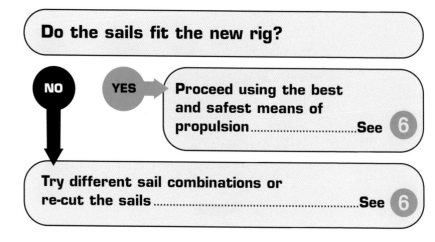

Fig. 1

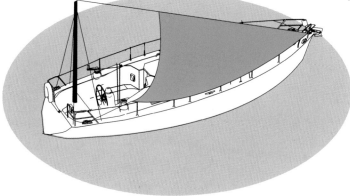

Fig. 2

Assessing the break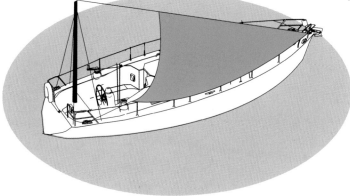

If the mast breaks at or near deck level, a different set of criteria apply. First see what is salvageable from the remains of your once noble spar. It may be possible to save stays, hardware, or a section of the spar itself. Before you decide what you will do, see what you have to work with.

Parts inventory

Having made an inventory of working materials—not forgetting oars, spinnaker and jockey poles, bunk fronts, etc.—sit below with a clean sheet of paper, some basic measurements (base of fore triangle, length of longest usable mast section, length of various salvaged wire, etc.), and a pencil and see what might be possible—what L. Francis Herreshoff called "thought experiments." It will be much easier than trying different combinations on deck in a seaway at night with the wind at Force 6. Perhaps the most important thing to remember is that the rig you design must be able to be created, hoisted, and used by the available manpower and the available skills. If you are within sight of land, turn on the engine! However, if you are mid-ocean you will want to devise something that will take you where you want to go on the available rations and water aboard in whatever weather you may reasonably expect to have.

Crew
4

Having decided on the solution, gather the crew, explain the jury rig
to them, and delegate one crew member to each task needed to raise
the rig. Collect and assemble all the necessary parts. Do as much as
possible with the new rig on deck. The less needed to do aloft, the
safer. Make sure, for example, that all the "mast-head" fittings are
secured, that the correct length wires and ropes are tied off. You don't
want to have to lower the whole mess if you can avoid it.

Raising the rig
5

Depending on size and
weight, raising the rig
can be a job for one
person with a winch
and a tripod
arrangement (figure 3)
or it can take the
muscles of 10 strong
men. Obviously, you
wish to get the thing
up with minimal effort.

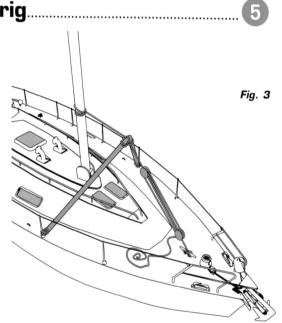

Fig. 3

Setting sail
6

Setting sail may mean adopting some odd and seemingly illogical
configurations. Jibs may be turned on end, or sewn together. Storm
sails may be the best driving sails for a reduced rig, and setting them
flying may be the best, and safest, means of propulsion. What is most
important is to devise a sail combination that will get you where you
wish to go. Quite often sprit sails, lateen rigs, make-shift schooners,
and squaresails will serve the purpose quite well if you know anything
about them. Unfortunately, the modern sailor has little use for working
sails of the past. The illustrations in figure 4 demonstrate their uses.

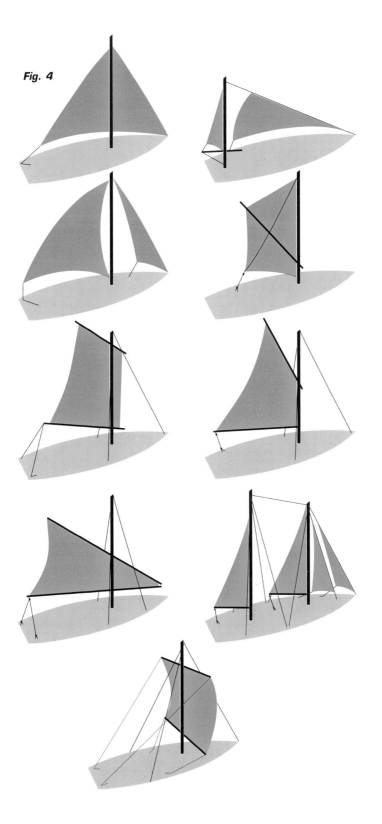

Fig. 4

JURY RIGS: Rudders

With a few exceptions, all boats are steered by means of their rudders. When a rudder gets stuck, bent, or broken, you may find yourself no longer in control of your ship. The majority of contemporary boats are equipped with hugely vulnerable spade rudders. Although these make maneuvering both quicker and more precise, they have the disadvantage of being supported only by the rudder shaft, tube, and bearings. Striking an underwater object with force will probably make the rudder inoperable. Additionally, since there is no support along the blade or at its foot, it is possible that the rudder will fall off completely.

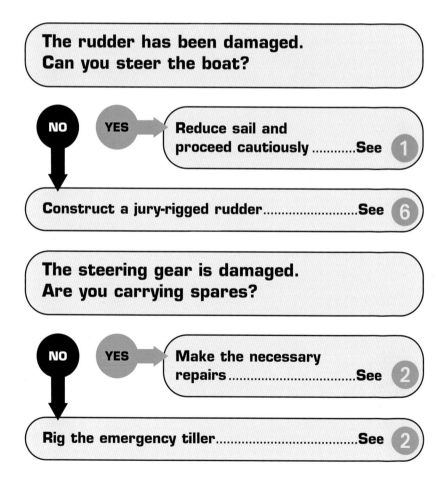

The rudder has been damaged. Can you steer the boat?

NO / **YES** → Reduce sail and proceed cautiously ....See **1**

Construct a jury-rigged rudder.........................See **6**

The steering gear is damaged. Are you carrying spares?

NO / **YES** → Make the necessary repairs ....See **2**

Rig the emergency tiller....................................See **2**

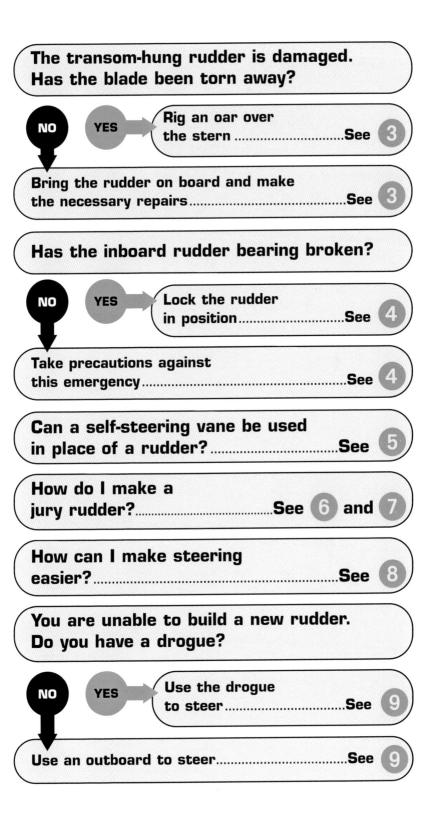

The transom-hung rudder is damaged. Has the blade been torn away?

NO

YES → Rig an oar over the stern ....**See** 3

Bring the rudder on board and make the necessary repairs ....**See** 3

Has the inboard rudder bearing broken?

NO

YES → Lock the rudder in position ....**See** 4

Take precautions against this emergency ....**See** 4

Can a self-steering vane be used in place of a rudder? ....**See** 5

How do I make a jury rudder? ....**See** 6 **and** 7

How can I make steering easier? ....**See** 8

You are unable to build a new rudder. Do you have a drogue?

NO

YES → Use the drogue to steer ....**See** 9

Use an outboard to steer ....**See** 9

Rudder damage ①

If steering becomes difficult or unresponsive, something is probably amiss with either the steering gear or the rudder itself. Either the rudder may be stuck to port or starboard, or the stock may be bent. Also, a cable or gear in the steering mechanism may be broken. If the rudder is inboard and the stock has been bent, ignore it. Instead, you will have to fashion a rudder or sweep to work off the transom. If the blade is damaged, it may still be possible to steer the boat, albeit with reduced sail. However, if the response is minimal and you are still some distance from port, some sort of jury-rigged rudder will have to be constructed.

Steering gear damage ②

Should the steering gear be damaged beyond repair, an emergency tiller should be aboard. Since many more yachts are wheel-steered now than even 20 years ago, essential spares should be carried—cable, clamps, sprocket wheels, gears, etc. However, parts of the gear may not be accessible without tearing out other equipment. You will have to weigh the pros and cons yourself. Obviously, you will never be covered for all contingencies. And, sooner or later, you will have to rig that emergency tiller. Accidents do happen which will incapacitate both wheel and rudder, in which case a jury rudder will be needed.

Transom-hung rudders ③

The simplest repairs are to a transom-hung rudder, which can be shipped and patched, or even replaced from parts fashioned from floorboards, hatchboards, etc. If the pintles and gudgeons are not bent or broken, repairs should be fairly straightforward, and if the rudder is wood, can be accomplished with screws and bolts (figure 1). If the rudder is fiberglass, the same methods can be used but reinforcement will be necessary in the form of load-spreading washers (of metal or wood) and lashings. However, if the major portion of the blade has been torn away, and the fastenings between rudder and hull are left without integrity, a new rudder assembly will have to be fashioned, or a long oar can be lashed over the stern.

Damaged area cut out

Fig. 1

Inboard rudders 4

Inboard rudders pose a different set of problems. If the rudder bearing has been broken, and the rudder is slamming back and forth, potential

Fig. 2

exists for major hull damage or rupture, especially in a seaway. Some means of locking the rudder in position, or even of shipping the entire assembly, will have to be devised. One good precaution is to drill a small hole in the trailing edge of the blade, with the foreknowledge that this will be used—should an emergency occur—to lead lines outboard and to the cockpit for steering (figure 2). If the blade can be set, a rudder aft will still have to be fashioned.

Fig. 3

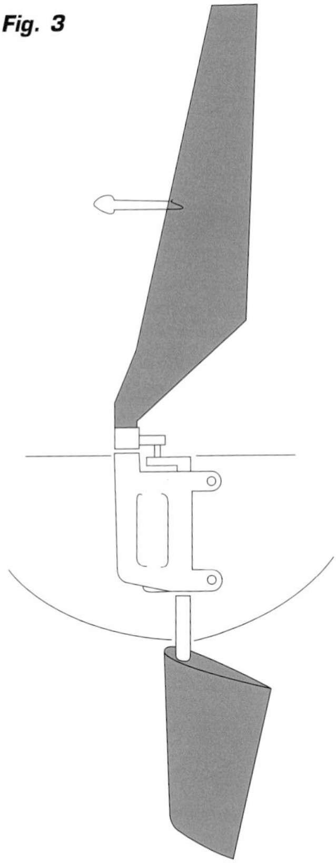

Self-steering 5

Some self-steering wind vanes can also act as an auxiliary rudder (figure 3). This potential might well be investigated when contemplating the purchase of a vane.

Making a jury rudder 6

To actually construct a new rudder, first gather the necessary materials: a pole or boom, spinnaker pole, or oar (if long enough); a blade substitute such as a hatchboard or section of floorboard; line, lashings, bolts, tools needed, etc. Fasten the pole to the blade with through bolts, U bolts, or anything that will produce a rigid structure. Next, determine how to attach the assembly to the stern. As long as the blade will be deeply immersed, any method will do. Stern shape will determine the most appropriate way of accomplishing this.

Mounting the jury rudder........................ 7

The easiest stern on which to mount your new rudder will be virtually plumb, utilizing the pushpit horizontals as fastening points, with stout lashings to hold the two together (figure 4). Reverse-counter transoms will demand a more deck-level approach with some fitting being used to hold the lashing. Traditional forward-sloping counters will do best to use the pushpit as above. Lacking guard rails aft, deck-level lashings will

Fig. 4

have to be used, remembering that with a single-point lashing some means will have to be devised to hold the blade in the water. Ballasting is one possibility (figure 5). Another is to run lines from a hole in the forward edge of the blade near the bottom, outboard, and forward to strong points on deck (figure 6). The backstay can also be used as a second lashing point for the pole/stock, remembering that any lashing used here will put enormous strains on the entire rig and should be used advisedly in heavy weather.

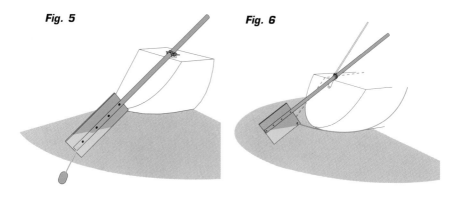

Fig. 5   *Fig. 6*

Ease of steering.. 8

There are several methods to ease steering. Lines can be led through snatch blocks attached to the pushpit at either outboard corner, or a spar can be lashed to the pushpit. In either case, lead lines from the new rudder "stock" through the blocks and thence to winches or cleats in the cockpit (figure 7). Despite advice to the contrary, it is always better to attempt to fix the tiller at the centerline. Even without a pushpit, some makeshift arrangement can be worked out on the afterdeck, usually by lashing a spar to the mooring cleats at the quarters and affixing the rudder stock to the spar.

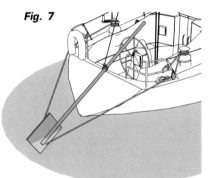

Fig. 7

Other means of steering .... ⑨

A drogue can be utilized for steering—tire, bucket, or proper drogue—with steering lines attached to the drogue line with rolling hitches (figure 8). To give the needed steering leverage, the ends of the steering lines should be led through blocks on either end of a fairly long spar lashed to the stern. Be sure to rig a tripping line for the drogue. You will find recovery difficult otherwise. Also, this arrangement, although the easiest to rig, will not offer the control of a jury rudder. Another possibility is to mount an outboard on the stern or boarding platform. You can move a surprising displacement with even a small outboard, slowly, to be sure.

Fig. 8

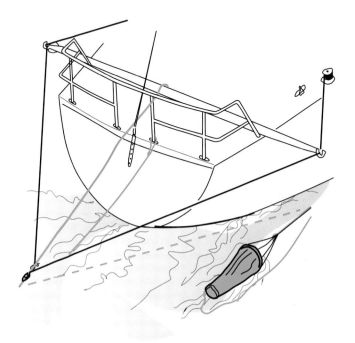

KEELS

Most sailboats and some powerboats have ballast keels. When they are fitted properly, with due concern for water-tightness and structural integrity, very little is likely to happen. However, depending on the type of keel and how it is attached to the hull, a grounding or sharp blow against an underwater obstacle can cause a leak or, horror of horrors, the loss of the entire keel.

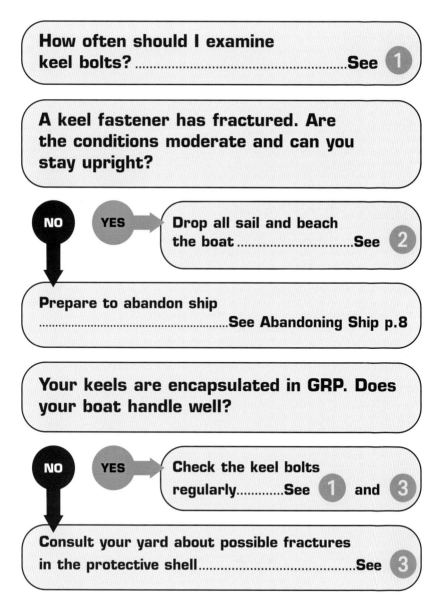

How often should I examine keel bolts?..See ①

A keel fastener has fractured. Are the conditions moderate and can you stay upright?

NO   **YES** ➤ **Drop all sail and beach the boat**..............................See ②

Prepare to abandon ship
....See Abandoning Ship p.8

Your keels are encapsulated in GRP. Does your boat handle well?

NO   **YES** ➤ **Check the keel bolts regularly**.............See ① and ③

Consult your yard about possible fractures in the protective shell..See ③

Keel bolt leaks 1

If a ballast keel is external, the constant movement of the boat in a seaway can loosen a bolt or cause the insulating gasket to dislodge. Keel bolts need to be examined regularly, more often if the boat is aging. This is not a problem in wooden boats, but GRP boats may have had the keel bolt heads hidden under moldings and furniture. It can be a messy and expensive project, especially if a bolt needs replacement. You can arrange to have the keel bolts x-rayed, though this is not cheap, and the boat must be hauled out.

Keel falls 2

Modern keels are usually rather deep and short fore-and-aft. The lateral strains imposed on them are very great. The chance exists that the fasteners—especially studs—can fracture, and it usually happens without warning. In relatively moderate conditions, you may be able to drop all sail and stay upright long enough to beach the boat. In heavy weather, chances are the yacht will capsize. Prepare to abandon ship. See Abandoning Ship p.8.

Encapsulated keels 3

Many fiberglass cruising boats have the ballast encapsulated in GRP (glass-reinforced plastic, or fiberglass). The ballast is dropped into the keel cavity and usually glassed over (figure 1). If the protective shell is fractured or pierced, water can lodge in the keel cavity. You may not notice initially. Iron ballast will start to rust and, as this worsens, you may notice that the boat no longer handles as it should—the rusting has made the ballast asymmetrical. This will not be noticeable with lead ballast, but any breaks must be fixed or the GRP may begin to delaminate. Consult your yard.

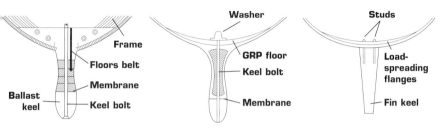

Fig. 1

Various keel attachment methods are shown above. The point of weakness is invariably the keel bolts or studs. These should be checked regularly.

LEAKS

Every boat, power or sail, will at some point develop a leak. It can be underwater or on deck. The first can be deadly; the second annoying in the extreme. Finding and stopping leaks can become a world-class sport! Water has an undeniable tendency to flow in hard-to-trace patterns.

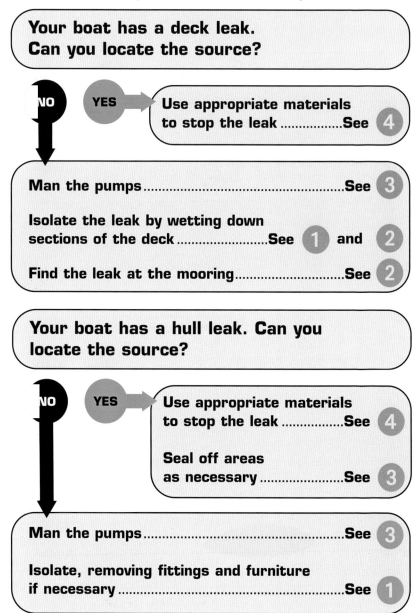

Your boat has a deck leak. Can you locate the source?

NO

YES → Use appropriate materials to stop the leak ....See **4**

Man the pumps...See **3**

Isolate the leak by wetting down sections of the deck ....See **1** and **2**

Find the leak at the mooring............................See **2**

Your boat has a hull leak. Can you locate the source?

NO

YES → Use appropriate materials to stop the leak ....See **4**

Seal off areas as necessary ....See **3**

Man the pumps...See **3**

Isolate, removing fittings and furniture if necessary ....See **1**

Locating the source 1

Locating a leak may be much more difficult than you might imagine. Likely spots are seacocks, rudder gland, stuffing box, keel bolts, hull-to-deck join, deck fittings—in fact anywhere the hull or deck has been drilled, cut, or opened to receive a fitting. In addition, tanks—water, waste, or fuel—may have developed a leak. Too often, the leak is far from the spot at which water, etc. collects. You may have to trace the course, and this may involve removing fittings or furniture.

Finding a leak logically 2

It is very difficult to find the source of a leak while underway. Better to mark off sections of the deck, starting with the lowest, and proceed to wet each section down. You will be able to close in on the source with greater speed. If water is coming aboard more than you can stop, be sure to pump regularly.

Hull leaks 3

A deck leak may be uncomfortable, but a hull leak, fitting or otherwise (skegs and keel sumps can crack from wracking strains in heavy seas), can be downright dangerous. Though the pumps may be able to cope, track it down. And don't forget the obvious: head intake hoses are usually not looped high enough. At rest this may be unnoticeable, but underway, especially when heeled, the head can overflow and cause a boat to founder. If the boat has sealed-off compartments, or if an area can be sealed off by makeshift means, do so until repairs can be safely effected.

Stopping the leak 4

Attempt to stop the leak with rags, caulking cotton, foam or neoprene, or plugs (figure 1, over the page). (Incidentally, all through hulls, even those with seacocks, should have a tapered softwood plug of appropriate size tied to the fitting with a lanyard, figure 2.) Rubber and silicone caulking will NOT adhere to wet surfaces. Underwater epoxy will, and should be kept aboard for such emergencies.

Fig. 1

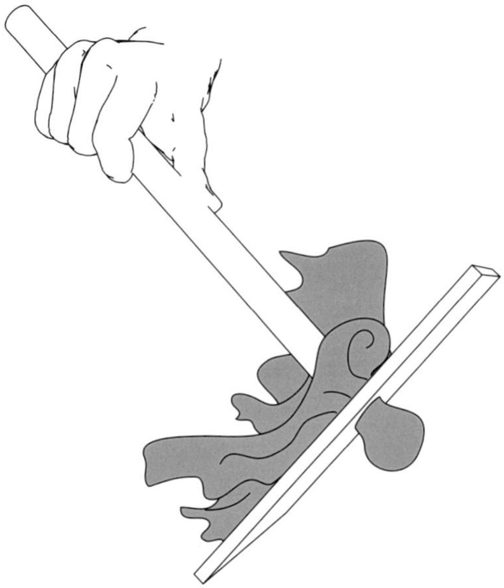

Fig. 2

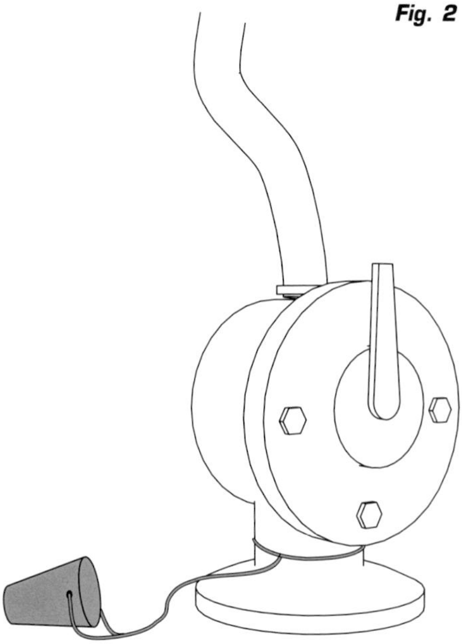

LEE SHORES

Onshore winds can be a godsend when you have to get back to port, but as the weather deteriorates, and no harbour of safety presents itself, any coast presents a danger. In the old days, before the advent of small, powerful diesels, a yacht's seaworthiness was judged by its ability to beat off a lee shore. If and when the engine fails, it is still a highly desirable trait.

Your boat is being driven into a lee shore. Can you anchor out?

NO   **YES** ➤ Anchor as far out as possible.........See **1** and **3**

Attempt to motor sail ....See **2**

Attempt to sail to windward ....See **4**

If there is no other option, abandon ship ....**See Abandoning Ship p.8**

Anchoring out **1**

Under most conditions a lee shore should be avoided only because of the possibility of heavy weather. If no choice exists, try to anchor as far out as is possible with safety. If you are singlehanding, deploy the kedge anchor from the stern (figure 1).

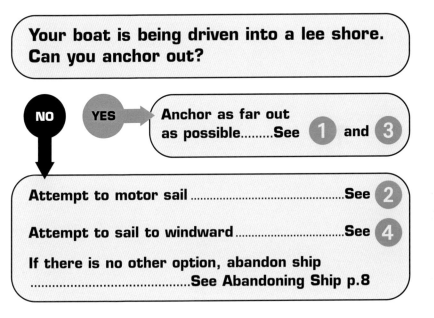

Fig. 1

Wind

To get underway again, secure the second anchor to a stern cleat (figure 2), bring up the stern warp so that the boat is beam-on the wind (figure 3), and raise the bow anchor. This can help position the boat more advantageously to power out of the situation, as well as allowing for sudden wind shifts. Buoy the kedge for later pickup (figure 4), and sail out to windward.

Fig. 2

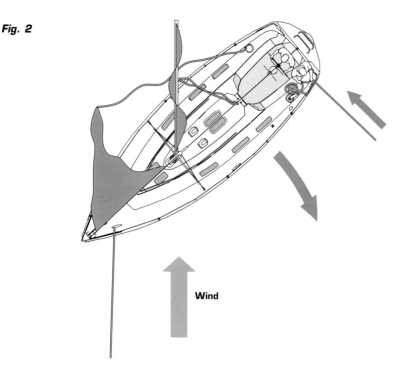

Wind

Fig. 3

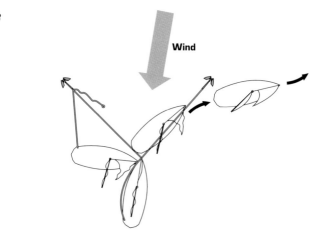

Wind

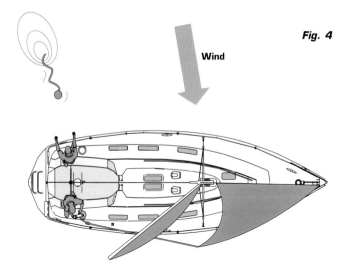

Fig. 4

Wind

Motor sailing.. ②

If the engine is powerful, motor sailing should be attempted before trying to leave under sail alone.

Multiple anchors.. ③

In truly horrendous conditions, boats have survived by sailing in a half-circle and dropping as many anchors as are on board. Under these conditions it will not be possible to set anything from the dinghy and no other choice will exist.

Sailing out.. ④

Careful planning and coordination from all the crew will be necessary for these maneuvers to work. It will be difficult to keep the headsail from flogging itself to death and the jib sheets from fouling. However, your safety depends on this, and a crew member should be stationed at what will be the leeward winch to haul in as soon as the anchor line has been released. Another must be stationed at the mainsheet, leaving the helmsman free to concentrate.

When alone or shorthanded, it may be an advantage to sail the yacht out under only one sail—whichever is most efficient—keeping the decks relatively clear. If you must lose an anchor, do so…it costs less than the ship.

LIFE RAFTS

Every boat going offshore should carry a life raft. Despite the cost, the need for regular servicing, and the stowage problems, there is no substitute for a proper life raft when all else fails. Ideally, the raft should be to SOLAS specifications, but that comes with a price. If the raft is to be exposed to the weather, a suitcase raft is advisable.

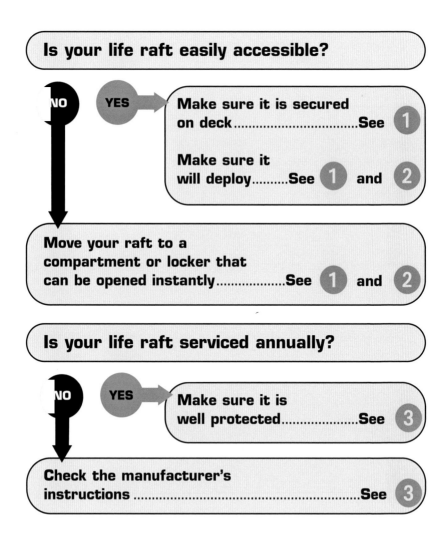

Is your life raft easily accessible?

NO   YES

Make sure it is secured
on deck..................................See **1**

Make sure it
will deploy..........See **1** and **2**

Move your raft to a
compartment or locker that
can be opened instantly.................See **1** and **2**

Is your life raft serviced annually?

NO   YES

Make sure it is
well protected....................See **3**

Check the manufacturer's
instructions ....See **3**

Has every member of the crew been instructed in life raft operation?

NO

YES → Make sure each crew member has a sharp, protected knife......................See **4**

Go through the complete drill while at moorings ....See **4**

Where should I tie off the painter?......................................See **5**

You need to inflate the raft. Is the raft clear of the ship?

NO

YES → Make sure the painter is free and tug firmly ....See **6**

Do **NOT** inflate the raft while it is on board...See **6**

You need to abandon the mother ship. Is everyone on board the life raft?

NO

YES → Make sure you have all the supplies you can carry and cut the raft free ....See **7**

Make sure the crew is aboard and safe...See **7**

Life raft stowage 1

It should be obvious that a life raft must be kept on deck or in a special raft locker. Nevertheless, many yachtsmen place it in a cockpit or lazarette locker where accumulations of gear and debris block access to it. Under-the-sole lockers are not recommended; too many people will be in the cockpit to make for easy access. The best location is either lashed to the coach roof (figure 1) or the base of the mast, or on the afterdeck (figure 2), or beneath the helmsman seat (figure 3). Newer boats have special recesses within the transom; these are fine if, in practice, you can get to them without endangering the crew. Best to keep all safety gear inboard if possible.

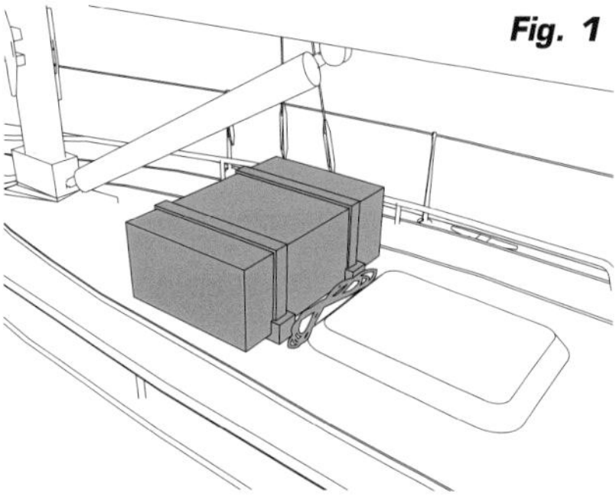

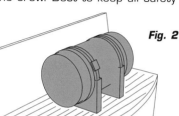

Fig. 1

Fig. 2

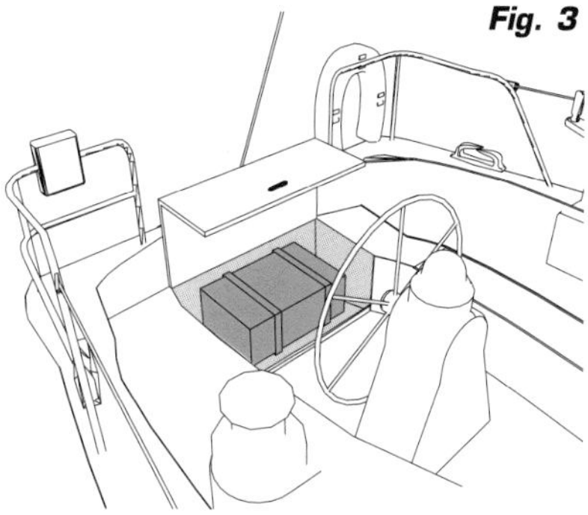

Fig. 3

Securing the life raft 2

Don't use lashings that end up like the Gordian knot. You must be able to release them with a single stroke of a knife, or with a single tug on a line—some variant of a slippery hitch, for example (figure 4). The lashings are best done up in natural cordage, as synthetics will slip too much.

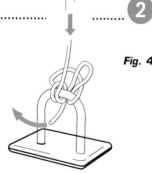

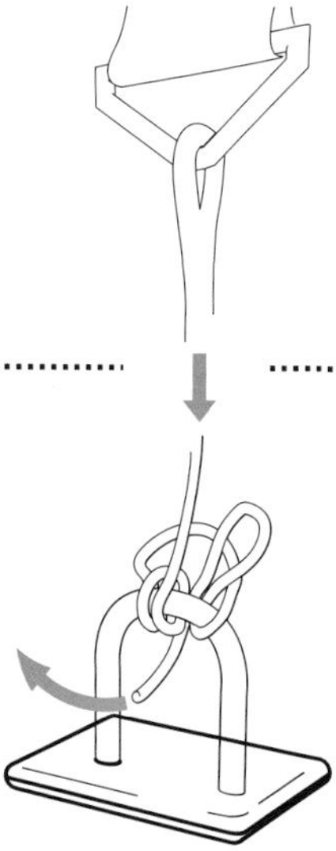

Fig. 4

Manila or hemp—if you can find it—are good. Patent hold-down systems (figure 5) can be acceptable, providing they are constantly checked for corrosion or chafe. Like anything mechanical they are liable to seizure and breakdown when most needed.

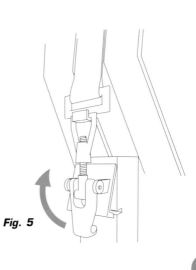

Fig. 5

Life raft service 3

Servicing is vital to life raft performance. Kept on deck, the raft, even in a fiberglass canister, is subject to moisture penetration, fabric deterioration, and valve failure. Yearly servicing by an authorized service center is ideal. Yes, it is expensive. Yes, you need to do it. Normally, manufacturers suggest servicing every two or three years. The choice is yours, but the inflation valves on CO_2 canisters have a tendency to corrode. If this happens, your and your crew's lives will be on the line. While we are on the subject, do buy a canister raft. Valises are too subject to kicks, seepage, and puncture. They should be avoided at all costs, no matter how well-protected you believe the raft to be. Also, if you can, pay more and get a raft that is up to SOLAS standards. The difference, especially offshore, is worth it both in terms of construction and materials specifications, and in terms of equipment.

Crew instruction 4

The crew, every member, must be given proper instruction in abandon-ship and life raft drills. Don't wait until it is too late. This is not to suggest you should inflate the raft to practice, but do use the dinghy to get the crew used to boarding a raft in rough seas and in a state of mock panic, something best done at one's moorings. Show them how to undo lashings, how to toss the raft overboard and how to inflate it. Make sure, when underway, that each crew member is supplied with a sharp—and properly protected—knife. Even if they are practiced sailors with long experience, go through the complete drill. People forget and not all rafts are the same!

Tying the painter.........................

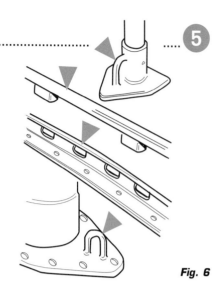

Depending on where the raft is located, the painter should be tied to a deck fitting which is through-bolted. The strains upon raft and painter in rough seas when thrown are great. Stanchion bases, mast step, coachroof rails, and pushpit are all appropriate choices (figure 6).

Fig. 6

Life raft inflation...

NEVER ATTEMPT TO INFLATE THE RAFT WHILE IT IS ON BOARD! What with rigging, deck gear, trampling crew, wheel or tiller, etc., you will never be able to get it into the water, and if you do, the chances are you will rip the fabric or tear off a fitting or two. Always throw the raft clear of the ship (figure 7). The painter can become tangled. First make sure it is clear, then tug firmly. The throw of the raft may start inflation, but it is always best to make sure by giving the painter the appropriate pull (figure 8). If the raft does not inflate, or only partially fills, get one person to attempt to start pumping. Make sure that individual is secure in a safety harness.

Fig. 7

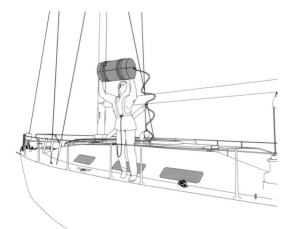

Fig. 8

Cutting free 7

Should abandonment of the mother vessel become imperative, make
sure all members of the crew are aboard the raft before cutting the
painter (figure 9). Rafts drift—especially in the conditions likely to prevail
when a raft is needed—at a remarkable rate. There is little or no
chance that contact can be re-established with the yacht. As tragic
experience has unfortunately shown, all too often, in panic, some crew
member cuts that figurative umbilical cord prematurely. Someone is
sure to be the worse for it.

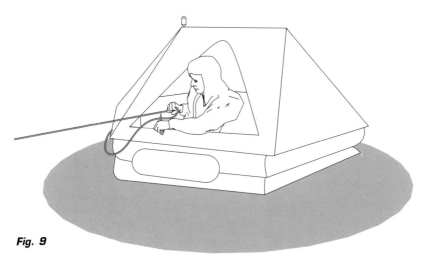

Fig. 9

LIGHTNING

Lightning is an electric charge of potentially fatal dimensions. Most yachts are not properly grounded—if at all—and in any electrical storm precautions must be taken to set up a path to dissipate the electrical energy that can easily fry your electronics, demagnetize the compass, burn a hole through the hull, or worse.

An electrical storm arises. Is your boat fitted with lightning protection?

NO

YES

Get the crew below ....See **3**

Anchor or heave to
the ship ....See **3**

Stay away from any
metal fittings ....See **3**

Do **NOT** use
the radio ....See **3**

Follow above and improvise a ground ....See **2**

Preventative action **1**

Lightning is unpredictable. Though it will rarely strike a yacht, enough cases exist, especially along the American eastern seaboard, to dictate all possible precautions. Since lightning will follow the most direct path to the water, it is up to you to provide such a path to help it on its way. Though copper wire #8 is generally recommended for a lightning ground, it is much better to use copper tubing, flattened at the ends, connecting the lightning rod at the masthead with a keel bolt (figure 1). In a boat with an encapsulated keel, a grounding plate should be attached to the hull as low below the waterline as is feasible.

Fig. 1

Improvised grounding........ .... ②

Since very few boats are fitted with lightning protection, in a sudden storm a length of chain, shackled to the cap (upper) shroud and dangled overboard (make sure it is long enough to remain under water) will act as a satisfactory substitute (figure 2). If time exists, tape the shackle end of the chain to the shroud to ensure positive contact.

Fig. 2

Personal protection .... ③

Obviously, the helmsman remains in greater danger than the rest of the crew, especially if steering with a metal wheel. If possible, anchor; when at sea, heave to and join the rest of the crew below. Under no circumstances hold onto rails, shrouds, or stays—these are all lightning conductors. Likewise, radio antennas are perfect lightning conductors and any strike will fry the radio, and possibly you!

LIGHTS

Sailing at night without showing the proper lights is a violation of maritime law. However, batteries die, engines fail to start, and short circuits occur. Under such circumstances, you will have to improvise to be seen by other ships.

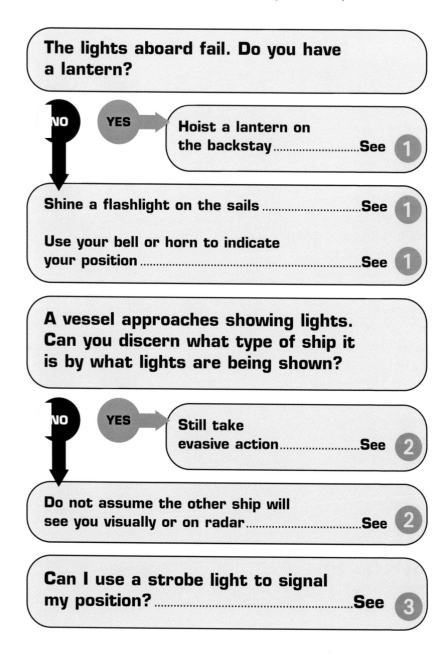

The lights aboard fail. Do you have a lantern?

NO / YES → Hoist a lantern on the backstay..........................See ①

Shine a flashlight on the sails..........................See ①

Use your bell or horn to indicate your position..........................See ①

A vessel approaches showing lights. Can you discern what type of ship it is by what lights are being shown?

NO / YES → Still take evasive action..........................See ②

Do not assume the other ship will see you visually or on radar..........................See ②

Can I use a strobe light to signal my position?..........................See ③

Staying noticed

Fig. 1

If the lights aboard go out, hoist a lantern, preferably on the backstay (figure 1). If hoisted to the spreaders, it will not be seen from leeward. A flashlight aimed at the sails will also act as a warning to other ships. If no lights are available, or the weather does not permit hoisting a light signal, sound signals can be used to indicate your position. Do not use flares unless you are in distress or another vessel is bearing down on you.

Other ships

Despite the International Rules, incorrect lights are often shown. Fishing boats are prime culprits, but yachts and merchants ships can also be offenders.

Always attempt to discern exactly what lights are being shown where on an approaching vessel before taking evasive action (figure 2). Likewise, even in approved anchorages, always hoist an anchor light.

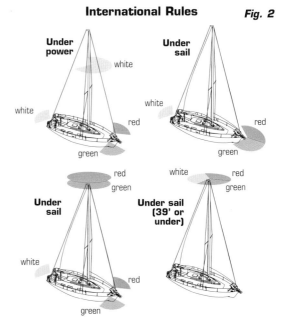

International Rules **Fig. 2**

Under power — white, white, red, green

Under sail — white, red, green

Under sail — white, red, green

Under sail (39' or under) — white, red, green

Strobe lights

Strobe lights, NOT in accordance with the International Rules, should be used only for distress and then only when necessary, as they can confuse a watch officer on the bridge of a large ship.

MAN OVERBOARD

Falling overboard is a terrifying experience for both the victim and crew. In any kind of seaway, just sighting the victim can be difficult, and in colder waters, immediate action is needed to prevent death by hypothermia. Assuming you keep the victim in view, recovery can be much more difficult than you imagine. There are no hard and fast rules for dealing with man overboard; you must modify your tactics and behavior to the existing boat and conditions. Under any circumstances, however, crew overboard is a threat to human life.

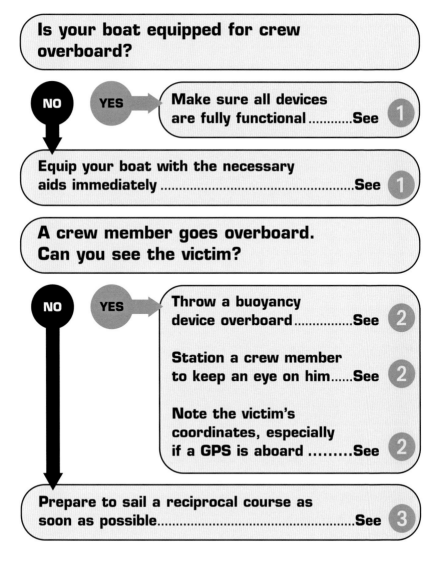

Is your boat equipped for crew overboard?

NO

YES ▶ **Make sure all devices are fully functional** ....**See** 1

Equip your boat with the necessary aids immediately ....**See** 1

A crew member goes overboard. Can you see the victim?

NO

YES ▶ **Throw a buoyancy device overboard** ....**See** 2

Station a crew member to keep an eye on him ......**See** 2

Note the victim's coordinates, especially if a GPS is aboard ....**See** 2

Prepare to sail a reciprocal course as soon as possible...**See** 3

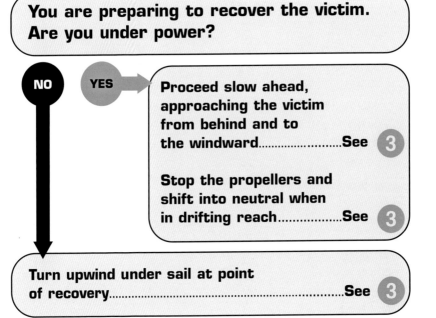

You are preparing to recover the victim. Are you under power?

NO

YES → Proceed slow ahead, approaching the victim from behind and to the windward.........................See ③

Stop the propellers and shift into neutral when in drifting reach.................See ③

Turn upwind under sail at point of recovery..See ③

Equipment.. ①

All boats should have a life ring with man-overboard pole, flag, whistle, light, and possibly a sea anchor attached (figure 1). A horseshoe buoy will be easier for the person in the water to slip into. For the pole to be sighted, it must be at least 8 feet (2.5 meters) long with a bright orange flag attached to the top. In heavy seas even this will be difficult to spot and a longer pole is not a bad idea. Equally, the flag should be as large as is practicable to aid in sighting. A whistle will help locate the

victim in any weather, while a light—preferably self-activating—will be a necessity in low-visibility conditions and at night. Sea anchors are often in bad repute, but a small cloth cone on a long bridle will certainly slow any drift and permit easier spotting and a more deliberate pick-up. No matter what the equipment, it should be mounted outboard of all rails, lifelines, and deck encumbrances. Nothing can be worse than to attempt to release the gear and have it foul where it may be impossible to release. Ideally, devices should be mounted both port and starboard, within reach and ready-release by the helmsman. The pole can

Fig. 1

be fitted into a special release socket or very lightly lashed to the backstay. Very lightly is important: the lashings must break only through the inertial pull of the life ring or horseshoe. Obviously, the idea is to have the entire kit in the water and close to the crew overboard as quickly as possible. Conditions exist where the shock of falling overboard will be enough to totally disorient and weaken the victim. It becomes absolutely necessary to get the flotation device to him or her as quickly as possible. In addition, the victim may have been hurt or possibly incapacitated in the fall. Finally, in heavy going and cold conditions, survival chances are greatly lessened, and the less activity required of the person in the water, the less the heat loss and the chance of hypothermia. See "Recovery" p.134.

Spotting the victim 2

As mentioned above, it is not easy to see someone in heavy seas. It is actually difficult to see a crew member overboard in almost any weather. The need for a crew member with good eyes and strong powers of concentration is obvious. But for such a person to be truly effective, he must be left alone, not bothered, not expected to do anything but keep an eye on the victim! This cannot be too highly stressed. If the crew in the water is lost sight of for just an instant, he may never be spotted again. Certainly, every sailor has practiced crew overboard drills, but usually in gentle conditions and without panic or the sense of urgency that results when a real living person goes over the side. It is a lot different in reality. If by chance a GPS is on board and the coordinates can be noted when the person goes overboard, this can relieve anxiety to a degree as well as limiting the area where the search will take place.

Maneuvering 3

Once the flotation materials are launched and a spotter is at work, then and only then should maneuvers to recover the person take place. Under sail, turn into the wind. This will allow the boat to keep way, yet slow her down long enough to prepare the crew for recovery measures. What you want to do is to get into a position to be able to pick up the man in the water from windward. (See Man Overboard: Pick-Up p.132.) Under power, there is less to do in working the boat, but perhaps greater potential danger to the victim. Proceeding "slow ahead," describe a circle in the water so that you approach the person in the water from behind and to windward (figure 2). When you are in drifting reach or just alongside (the forward third of the hull), STOP THE

Fig. 2

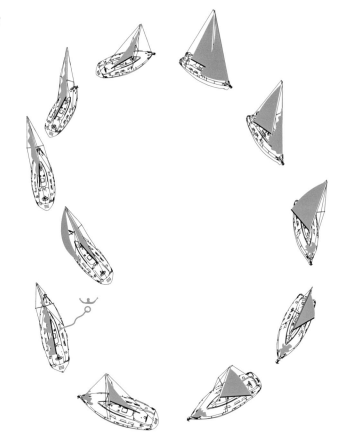

PROPELLERS FROM TURNING. One way is to throw the gears into neutral. In calm weather, shut off the engine if you are in clear water.

The danger from the propellers is frightening, and cases are on record of persons being dismembered or killed by a fast-turning propeller (figure 3). On a powerboat, the freeboard, even aft (except on a fishing boat) will be appreciably higher than aboard a similar-length sailing vessel. If a stern door or swim platform is available, the person can best be hauled up from there. However, getting a soaked body up a meter or more of slick topsides is a maneuver that demands some forethought.

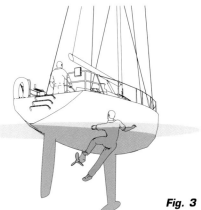

Fig. 3

MAN OVERBOARD:
Pick-Up

Finding a crew member overboard is difficult enough. Getting him or her back on deck can be frustratingly difficult. A fully-clothed body in the water gains weight very quickly, sometimes as much as 45–90 lbs (20–40 kg). Also, modern yachts usually have high topsides, and the dead weight of the victim may make it impossible to haul him aboard without some mechanical help.

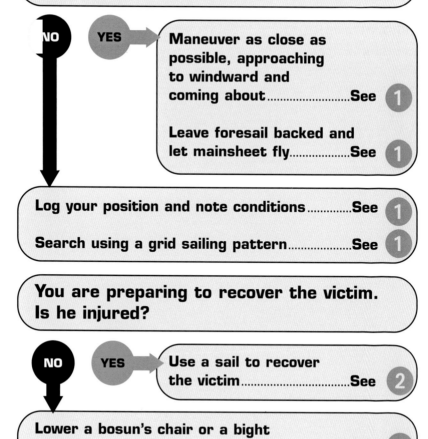

A crew member has gone overboard. Can you locate the victim?

NO **YES**

Maneuver as close as possible, approaching to windward and coming about........................See ❶

Leave foresail backed and let mainsheet fly..................See ❶

Log your position and note conditions..............See ❶

Search using a grid sailing pattern...................See ❶

You are preparing to recover the victim. Is he injured?

NO **YES**

Use a sail to recover the victim................................See ❷

Lower a bosun's chair or a bight of rope...See ❷

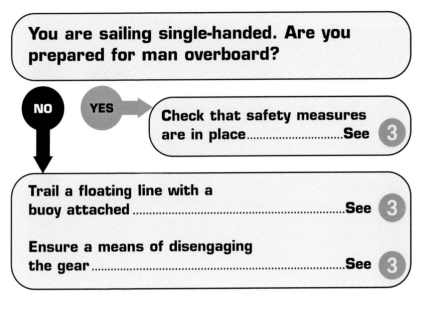

You are sailing single-handed. Are you prepared for man overboard?

NO **YES** ➡ Check that safety measures are in place............................See ③

Trail a floating line with a
buoy attached ....See ③

Ensure a means of disengaging
the gear ....See ③

Maneuvering .... ①

Depending on what course you are following at the time of the accident,
different maneuvers are more or less appropriate for successful
positioning of the boat. If running downwind, you will have to beat
back to the approximate location, or motor on a reciprocal course.
If the weather is foul or shows signs of deteriorating, begin a search
from upwind of the approximate position you lost your crew member
(figure 1). Keep records of time and distance sailed, and take into

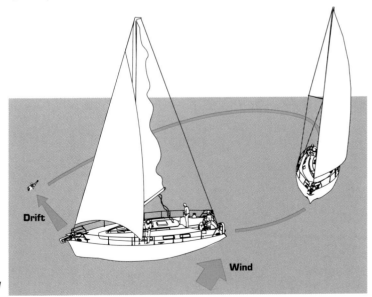

Drift

Wind

Fig. 1

account current, tides, and wind speed—all of which will affect the drift of the person in the water to a much greater degree than the ship. The search may be carried out to windward, on a reach, or running. In each case you will have to tack back and forth, running parallel lines over the search area (figure 2).

Fig. 2

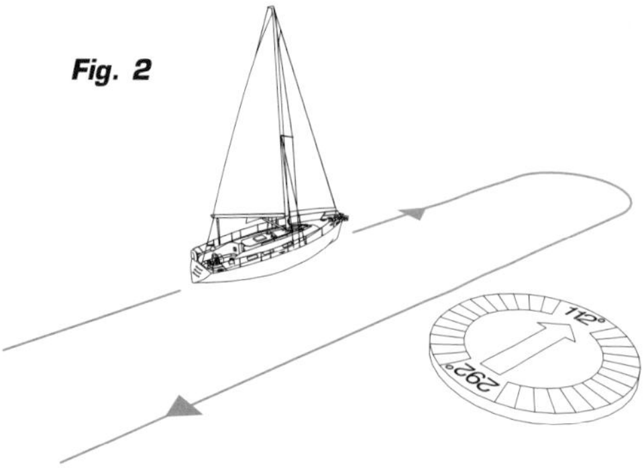

It is a good idea to log your position as soon as the alarm is raised (figure 3). As mentioned above, a GPS reading can be invaluable.

Fig. 3

Time 17.35
Distance sailed   3/4 m
Current   Westerly
Wind speed   15 knots
Direction   SSE
Tide   35 m to high

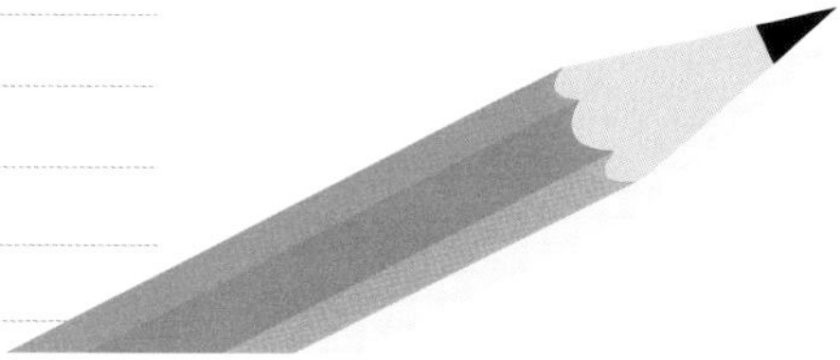

Recovery .... ②

Once you have him spotted, and the boat is under control, you must be prepared to get him into the boat. An average adult, in foul weather gear and several layers of clothing, will add as much as 50 lbs (23.5 kg) to his or her dry weight with immersion. This is not inconsiderable, and must be taken into account in any maneuver to get him back on board.

NOTE: The crew member in the water should practice a few precautionary measures to prolong his strength and chances of survival. He must keep his clothing on to conserve body heat. He must not scream or attempt to swim toward the boat. It will only confuse the crew and deplete his strength resources. He should utilize the gear thrown to him if possible and wait, using the whistle when the mother ship is in sight. Above all, do not panic!

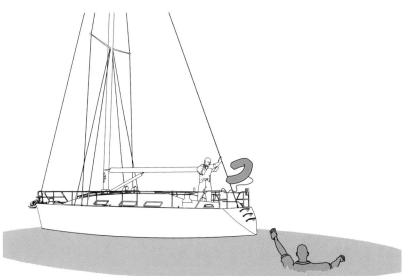

Fig. 4

To get the survivor on board, several methods are possible. If he is injured or exhausted, lower a sail with all corners secured by lines to the ship. If he can do some of the work himself, a bosun's chair or bight of rope can be lowered to swing around his arms, allowing him to sit in it and be winched aboard (figures 4 and 5). Patent devices, such as the Lifesling, can be deployed. If a platform or boarding ladder is permanently attached to the stern, have him grab a bight of rope and maneuver him to the stern with a crew member on each quarter to assist boarding. In boats with transom-mounted rudders, a set of steps can be installed on the rudder blade from below the water line to allow easier boarding. *Do not attempt to haul a victim aboard by his arms!*

Fig. 5

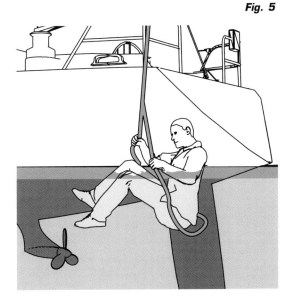

Single-handing

Single-handed sailors have the most to worry about in crew-overboard situations. You must always trail a poly (floating) line with a buoy attached to the end of it. This should be about 85 feet (25 meters) long. If you are sailing under self-steering gear, some means of disengaging the gear is necessary. One possibility is suggested in figure 6. A permanently mounted ladder with a lanyard attached to release the lower half, or the transom steps mentioned above, should be included in fitting out the boat. In power boats, the trailing line must be bridled to avoid fouling the propeller and might be rigged either to shift the gears into neutral or shut down the ignition when given a sharp jerk.

Fig. 6

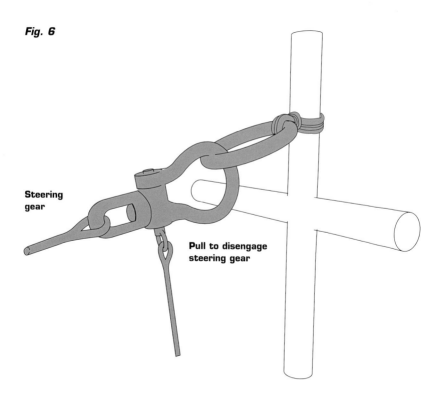

Steering gear

Pull to disengage steering gear

MAST PROBLEMS

Every component on a mast is subject to failure, and most can be fixed at sea. The repair process is not for the faint hearted. Being aloft in a seaway is both frightening and dangerous, and all precautions must be taken to avoid injury.

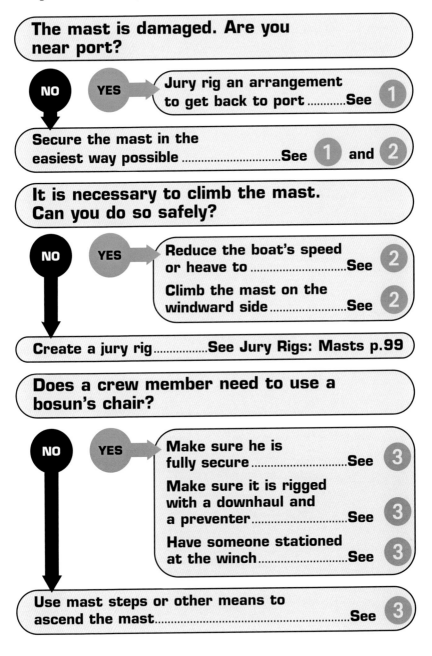

The mast is damaged. Are you near port?

NO   YES → Jury rig an arrangement to get back to port ....See **1**

Secure the mast in the easiest way possible ....See **1** and **2**

It is necessary to climb the mast. Can you do so safely?

NO   YES → Reduce the boat's speed or heave to ....See **2**

Climb the mast on the windward side ....See **2**

Create a jury rig................See Jury Rigs: Masts p.99

Does a crew member need to use a bosun's chair?

NO   YES → Make sure he is fully secure ....See **3**

Make sure it is rigged with a downhaul and a preventer............................See **3**

Have someone stationed at the winch..........................See **3**

Use mast steps or other means to ascend the mast...See **3**

Deck fixes 1

First ascertain if there is a way to free the line or ignore the damage without going up. If you are near port, you may be able to jury-rig an arrangement to get you in without trying to work in a seaway at the masthead. Remember, the pitching moment is much greater high up, especially if 165 lbs (75 kg) of mass is suddenly hanging on for dear life. Most repair jobs at the top are two-handed affairs, and for effective work both body and legs must be secured and braced. If any possible way exists to carry on without clambering up, take it, unless the crew or ship will be endangered through failure to take action. If a shroud parts, tack immediately. You may not get where you want to go, but you will save the mast. A spare halyard can be run to a block or chain plate, and then to a winch to temporarily replace the broken shroud.

Safety aloft 2

Tearing along at hull speed will in no way aid the crew member who must be at the masthead, either once there or when climbing. Lower the boat speed as much as possible while maintaining steering way. A reach will steady the boat and, depending upon the tack, can actually provide a more secure position at mast top. The sail may have to be reduced.

Bosun's chairs and tools 3

Fig. 1

The traditional bosun's chair is both uncomfortable and potentially dangerous (figure 1). The wood seat can slam into the mast, causing more damage. The newer, all-cloth models with restraining straps and tool pockets can be both safer and allow for more efficient and quicker work. The crew member who has volunteered to go up must be totally secured before ascending. A downhaul must be rigged to the chair, and a line with snap hook or some other expedient means of wrapping around the mast as a preventer to keep the occupant in position should be affixed, preferably around the person, not just to the seat. A safety harness can be employed, providing that the tether is not too long. All the tools that might be needed should be secured by lanyards. In fact, it is a good idea to keep basic tools permanently ensconced with the bosun's chair: vise grips, screwdriver, marlinspike, adjustable wrench, etc.

Rigging the chair on a spare halyard demands some forethought. Spinnaker halyards may be too light to be safe, the main halyard may be jammed, and the jib needed to maintain forward motion. In such a situation, it may be wise to use the spinnaker halyard as a messenger to carry a heavier line through its masthead sheave. In a fractionally rigged boat, a spare main halyard might well be permanently rigged.

Hauling the man aloft demands a strong person to man the winch, enough turns (at least four) around the winch and a good braking turn around a cleat. The point is to get someone up safely, not fast. A second crew member on the deck should handle the downhaul, keeping it taut and making sure that swing is kept to a minimum (figure 2). When the main is down, the safety line should be secured at the spreaders to help stabilize the man aloft.

Frankly, the precautions mentioned above should be adhered to in all weathers. At night, a flashlight should be carried aloft, possibly taped to the upper arm with gaffer's tape. Gloves are another recommendation, but they must be full-fingered and leather. Anything else will either chafe or slip. Deck boots will protect the legs and a foam-filled life vest will help absorb bumps while not overly hindering the wearer's movements.

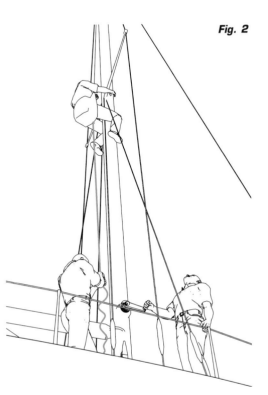

Fig. 2

Other means of mounting a mast....... 4

If for some reason the bosun's chair is not usable or one isn't on board, a substitute will have to be devised. Lots of possibilities exist, of course, but whatever is used must be of irreproachable integrity: a bowline on a bight or an emergency boarding ladder. Do not use a fender unless it is the type that allows the line to run through it; standard inflatable fenders are not reliable enough in their grommeting to hold a man's weight under stress conditions. And, if you use one of the other alternatives, remember to pad it well. Raw wood or rope can cause serious injury aloft in high winds and rolling conditions.

There will be times when no halyard is available for hauling a bosun's chair. A rope or plastic ladder, or a wood and rope ladder, can be used but demands much vigilance and agility as well as a messenger line to haul it up: it's usually far too much bother and too time-consuming when you need it. The main can be slacked slightly (only in fairly large boats) and used as a ladder (figure 3). However, the slides must be metal. Plastic

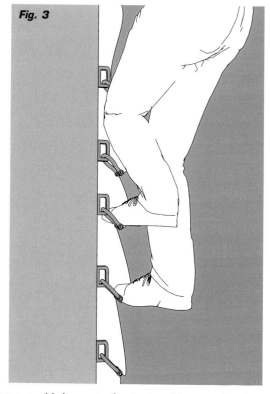

Fig. 3

slugs can fracture, causing a rapid descent of catastrophic speed and force. Remember to follow the safety precautions!

Finally, if you are planning to go offshore, it is a good idea to install mast steps. Various types are available, but all must provide a flat footbed and be designed so as not to catch sails and lines.

MEDICAL EMERGENCIES

Any accident or injury at sea is potentially dangerous. You should always carry an up-to-date medical kit suited to the type of cruising you are undertaking. Obviously, if going offshore you will need far more in the way of medications and equipment than you will for coastal hopping. In other words, you must be able to handle disasters that a hospital would treat ashore. Luckily, with radios, satellite communications, and e-mail, advice and treatment options are much improved compared to the days when you had only a first aid book on which to rely.

- **Do you need to save a life?**
- **Do you need to prevent the situation from getting worse?**
- **Must you relieve pain and suffering?**
- **Do you need outside assistance?**

Preliminary 1

The above questions are not meant to solve any specific problem, but they must be asked in any situation concerning injury or sickness. Though most accidents aboard will be minor—cuts, seasickness, sunburn, colds, and flu—many others will require more than two aspirin and a cup of tea. You must be prepared to cope with anything short of major surgery, especially if you intend a transoceanic passage of any length. To this end, every yacht should be equipped with an up-to-date and constantly renewed first-aid kit, including medications that are appropriate for the areas to which you plan to travel. Also aboard must be a modern first-aid manual that has been read by at least two crew members. Any member of the crew who has a specific chronic ailment, drug allergy, or medication requirement should inform the captain of such before setting sail. It is up to the captain to assess the situation and make any decision about the crew member's suitability based on the remoteness of the land-fall, the conditions likely to be encountered, and the general physical condition of the crew member.

Stopped breathing .... (2)

If the person has stopped breathing or has no discernable heartbeat you must act immediately to save that person's life. Bleeding will kill a person much less quickly—unless it is a major hemorrhage of a major artery—than lack of oxygen or heart failure.

Potential complications .... (3)

If the person is not subject to any immediate threat, you must decide if the condition might worsen. Many injuries and illnesses can get more serious, but the most common might include burns, infections, exposure, poisoning, concussion, fractures, unconsciousness, open wounds, and chest pain. If you decide that the person is in no immediate danger, continue to port. Otherwise, consult your medical guide.

Anxiety .... (4)

The greatest concurrent problem with any injury at sea may be fear. You must not only take appropriate medical action, but reassure the injured person. Care, concern, and will can play as important a part as anything to help alleviate distress and aid someone on the path to recovery.

Stabilizing .... (5)

Can you cope? Certain medical conditions will be beyond your ability to treat. If you are far from shore, you must use your judgment and common sense, and do everything in your power to aid the patient with what you have at hand. Certain infections can be held at bay with antibiotics. Certain fractures can be immobilized until a doctor is at hand. But it may be impossible to do much about other conditions. Internal hemorrhaging, heart attack, certain types of poisoning, or extreme hypothermia may be beyond you.

Steps to take .... (6)

The following are some basic general guidelines for diagnosis and treatment. They should be used in conjunction with a reliable medical first-aid manual. They are not infallible, and any responsibility is in the hands of the person administering the first aid.

Abdominal pain

This can be mild or severe. Until the cause is clear:
- *Put the patient to rest.*
- *Allow neither food nor liquids.*
- *Do not give laxatives.*
- *Give pain medication if required.*

If pain is persistent, vomiting frequent, diarrhea severe, and the abdomen firm and sensitive, seek medical assistance. Severe pain accompanied by a very hard, sensitive abdomen can indicate ruptured appendix, ulcer, or ovarian cyst. Infection is possible and antibiotics every six hours should be considered until professional advice is secured.

Antibiotics

Antibiotics are useless against viral or fungal infections. Follow a doctor's recommendations closely regarding dosage and types to carry aboard. Duration of treatment should be no more than one week to 10 days.

Cautions:
- *Avoid sunlight.*
- *Never give to pregnant women or children under eight without specific medical advice.*
- *Allergic reactions or lack of response should indicate a need for immediate medical consultation.*

Bleeding

Use sterile, soft, absorbent material and apply pressure. Small cuts will usually stop bleeding after a short while (figure 1); material should be taped over larger cuts until further action can be taken. Cleanse cuts with soap and water or hydrogen peroxide. Only use a tourniquet in extreme, heavy-bleeding emergencies.

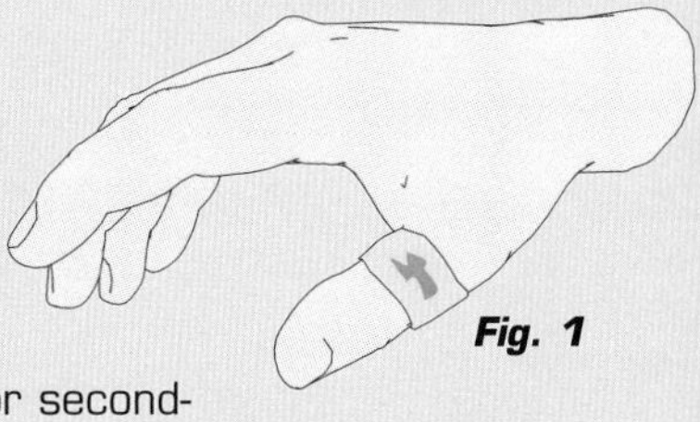

Burns

For all burns, immediate treatment is to apply cold water liberally. Use cloths soaked in either fresh or salt water. Avoid running water and ointments, creams, or sprays. For second-

Fig. 1

and third-degree burns, cover with sterile petroleum jelly, gauze, and a sterile dressing, and seek immediate medical attention. Life-threatening burns can cause shock and there is a danger of infection. Give oral fluids, keep dressings in place, and give pain killers and antibiotics if more than 24 hours will elapse before a doctor can care for the patient.

Cardiopulmonary arrest

Heart attack or lung malfunction. Follow these steps:

- *Determine consciousness.*
- *Open the airway, tilt back the head with the neck lifted.*
- *Give mouth-to-mouth resuscitation; if after four breaths the chest doesn't move, attempt the Heimlich maneuver (see below).*
- *Feel for a pulse. If there is a pulse but the person is not breathing, start mouth-to-mouth resuscitation at one breath per five seconds.*
- *If there is no pulse, start CPR (see below).*

CPR

Your local Red Cross offers training in this lifesaving technique. If you haven't taken the course, follow the steps below only if the situation is genuinely desperate:

- *Place the casualty on a hard surface.*
- *Place the heel of your hand over the casualty's sternum about 2 inches from the lower tip.*
- *Place your other hand at right angles on top of the first and press down hard enough to depress the breast plate an inch or two (figure 2). Release.*
- *Pause. Repeat.*
- *Give the casualty two breaths after every 10 to 15 depressions. This is about the correct rate.*

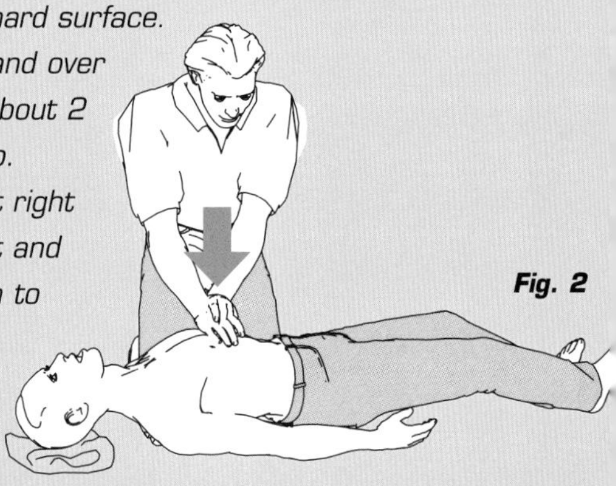

Fig. 2

Choking

Use the Heimlich maneuver:

- *Deliver back thumps with a closed fist between the casualty's shoulder blades.*
- *With your hands clasped around the casualty, make abdominal thrusts between the breastplate and the navel—four thumps, four thrusts (figure 3).*
- *Continue until choking is relieved.*

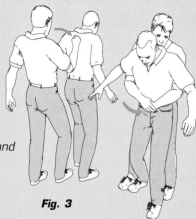

Fig. 3

Cold

Wear layers of loose-fitting, warm clothes; keep hands, feet, and head covered. Get out of wet clothes as soon as possible. Drink and eat warm substances. Do NOT drink alcohol.

Frostbite

Warm the affected part in 104–108°F (40–42°C) water (not hot). Pain medication may be needed. Seek medical assistance. If unavailable, soak the affected area in warm water twice a day. Applying clean dressings and separating toes and fingers will prevent tissue deterioration.

Constipation

Eat lots of fruits, vegetables, and roughage. Mild stool softeners are usually effective and convenient to take. Avoid laxatives if possible. A glycerine suppository or a warm-water enema may be best for prolonged constipation.

Cuts

Use strip or butterfly bandages to close the cut, apply pressure, and keep it clean (figure 4). Larger cuts will require stitching and prompt medical attention. If infected, use antibiotics.

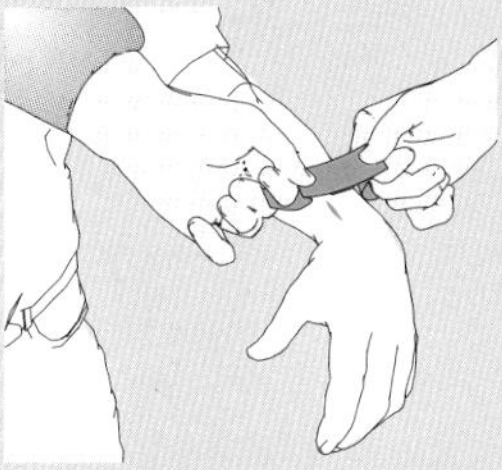

Fig. 4

Diarrhea

Keep up fluid intake; most patent medicines will make the patient feel better but will not cure the cause. Over-the-counter medications are available. If the diarrhea is accompanied by a high fever or bloody stools, use a broad-range antibiotic as per directions. Seek medical care as soon as possible as complications are possible.

Eyes

For eye irritations from glare or foreign bodies, wash with fresh water and cover the eye with loose-fitting bandages. Seek medical care if pain or visual impairment persists. Always wear sunglasses.

Fever

Take aspirin or acetaminophen, but no more than 375 mg every four hours after an initial 750 mg. Do NOT increase the dosage. Cool sponge baths can reduce fever. Dress the patient lightly unless suffering from chills. If fever is high and persists, infection is possible and antibiotics are called for. If there is no change after 48 hours, seek medical attention.

Fractures

Immobilize the patient immediately, apply ice packs if possible, and give pain medication. Do NOT try to set the fracture, but keep it from moving with splints, bandages, or inflatable casts (figure 5). Keep the splint tight, but not so tight as to stop or hinder circulation. Seek medical aid immediately. Compound fractures—where skin has been broken—will require cleansing of the wound and antibiotics.

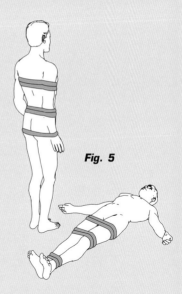

Fig. 5

Heat

Keep protected from the sun, even on cool days. Drink what you need to feel comfortable. Do NOT ration water. The body can store water and the old saw about rationing has been fairly convincingly disproved by U.S. Army Survival School studies. If heatstroke occurs, intensive, rapid cooling is called for. Put the casualty in a cold-water bath (plugged cockpit) or wrap him in soaked sheets. Sea water works well. After the casualty's body temperature has dropped to 102°F (40.6°C), cease cold treatment. Massage the casualty's arms and legs to promote cooling circulation. As soon as possible, start feeding the casualty cool liquids by mouth. Follow-up medical care is necessary as potentially serious damage can be inflicted on internal organs.

Pain

Pain is a symptom. Specific medication will not cure the cause unless the cause is known. For relief, take aspirin or acetaminophen. For medium pain your doctor can prescribe medication. Ask your doctor for specifics. For severe and persistent pain, take morphine or Demerol. These are dangerous drugs and should be avoided for all but the transoceanic passagemaker. Ask for specifics from your doctor.

Poisoning

For internal poisoning, cause vomiting as soon as possible, except for poisoning by petroleum products. When vomiting stops, feed the victim milk, mineral oil, or bread to absorb the poison and keep it from entering the system.

For poisoning through skin contact, remove clothing and wash the area thoroughly with water. Get into fresh air immediately. As so many poisons exist it is advisable to contact a doctor by radio as soon as you are able to receive further help. If the victim is comatose, get to land immediately, even if it means calling for an air rescue.

Respiratory infections

Respiratory infections cure themselves. Flu, colds, sore throat, and bronchitis are best treated with rest, lots of fluids, aspirin, decongestants, etc. In cases where fever develops or persists and no improvement is seen, antibiotics may be called for. They should be kept up, using the entire recommended dosage, even after symptoms have disappeared.

Seasickness

Seasickness affects different people in different ways. As many patent medications are available, as well as pressure patches, consult your doctor. Patent medicines work or don't work according to the individual. Chronic seasickness must be dealt with in the best way possible. Focusing on a distant horizon, keeping blood sugar levels up, and avoiding interiors or an exaggerated sense of motion can often cure milder forms of seasickness.

Shock

You can help prevent shock by keeping the casualty warm, dry, reassured, and breathing regularly. If the casualty goes into shock, there is little that can be done without transfusion and medical facilities.

Urinary tract infections

For non-specific infections, drink lots of fluids. Consult with your doctor, as new medications are available with some frequency. If you suffer from a chronic condition, consult your doctor before venturing on a long passage.

Symptoms of gonorrhea—discharge, burning urination—can be treated with antibiotics and a medical follow-up. Syphilis can be diagnosed as a painless ulcer at the point of sexual contact. Seek medical advice immediately. Syphilis is a complicated disease and is beyond the scope of any first-aid treatment.

PROPELLER PROBLEMS

An engine without a functioning propeller is nothing but ballast. Should the propeller foul, become damaged, or heaven forbid, fall off, all motive power ceases. Replacing a lost propeller is usually a job for a boatyard, although it can be accomplished by careening the boat. Thus, any passage-making powerboat should probably carry a spare propeller.

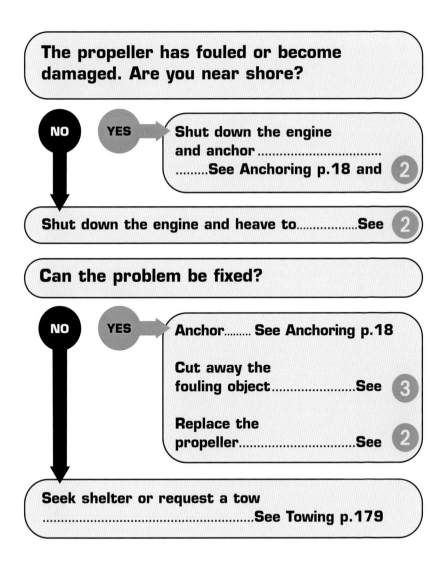

The propeller has fouled or become damaged. Are you near shore?

NO

YES → Shut down the engine and anchor ....See Anchoring p.18 and **2**

Shut down the engine and heave to..................See **2**

Can the problem be fixed?

NO

YES → Anchor........ See Anchoring p.18

Cut away the fouling object......................See **3**

Replace the propeller..............................See **2**

Seek shelter or request a tow ....See Towing p.179

Telltale signs

1

Ropes and plastic bags are the most common items to become entangled in propellers. Usually, these objects become wrapped around both the propeller and shaft. Failure to shut down the engine immediately could cause damage to the gearbox. As the propeller and shaft turn more slowly, the engine will begin to overheat—which is easily discovered by checking the engine temperature gauge(s).

Damaged propeller

2

If you have hit a submerged object, the propeller may be bent or have a blade torn off. The loss of balance will cause odd sounds beneath the hull, and the change in torque can actually shift, and perhaps unseat, the engine. Stop the engine immediately. You will probably have to visit a yard to have the propeller replaced. If you are on a long passage, you will either have to careen the boat to replace the propeller or dive (a very difficult task indeed) using underwater breathing apparatus.

Clearing obstructions

3

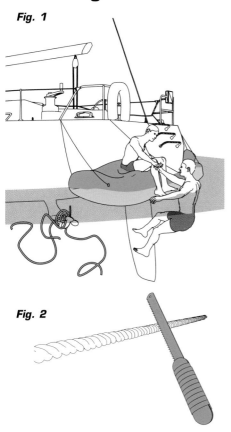

Fig. 1

Fig. 2

Since a crew member will have to dive to clear the obstruction, follow the methods set out in the section on Diving p.48. Stopping the vessel will greatly aid repair.

It may help to raise the stern of the boat by concentrating weights forward. Also, a partially inflated dinghy can make a useful work area as well as cushioning the stern in any sort of swell (figure 1).

It will probably be easier to saw rather than cut the rope turns on the propeller. A hacksaw blade or keyhole saw is most effective and can be lashed to a makeshift wood handle (figure 2).

PUMPS

Modern boats are equipped with pumps for engine cooling, drinking water, showers, bilges, wash downs, and more. With very few exceptions, these are impeller or diaphragm driven and extremely reliable. However, diaphragms and impellers are made of synthetic rubber or neoprene and they can rupture, tear, or even disintegrate. Pumps can clog, and hose clamps can come undone.

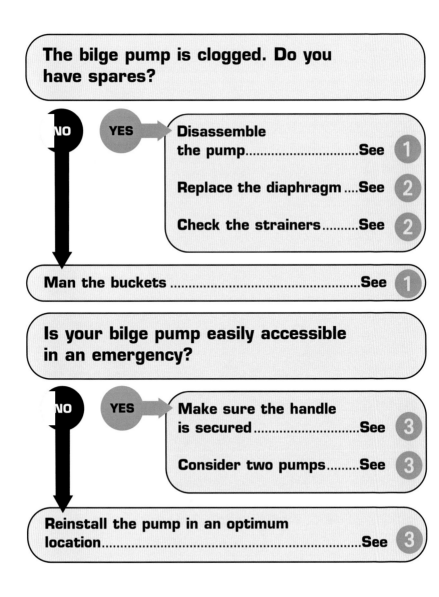

The bilge pump is clogged. Do you have spares?

NO

YES

Disassemble the pump..............................See **1**

Replace the diaphragm ....See **2**

Check the strainers..........See **2**

Man the buckets ....See **1**

Is your bilge pump easily accessible in an emergency?

NO

YES

Make sure the handle is secured..............................See **3**

Consider two pumps.........See **3**

Reinstall the pump in an optimum location...See **3**

The engine is overheating. Are you equipped to replace the engine cooling pump impeller?

NO   **YES** → Shut down the engine and replace ....See **4**

Always carry spare parts ....See **4**

Consider installing an easily removable cap ....See **4**

Bilge-pump clogging **1**

Most modern bilge pumps are of the diaphragm type. These will function in situations where older pumps would have long failed or clogged. However, even a pump that has a capacity of moving 30 gallons (115 liters) of water per minute will not be very effective with a major hull breach. In such a case, only an engine-driven pump will suffice. And if the engine ceases to function, a bucket brigade will do far more than either.

Spares **2**

Always carry spares for all pumps. A new diaphragm can be installed in approximately five minutes, providing access is reasonable (figure 1). The same is true of strainers; you must be able to reach them.

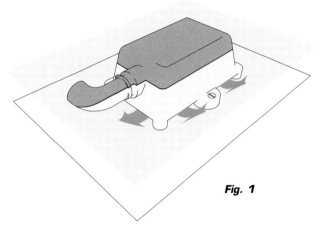

Fig. 1

Pump locations

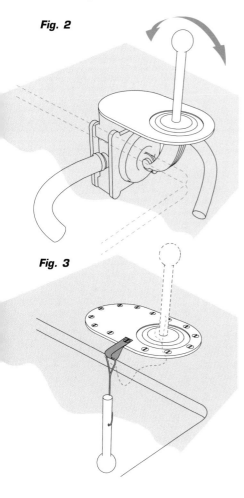

Fig. 2

Fig. 3

Installation is vital to proper pump efficiency and safety. Too often, bilge pumps are mounted so that a cockpit locker lid must be opened to operate them. Mount the cockpit pump with a through-deck fitting, properly capped and watertight, and accessible to the helmsman. Any offshore boat should have a second pump operable from below. Most stock boats are equipped with pumps of much too small a capacity. The minimum capacity should be 25 gallons (95 liters) per minute.

Pump handles will break. Either keep a factory spare, make sure the interior and exterior pumps have identical handles, or carry a hardwood dowel of the correct dimensions. Also, it is a good idea to drill a hole through the handle and tie it with a light lanyard to a spot where it is always at hand, near the pump. A spring clip will also work well (figures 2 and 3).

Engine cooling pumps 4

The cause of most engines overheating is the wear or fracture of the pump impeller. If the engine shows signs of overheating, or the cooling water discharge stops, immediately shut down the engine. Check the pump impeller. Spares should always be carried. A cap for the pump housing is now made that allows replacement of the impeller simply by means of removing thumb screws—so there is no need for wrenches.

RADAR

If you can afford it, radar can be an immensely valuable tool on the water. Not only can it help nighttime and low-visibility navigation, but it serves as an effective warning of other ships in the vicinity, allowing you to make defensive course changes. However, it takes much practice to learn to differentiate objects on the screen.

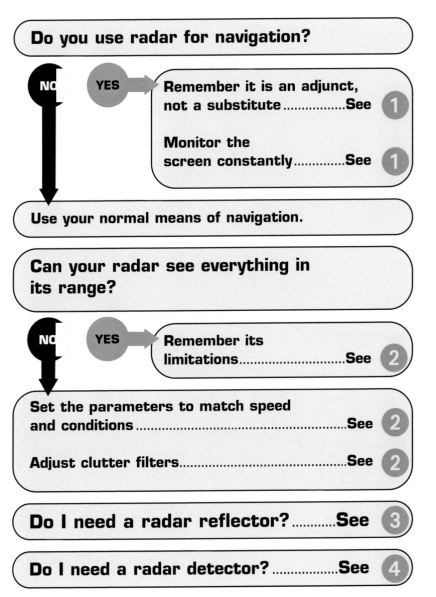

Do you use radar for navigation?

NO

YES → Remember it is an adjunct, not a substitute................See **1**

Monitor the screen constantly..............See **1**

Use your normal means of navigation.

Can your radar see everything in its range?

NO

YES → Remember its limitations............................See **2**

Set the parameters to match speed and conditions..See **2**

Adjust clutter filters..See **2**

Do I need a radar reflector?............**See** **3**

Do I need a radar detector?................**See** **4**

Radar for navigation

Radar navigation can be a valuable aid in low-visibility (figure 1). However, it is only as reliable as the operator. Screen clutter can be confusing, especially in rain and gale conditions. False echoes, blind sectors, and interference can cause identification problems. Only practice will allow you to both fine tune the radar, and distinguish targets with greater precision. Some radar can be interfaced with chart plotters.

Fig. 1

Ranges

Ranges can vary depending on the power of the radar set and the size of the antenna (figure 2). Most modern radar has adjustable ranges, which are most useful when approaching a headland or landfall. Basic filters can reduce clutter to the degree of recognizing landmass.

Fig. 2

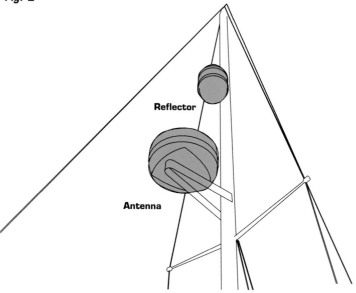

Reflector

Antenna

Radar reflectors .... ③

Any boat venturing into shipping lanes should carry a radar reflector, properly mounted. The old folding metal reflectors are not particularly viable in that their surface area is only exposed to radar signals randomly and may not present enough area to be seen. Masts and rigging are not good reflectors. Modern reflectors, though not cheap, are containers filled with a complex set of reflecting materials and are far more effective.

Radar dectectors .... ④

Radar detectors (figure 3) are similar to those used in cars to avoid a speeding ticket. They are passive devices that will only alert you to the presence of ships' operating radar. Whether they are necessary depends on your cruising ground. In areas of heavy shipping traffic, they can be invaluable.

Fig. 3

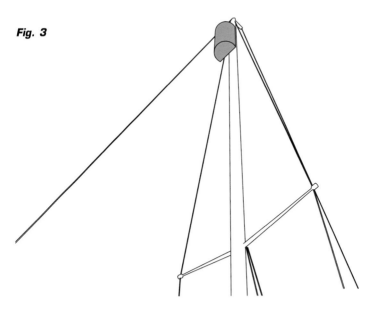

RADIO

No prudent skipper goes to sea without at least a VHF radio. Compared to the old days, when communication was by means of flag signals and flares, today's small, powerful radios allow reliable voice-to-voice communication with other ships, harbormasters, and lock and bridge tenders. A marine radio is not a toy. Use it only when you need to: don't clutter the airwaves with pointless chatter. Save that for your cellphone!

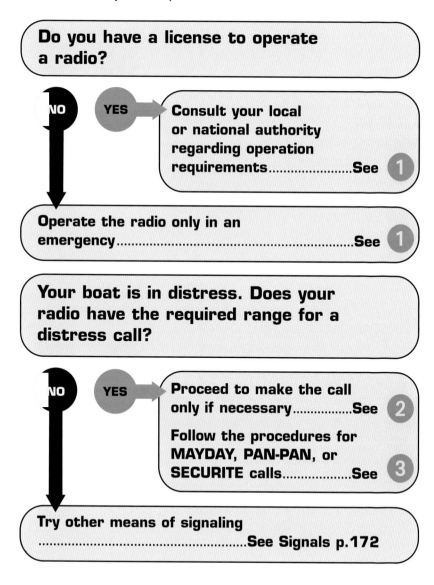

Do you have a license to operate a radio?

NO / **YES** → Consult your local or national authority regarding operation requirements...................**See** 1

Operate the radio only in an emergency..**See** 1

Your boat is in distress. Does your radio have the required range for a distress call?

NO / **YES** → Proceed to make the call only if necessary................**See** 2

Follow the procedures for MAYDAY, PAN-PAN, or SECURITE calls...................**See** 3

Try other means of signaling
....**See Signals p.172**

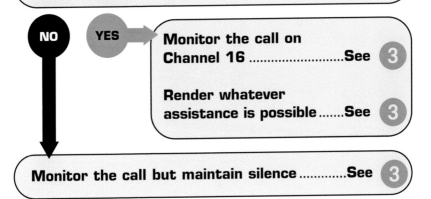

You hear a **MAYDAY.** Are you able to assist?

NO

YES ➡ Monitor the call on Channel 16 ....See ③

Render whatever assistance is possible ....See ③

Monitor the call but maintain silence ....See ③

Licenses .... ①

Different nations have different requirements for the operation of radios, depending on the type. In the UK, you must apply for and pay for a radio license for all types of marine radio. In the USA, you may operate—as a recreational user—a VHF marine radio, EPIRB, and marine radar without an FCC ship station license. However, under US regulations, if you travel internationally, you must obtain and carry an FCC ship station license. Under emergency conditions, you may operate a radio.

Range .... ②

VHF has a line-of-sight range of about 25 miles; handheld sets, having less power, will be less. For ship-to-ship and coastal communications, VHF will work satisfactorily. For greater distances, the options are SSB, satellite, or ham radio. SSB and satellite communications are expensive, though generally effective. Satellite e-mail can be a godsend, but in emergencies you need someone monitoring at the other end. VHF radios usually monitor channel 16 automatically. Thus, any distress call will most likely be heard by someone.

MAYDAY .... ③

In any life-threatening emergency, you should broadcast a **MAYDAY**. Do not send a MAYDAY if your engine breaks down, or if you cut your finger! You will be wasting time, money, and resources. Also, if you broadcast a hoax, you will be legally liable for the costs of search and rescue. Think before you act!

If you hear a MAYDAY, monitor the call carefully, noting all information. If Coast Guard or lifeboat services respond, continue to monitor the call, but keep radio silence. If these agencies do not respond, attempt to pass on the information to the authorities or to any ships in the area. If possible, render assistance without, however, putting your own boat and crew in danger.

PAN-PAN calls are used when the safety of a boat or person is in jeopardy. This is the signal to use for crew-overboard situations when you need assistance in recovery.

SECURITE messages are used to relay navigation information and weather warnings.

DSC (Digital Selective Calling) is now becoming the legal standard for marine radio systems. It is a paging system used to automate distress alerts over marine radio. When the DSC radio is interfaced with a GPS, it will automatically broadcast the position of your ship. Since your ship's address and identification are programmed into the DSC, the chances of quick identification and location are much greater, and the speed of aid and/or rescue greatly increased.

To make a MAYDAY call:

1. Say, "MAYDAY, MAYDAY, MAYDAY."
2. Say, "This is (name of boat three times, call letters once)."
3. Say once more, MAYDAY and your boat's name.
4. Report your position.
5. Report nature of the emergency.
6. Report type of assistance required.
7. Report number of crew and condition of any injured.
8. Describe the boat and its current state.
9. Say, "Over."

RIGGING

Unless you sail a freestanding rig, your mast will be held up by rigging—wire rope, rigging screws (turnbuckles), toggles, spreaders, chain plates, pins, vangs, and assorted bits and pieces. If one single element or parts of the rig are damaged, the entire rig is in danger. Pre-season examination is mandatory, along with tuning. Look out for cracks in rigging screws and chain plates, broken wire rope, kinks, and corrosion.

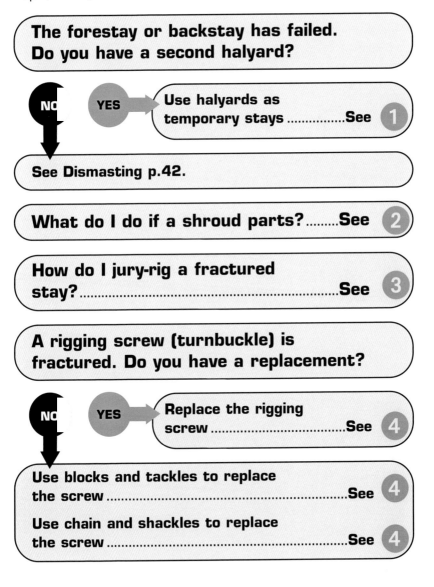

The forestay or backstay has failed. Do you have a second halyard?

NO

YES → Use halyards as temporary stays ....See ①

See Dismasting p.42.

What do I do if a shroud parts?.........See ②

How do I jury-rig a fractured stay?...See ③

A rigging screw (turnbuckle) is fractured. Do you have a replacement?

NO

YES → Replace the rigging screw ....See ④

Use blocks and tackles to replace the screw...See ④

Use chain and shackles to replace the screw...See ④

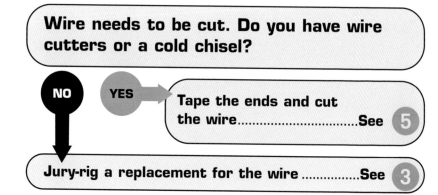

Wire needs to be cut. Do you have wire cutters or a cold chisel?

NO   **YES** →   Tape the ends and cut the wire...............See **5**

Jury-rig a replacement for the wire ....See **3**

Forestay and backstay............................ **1**

Depending on conditions, you can continue sailing if the forestay or backstay fails. If the forestay fails, do not risk the chance of the mast falling aft into the cockpit. Use the foresail halyard as a temporary stay (figure 1). If you have a second halyard—a spinnaker, for instance—double the halyards to the stem head fitting. When things start getting rough, strike the sails. If the backstay breaks, lead a halyard aft and tension with a Spanish windlass or block and tackle—the vang, perhaps. You will head up during this process. If the halyard is long enough, it can be led aft to a winch for greater tensioning (figure 2).

Fig. 1

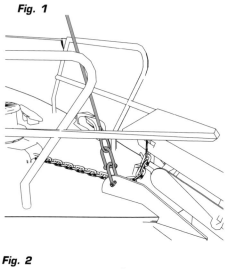

Fig. 2

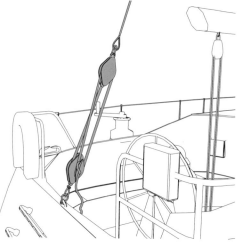

Broken shrouds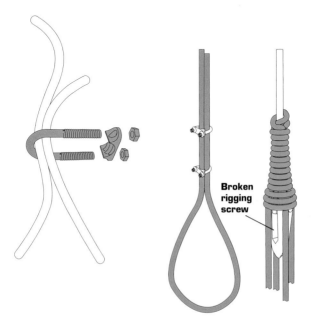

2

Should a shroud fail, immediately tack—gybing will place undue strain on the rig, and could carry it away—and head off so as to put the least strain on the failed part of the rig. Try to take sea state into account, as undue pitching and rolling can cause almost as much damage as the original fitting letting go. Run a spare halyard to temporarily replace the leeward shroud. In anything but light weather, strike sails.

Jury-rigging fractured stays

3

Your most useful equipment for jury rigging, besides a spare halyard, will be wire rope or bulldog clips. These should be galvanized, and not stainless steel, which has a tendency to slip. If a stay has fractured at the turnbuckle fitting end, form a bight or loop with the wire and use at least two clips to form an eye, which may be lashed or shackled to the turnbuckle or attached directly to the chainplate with a block and tackle (figure 3). If the stay has broken at the masthead, sooner or later someone will have to go aloft. If no spare length of wire is aboard, the eye should be made at the end of the wire aloft (do this while still on deck), which can then be shackled to the masthead fitting or tang. The now shorter stay can be attached to the chainplate or turnbuckle with shackles and a length of chain or low-stretch fiber rope. If the wire has broken midway, make two eyes and fasten them with shackles, lashings, or chain.

Fig. 3

Broken rigging screw

Turnbuckles (rigging screws) 4

Rarely does it occur, but when a turnbuckle fractures or lets go the solution is actually much simpler than when the shroud or stay breaks. Either replace with another turnbuckle, use a tackle arrangement, or use a length of chain and shackles to replace the turnbuckle. There will be times, however, when the turnbuckle is frozen tight. This is the result of lax maintenance, and you should curse yourself soundly. Since you are presumably sailing on a tack that takes the strain off the fitting, remove the offender by slipping a clevis pin, lash the stay temporarily, and use two mole wrenches to break the freeze. Then replace the turnbuckle.

Cutting wire 5

Should wire need to be cut, use either wire cutters or a cold chisel. However, whip or tape the wire to either side of the proposed cut first to prevent unlayed strands or eye-damaging bits of flying steel (figure 4). Wire rope is prone to a life of its own, and another crew member should hold it fast. If you lack the personnel, lash the wire with light stuff to keep it in place.

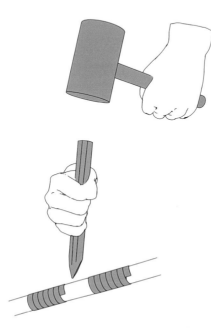

Fig. 4

SAIL REPAIR

Sail making has advanced more in recent years than at any time since the introduction of synthetics. Computer-directed sail cutting, hi-tech adhesives, in-mast and in-boom reefing, furling headsails—the list is long and, for the most part, good for the sailor. Most sails—unless you are a fervent and relatively wealthy racing sailor—are still sewn from numerous panels of synthetic cloth with synthetic thread. Tears can occur and repair will be necessary.

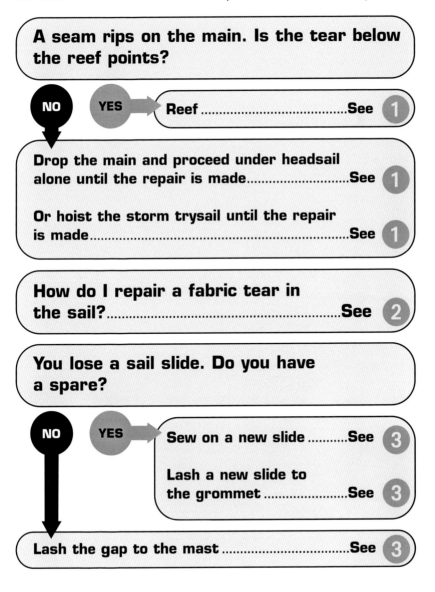

A seam rips on the main. Is the tear below the reef points?

NO YES ➡ Reef ....See ①

Drop the main and proceed under headsail alone until the repair is made...........................See ①

Or hoist the storm trysail until the repair is made...........................See ①

How do I repair a fabric tear in the sail?...........................See ②

You lose a sail slide. Do you have a spare?

NO YES ➡ Sew on a new slide ....See ③

Lash a new slide to the grommet ....See ③

Lash the gap to the mast ....See ③

> **There is a tear in the bolt rope. Can you patch the sail around it?**

NO · **YES** →

Sew a patch around the sail ....See **4**

Temporarily tape the tear ....See **4**

> Drop the sail to make permanent repairs ....See **4**

> **What do I do if the clew fitting goes by the board?** ....See **5**

Mainsail seams **1**

If the main rips along a seam or the stitching comes undone, and the tear is below the reef points, reefing is the simplest immediate solution (figure 1). If the tear is high up, lower the sail immediately and continue to sail under foresail alone. Another option is to hoist the storm

Fig. 1

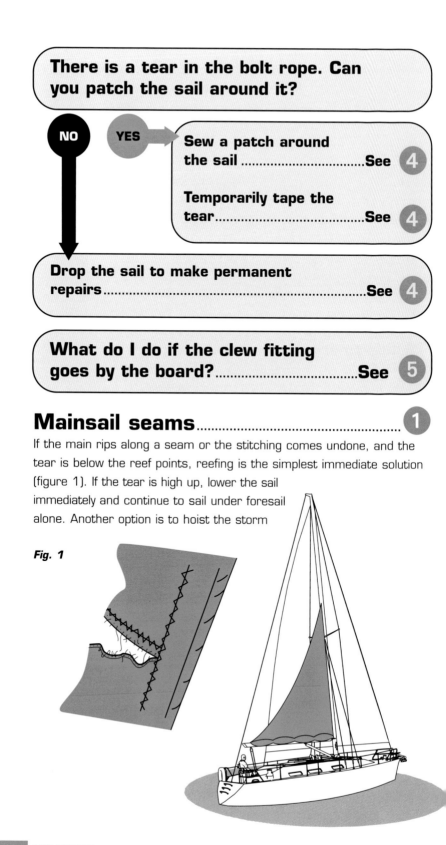

trysail in its place until repairs can be effected. With roller reefing, there is greater latitude in just how large or small the reef can be, but after a certain point the main will lose any efficiency, driving power, or ability to balance the foresail, and should be dropped and replaced.

Cloth tears .... ②

Should the sailcloth, not a seam, tear, it is best to patch it on both sides, either with rigging tape or, a better option, the special self-sticking sail-repair patches sold for this purpose. In calm conditions, patches of sailcloth and instant waterproof glue can effect a temporary repair. The best solution is to drop the sail, replace it with another, and have the sail sent below for a proper stitched repair.

A stitched sail repair requires, in synthetic cloths, fine needles—not the canvas-piercing monsters of old—Terylene/Dacron thread, and a comfortable sewing palm. Beeswax is not really necessary with modern materials. Double the thread, knot the two loose ends, and close the tears with a series of herringbone stitches. With synthetic cloth, anything from six to ten stitches per inch (2.5 cm), depending upon the weight of cloth, thread, etc., should be adequate. If you can fit your four fingers through the tear, it should be patched. A patch can be done in several ways. Use approximately the same weight cloth as that of the sail. Use two layers—one on either side—of lighter cloth. Seal or fold under the edges. Tape the patch in place. Fasten using a seam stitch. **Note:** try to line up the weave of the sailcloth and the patch if possible. With very large rips this may not be achievable with the materials at hand. Any patch is better than none.

Adhesive-backed sail-repair patches are sold for small jobs (figure 2). These will usually work for a while, but are neither permanent nor particularly suited for heavy weather. They can be used temporarily until you or your sail maker makes a permanent repair.

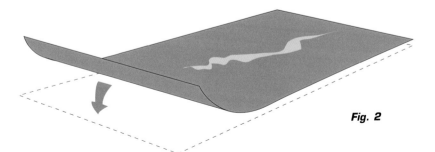

Fig. 2

Sail slides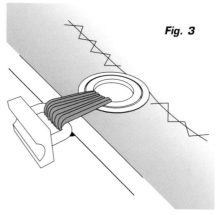

Lost sail slides are common, especially with plastic and nylon. A few spare slides should be carried on board. These can easily be sewn on or, if the sail has been grommeted along its luff, they can be lashed with light synthetic twine or tape (figure 3). If no spare slides are onboard, lash the gap directly to the mast, but with a loop that is loose enough to allow lowering the sail.

Fig. 3

Bolt ropes

Bolt-rope tears are easily repaired with a patch around the rope on either side, extending several inches outward from the rope (figure 4). Sew through on both sides, remembering to keep the patch around the rope as tight as possible, increasing the diameter as little as possible and thus avoiding jams. Tape can be used for a temporary patch. If you cannot effect an immediate repair, drop the sail.

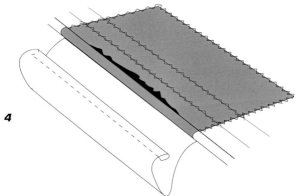

Fig. 4

Clew fittings

If the clew fitting goes by the board, a stout lashing will temporarily suffice (figure 5). More permanently, sew in a new grommet, sew in a rope grommet, or stitch in a D-ring or O-ring replacement. In any case, make sure that the corner of the sail is heavily reinforced, and that the stitching is doubled or quadrupled. All sewn repairs are similar. If overlap is possible, do it. If you can double the stitching, do it. If both sides can be patched, do it.

Fig. 5

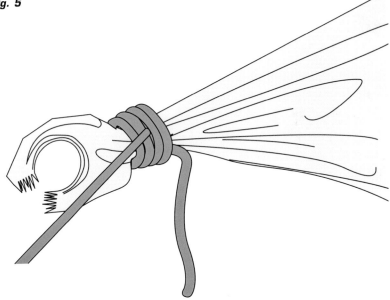

SALVAGE

Salvage claims are fraught with hidden danger. Be sure you understand what is involved before signing any forms. Also, be certain that all terms are agreed upon before any action is taken by the salvor. Included below is an internationally accepted salvage agreement.

Salvor's claims .... ①

A salvor must establish certain proofs to make a claim: 1) The vessel was in peril; 2) He made a voluntary decision to aid the distressed vessel; 3) He risked his life and vessel to save the distressed vessel; and 4) He achieved his aim and succeeded in aiding.

Vessel-owner's rights .... ②

Make a contract beforehand if possible. If a contract is agreed upon before rescue efforts commence, no further claims can be made. A verbal agreement with witnesses present is legal and binding. No matter what, few claims are settled without court or arbitrator attentions. Be prepared for a long and complicated procedure. Seek legal advice, specialized if necessary. The procedures are not related to land law and can easily overwhelm an amateur. Accepting tows or aid does NOT entitle the aiding party to claim salvage, nor claim ownership of property. Consult an attorney or solicitor to determine the extent of claims or damages.

International Conventions on Salvage, 1989

Criteria for Fixing the Reward

1. The reward shall be fixed with a view to encouraging salvage operations, taking into account the following criteria without regard to the order in which they are presented below:

(a) the salved value of the vessel and other property;

(b) the skill and efforts of the salvors in preventing or minimizing damage to the environment;

(c) the measure of success obtained by the salvor;

(d) the nature and degree of the danger;

(e) the skill and efforts of the salvors in salving the vessel, other property and life;

(f) the time used and expenses and losses incurred by the salvors;

(g) the risk of liability and other risks run by the salvors or their equipment;

(h) the promptness of the services rendered;

(i) the availability and use of vessels or other equipment intended for salvage operations;

(j) the state of readiness and efficiency of the salvor's equipment and the value thereof.

2. Payment of a reward fixed according to paragraph 1 shall be made by all of the vessel and other property interests in proportion to their respective salved values. However, a State Party may in its national law provide that the payment of a reward has to be made by one of these interests, subject to a right of recourse of this interest against the other interests for their respective shares. Nothing in this article shall prevent any right of defense.

3. The rewards, exclusive of any interest and recoverable legal costs that may be payable thereon, shall not exceed the salved value of the vessel and other property.

Special Compensation

1. If the salvor has carried out salvage operations in respect of a vessel which by itself or its cargo threatened damage to the environment and has failed to earn a reward under article 13 at least equivalent to the special compensation assessable in accordance with this article, he shall be entitled to special compensation from the owner of that vessel equivalent to his expenses as herein defined.

2. If, in the circumstances set out in paragraph 1, the salvor by his salvage operations has prevented or minimized damage to the environment, the special compensation payable by the owner to the salvor under paragraph 1 may be increased up to a maximum of 30% of the expenses incurred by the salvor. However, the tribunal, if it deems it fair and just to do so and bearing in mind the relevant criteria set out in article 13, paragraph 1, may increase such special compensation further, but in no event shall the total increase be more than 100% of the expenses incurred by the salvor.

3. Salvor's expenses for the purpose of paragraphs 1 and 2 means the out-of-pocket expenses reasonably incurred by the salvor in the salvage operation and a fair rate for equipment and personnel actually and reasonably used in the salvage operation, taking into consideration the criteria set out in article 13, paragraph 1(h), (i), and (j).

4. The total special compensation under this article shall be paid only if and to the extent that such compensation is greater than any reward recoverable by the salvor under article 13.

5. If the salvor has been negligent and has thereby failed to prevent or minimize damage to the environment, he may be deprived of the whole or part of any special compensation due under this article.

6. Nothing in this article shall affect any right of recourse on the part of the owner of the vessel.

SELF-STEERING

Sailing shorthanded or voyaging far usually demands self-steering. The choice is between vane-activated self-steering or an autopilot. The vane is obviously only for sailing yachts; autopilots can be used in both sail- and powerboats. No matter which option you choose, there are eccentricities that must be worked out.

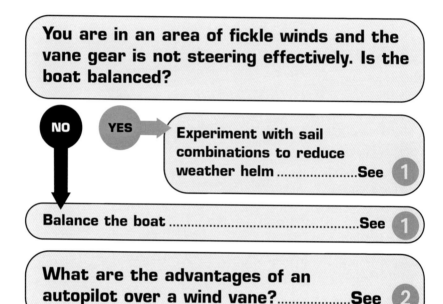

You are in an area of fickle winds and the vane gear is not steering effectively. Is the boat balanced?

NO   **YES**   **Experiment with sail combinations to reduce weather helm** ....**See** **1**

Balance the boat ....**See** **1**

What are the advantages of an autopilot over a wind vane?.................**See** **2**

Vane gears **1**

There are many types of vane gear available. All types work on the principle that the vane will transmit force to the rudder or auxiliary rudder, steering the boat relative to the wind direction (figure 1). In areas of fickle winds, vane gears will not perform particularly well. Much depends on the natural ability of the boat to get into a groove on its own. If the boat is easily balanced, a vane gear will generally perform much better.

If the vane does not perform to expectations, a certain amount of experimentation will be needed to find the right combination of sails to reduce weather helm. This may involve re-cutting sails or repositioning the mast (in extreme cases). Vanes can be temperamental, and trial and error is the only way to get them to work effectively. Should the vane malfunction at sea, repairs can be dicey, as it is, after all, hanging off the stern. A spare vane should be carried, as well as bushings, steering lines, possibly a spare rudder, and other parts. Mounting a vane is usually a custom job, as each yacht has a different stern.

Fig. 1

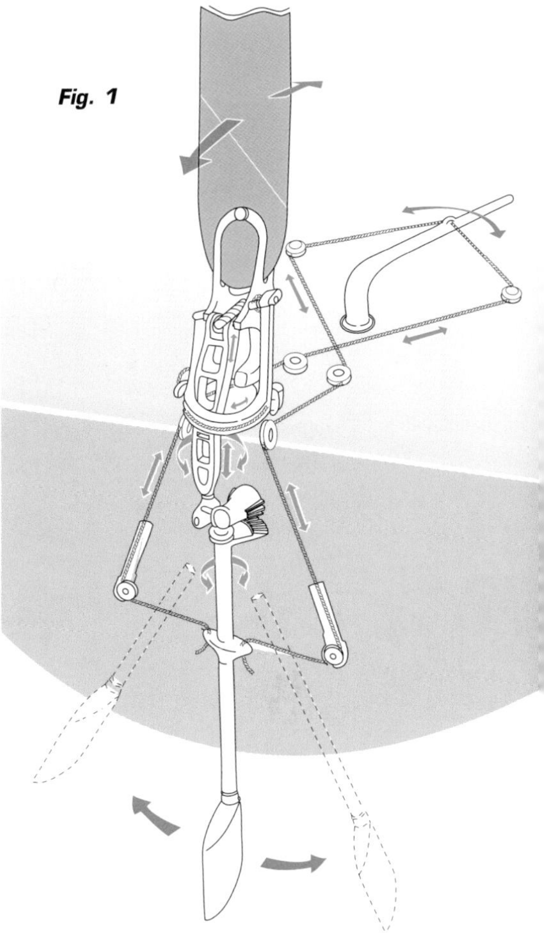

In this typical servo vane, the force of the wind activates an underwater paddle which then transfers the motion to the tiller by means of lines, correcting the course in relation to the wind direction.

Autopilots..2

Autopilots have long been standard on powerboats—after all, they are not dependent on wind direction to get somewhere. Autopilots for sailing yachts are certainly effective, but only in steady winds or under power. Since they maintain a compass course, wind shifts will luff or back the sails, besides which they draw considerable power from the batteries. With the exception of tiller-mounted autopilots, installation by a professional is a good idea. The one great advantage of an autopilot is that it can be interfaced with a GPS, providing an accurate course made good to a waypoint or a series of waypoints.

SIGNALS

Signaling is not for episodes of distress only. Signals can be sent to harbor authorities, passing ships, and planes to relay positions, for navigation and weather information, and for warnings. Here we are concerned with distress signals.

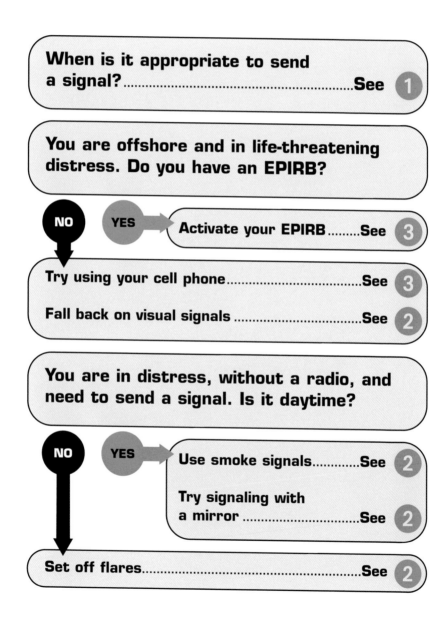

When is it appropriate to send a signal?..**See** **1**

You are offshore and in life-threatening distress. Do you have an EPIRB?

NO | **YES** → **Activate your EPIRB**........**See** **3**

Try using your cell phone...................................**See** **3**

Fall back on visual signals ....**See** **2**

You are in distress, without a radio, and need to send a signal. Is it daytime?

NO | **YES** → **Use smoke signals**............**See** **2**

Try signaling with a mirror ....**See** **2**

Set off flares...**See** **2**

When to send distress signals........... ①

Far too often distress signals are sent for inappropriate reasons, or for no reason at all. If you are becalmed or the head won't flush, you have no excuse for sending a signal. Doing so costs rescue services time and money that is better spent on real emergencies. Define your situation carefully before even attempting to signal.

Flares and smoke signals .... ②

Don't use flares in the daytime or smoke signals at night. No one will see them. All pyrotechnics are dangerous (figure 1). Be sure you know how to operate them: you don't want to set the boat on fire. Be sure to renew flares when they expire. They may well work, but you have no guarantee. Dispose of unused flares safely: contact your local authority.

Fig. 1

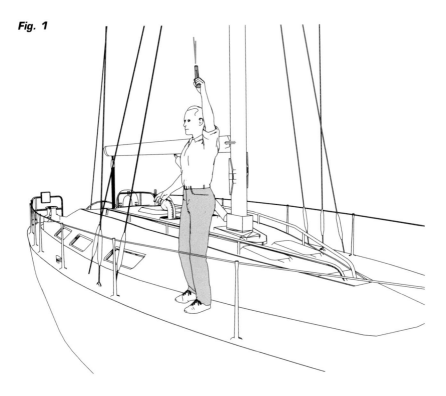

In a pinch, a metal bucket of burning rags (figure 2), a gun fired, and most importantly a signal mirror can work. Obviously, burning materials must be used with extreme caution and are not advised aboard GRP boats. A signal mirror, even if torn from the head's bulkhead, can, providing the weather cooperates, be extremely effective. It can be seen from the bridge of a large ship with greater ease than dye markers or other daytime visual signals (figure 3).

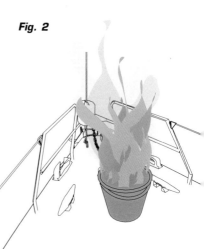

Fig. 2

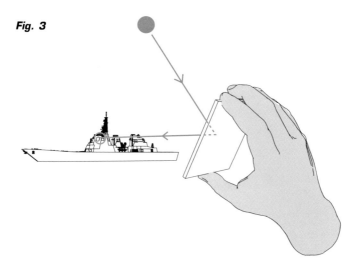

Fig. 3

EPIRB .... ③

Boats venturing offshore should carry an EPIRB (Emergency Position Indicating Radio Beacon). When activated, an EPIRB will send a continuous radio signal that rescue craft and planes can home in on to a remarkable degree of accuracy. Don't skimp: a good EPIRB is expensive and those certified to SOLAS standards are preferable.

Other possibilities include cell phones, VHF (if range permits), and SSB. MAYDAY calls are discussed under Radio p.156.

STEERING GEAR

Steering gear can be as simple as a tiller attached to the rudder post or as complicated as a dual rudder hydraulic system. Since any gear is subject to constant movement and strain, malfunctions and breakages can occur.

The cheeks at the rudder head are damaged. Is there any scrap plywood on board?

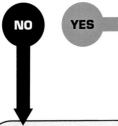 NO

YES 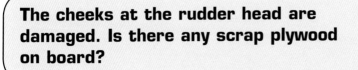 Use anything that can be fit between the rudder cheeks and is long enough for leverage.........................See **1**

Rig lines from the rudder head through locks...See **1**

How do I replace a tiller fitted to a socket?...See **2**

The wheel steering has failed. Can the problem be repaired?

NO YES Determine which wheel steering system you have and make appropriate repairs...........See **3**

Attach emergency tiller ....See **3**

Cheeks .... ①

If the outboard rudder is broken, jam a section of boathook or an oar between the rudder cheeks and lash in place (figure 1). If the cheeks at the rudder head are damaged, scrap plywood can be used as reinforcement on either side, lashed temporarily (figure 2). Later, when time permits, drill three staggered holes through ply and rudder cheeks and through bolt. A makeshift tiller can still be lashed between the new

Fig. 1

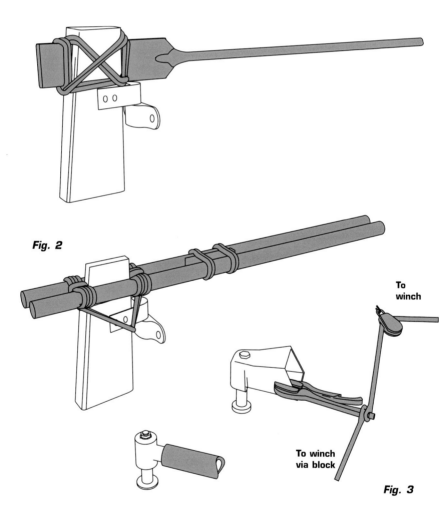

Fig. 2

To winch

To winch
via block

Fig. 3

cheeks or else drilled and then through-bolted, making for a stronger, more responsive jury tiller. If nothing else is at hand, use two long fiddles, such as are often found to keep settee cushions in place. These are usually fastened with self-tapping screws and can be easily re-fitted later; they make an elegant, either-side-of-the-rudder-head tiller.

If no replacement is possible, try running lines from the tiller head or socket through blocks, port and starboard, using cockpit winches if necessary, to steer the boat (figure 3).

Cheek fittings are usually bronze or stainless steel and the wood may have swelled between them, the tiller having broken slightly above the fitting. Knock out retaining bolt and swelled wood fragments. This will require a chisel and mallet. The same tools can be used to shape the wood replacement. Remember, any jury tiller will be weaker and offer a less-than-ideal position for maximum leverage. Go easy.

Socket-fitted tillers................................ 2

Socket fittings are usually impossible to clear quickly. A possible solution is to use a section of whisker/jockey pole or any strong tubing over the socket fitting. Another possibility, if you can clear the socket, is to use a spare stanchion—chilly to touch but of unrivaled strength.

Wheel steering...................................... 3

The majority of steering gears using wheels are either cable, direct linkage, or rod and hydraulic (figure 4, over the page). Each has specific problem areas. Cable systems usually suffer from either a broken cable or the failure of the clips holding the cable in place. Repairing this is not difficult if you can access the quadrant and cable. Non-stretch rope can sometimes be utilized as a temporary repair.

Rod steering breaks often happen at the linkage points. If you have no way to reattach the linkage, either jury rig an attachment or break out the emergency tiller.

Hydraulic systems can suffer a drop in hydraulic pressure due to a leak; the pump may stop functioning or a hose may split. Without specialized tools and replacement parts this may be unfixable.

Looseness in the steering can usually be corrected by tightening cables or adjusting linkages; in a hydraulic system, it can be caused by a loose or leaking hose connection or fitting. The system will probably have to be bled.

In all boats equipped with wheel steering, an emergency tiller should be available.

Fig. 4

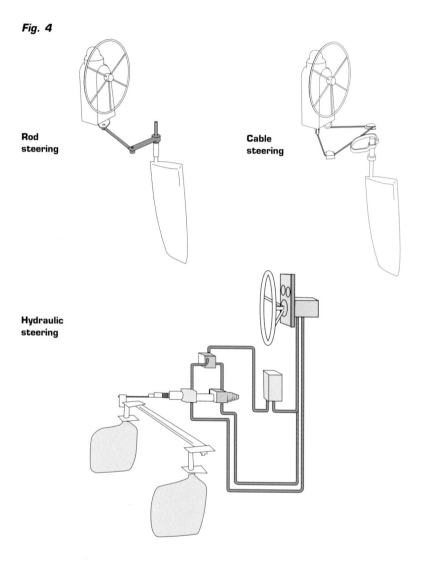

Rod steering

Cable steering

Hydraulic steering

The three most common types of wheel-steering mechanisms are cable, rod, and hydraulic. The linkages that transfer the wheel's movement to the rudder are most likely to fail due to wear and tear (cable and rod) or leaks (hydraulic).

TOWING

There are times when the engine dies, the rudder is lost, the sails are ripped, or some other catastrophe has overcome you and your ship. If may be necessary to be towed to or to offer a tow to another boat. To avoid en-route disasters, some of the following points may be useful.

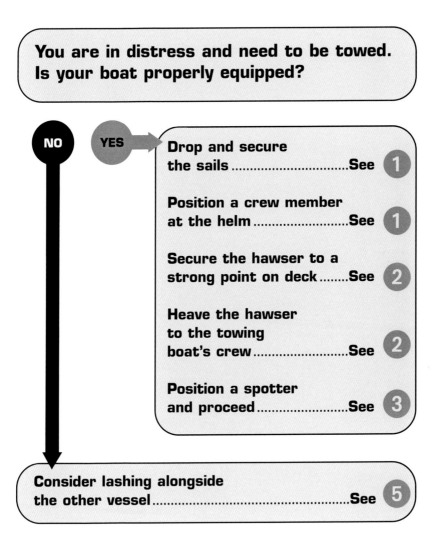

You are in distress and need to be towed. Is your boat properly equipped?

NO   YES

Drop and secure
the sails ....See **1**

Position a crew member
at the helm ....See **1**

Secure the hawser to a
strong point on deck ....See **2**

Heave the hawser
to the towing
boat's crew ....See **2**

Position a spotter
and proceed ....See **3**

Consider lashing alongside
the other vessel...See **5**

You are preparing to tow another boat. Are you under sail?

NO

YES →

Pass the disabled vessel's bows from leeward.....................See **1**

Heave the towline as you pass her bows ....See **2**

Head off on a reach or run...................................See **4**

Approach from leeward..See **1**

Pass or accept a hawser when crossing her bows...See **2**

Attach the hawser to spread the strain ....See **2**

Position a spotter ....See **3**

Proceed ahead slowly, handing out the towline until taut...... ....See **3**

Approach.. **1**

In a disabled yacht, drop sail before accepting a tow. However, if there is a sea running, a very small steadying sail aft may make steering easier for the towed boat and maneuverability greater for the towboat.

The crew should be positioned at the helm, forward, and on standby. All crew members must be ready for immediate action, especially as this might concern recovery of the towline.

The towing vessel should always approach from the leeward side of the disabled vessel (figure 1). It will then be able to avoid either drifting down on the vessel or overshooting it.

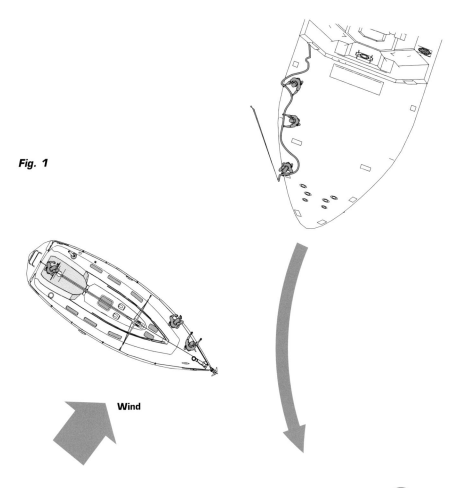

Fig. 1

Wind

The towline..2

The disabled boat should secure the bitter end of the hawser to a strong point on deck. Whether you should accept a towline or pass over your own is not a clear point of maritime law. See Salvage p.168.

Many contemporary boats do not have adequate foredeck cleats. A towing hawser handed by a commercial vessel will be quite large, and even if the cleats were enormous it is very likely they would only be through-bolted to a backing pad. Decks have been ripped up. The ideal foredeck attachment point will be a samson post properly locked into the keel or stem (figure 2, over the page). Lacking this, it is perhaps best to secure the towline around the base of the mast, or on a powerboat, around the entire deckhouse (figure 3, over the page). Alternatively, the towline can be attached to a bridle led either side of the deckhouse to the cockpit winches and then cleated. In any case, it is a good idea to bend a piece of (comparatively) light stuff to the hawser and tie its bitter end to a deck cleat; the bend to the hawser should be forward of the stemhead. In case the towline slips or chafes through at the stem, this line will make it that much easier to retrieve it.

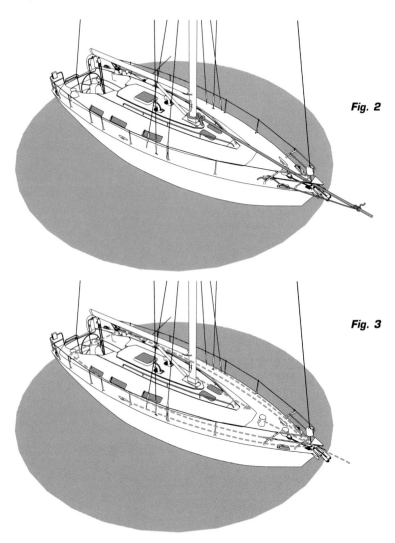

Fig. 2

Fig. 3

If you are the towing vessel, try to fasten the towline to strong points forward of the rudderpost to aid in maneuverability. A bridle, carrying the towrope to either quarter or to the winches, will enable you to maintain a straighter tow and allow for more fluid handling, as well as keeping the rope clear of the propeller (figure 4). It will prevent your vessel from skewing from side to side and will distribute the towing strains better.

Fig. 4

Proceeding 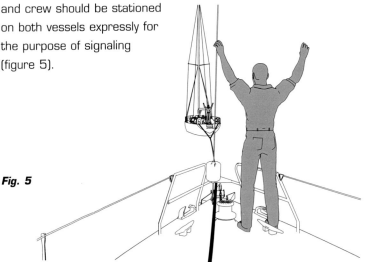 ⓷

All tows must be undertaken at slow speed. Quite often, commercial ship operators do not fully understand the limits that can be imposed safely upon a yacht under tow. What happens is either the towrope snaps or your foredeck has a good chance of disintegrating.

Hand signals are the only way to communicate properly during a tow. These must be arranged prior to the actual commencement of towing, and crew should be stationed on both vessels expressly for the purpose of signaling (figure 5).

Fig. 5

Towing under sail 4

Under sail, tows can be very efficient. They also allow for better communication between vessels and more precise handling, believe it or not. Since the sails can be trimmed to help steer the boat, there will be less strain on the rudder assembly. Also, there will be little chance of dragging the disabled vessel at imprudent speeds. The towing vessel should approach from windward, secure to the disabled vessel, and proceed on a reach (figure 6).

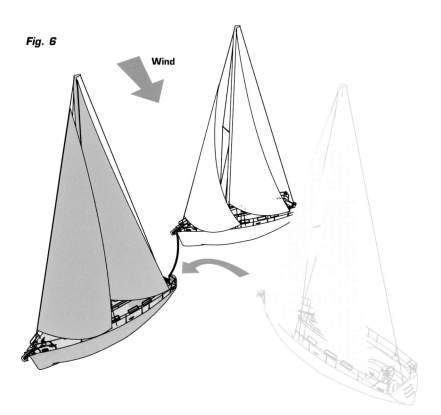

Fig. 6

Wind

When towing is impracticable 5

There are times, especially in calm conditions, where it may be better to lash the boats together, with the able ship slightly astern of the disabled one. Well-fendered fore-and-aft lines, as well as spring lines, will allow for greater control of both vessels.

WATER

Drinking water can run low on long passages. You will have to learn to conserve. However, even full tanks can be contaminated and rendered unsafe to drink. Here are a few ideas to keep in mind when planning a voyage.

Rainwater.. 1

Rainwater can be caught in awnings, buckets, from the mainsail, etc. Allow it to run for a few minutes to rinse off any salt adhering to the

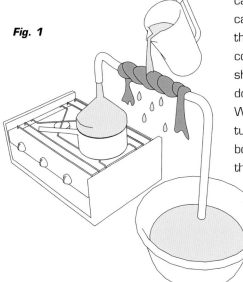

Fig. 1

catchment. Distillation can be carried out using a large pot on the stove with a funnel-like cover secured over it. A tube should run up and over, then down to another container. Wrap the central portion of the tube with rags. As the water boils, pour cold seawater on the rags; this will condense the steam in the tube and leave the salt residue in the pot, producing reasonably salt-free water (figure 1).

Purifying water.. 2

Household bleach can be used to purify and make palatable drinking water that may be tainted or old. Use two drops per quart or liter of clear water, double if the water is cloudy. Iodine (2%) can be used instead in the ratio of five drops per quart or liter of clear water, double if the water is cloudy. Let the water stand for an hour before using and aerate by pouring back and forth between containers.

Desalinization 3

Small, hand-operated membrane desalinating pumps are available at chandlers and camping-supply stores. Though they will not produce great volumes of water, they can be vital in emergencies.

APPENDICES

APPENDIX A

Spares and Tools

Following are three lists, of spare parts, tools, and oddments that might well be carried aboard any boat, but especially offshore, when you have no one but yourself to undertake repairs.

For boats under 30 feet

TOOLS
adjustable wrench
medium-sized pliers
medium-blade screwdriver
vise grips
pocket rigging knife with spike
Dacron pouch or waterproof bag
  to carry tools

SAIL REPAIR KIT
scissors
sailmaker's wax
palm
seam ripper
hot knife
three spools waxed polyester
needles (5 each #s 15 and 17)
one roll Rip-stop tape
piece of adhesive stickyback
  Dacron/Terylene
light thread for spinnaker repair,
  telltale yarn
nylon dittybag containing all of
  the above

SPARE PARTS
assorted stainless steel nuts,
  bolts, washers, sheet metal
  screws
bulbs for compass and running
  lights
winch pawls and springs
cam cleat springs
cotter pins (stainless steel, two of
  each size used and split rings)
small clear plastic tackle box to
  contain above

ODDS AND ENDS
one roll of silver duct tape
tube of clear silicone seal
one can penetrating lubricant
small can machine oil
felt-tip marker pen (black)
can Never-Seize
nylon dittybag to hold the above

For boats from 30 to 45 feet

TOOLS
Allen wrenches
chisels (one cold)
drills (hand drill plus set of bits)
files (8" mill bastard, one medium
  size rattail, one triangular)
hammer (medium ballpeen)
measuring tape
nail set
oil stone
pliers (channel locks, needle nose,
  2 regular)
saw (hacksaw plus at least 10
  high-speed blades)
screwdrivers (6 assorted sized, 2
  Phillips head, 1 jeweler's set)

vise grips
wire brush
wire cutters
work gloves
wrenches (set of combination—
  open end and box)
tool box or dry organized area to
  store all of the above

ELECTRICAL PARTS
spare bulb for each light aboard
three each spare fuses for each
  kind aboard
assorted wire crimps
wire stripper/crimper
flashlight batteries and bulbs
continuity tester
black electrical tape

ENGINE AND MECHANICAL SPARES
three cans of oil for hydraulics
hydraulic hose and assorted end
  fittings
transmission fluid
set of engine filters
assorted grits wet/dry sandpaper
complete set engine belts
enough oil for oil change
new voltage regulator for each
  alternator
canvas drop cloth with grommets
assorted hose clamps
drift punch

SPARES
assorted nuts, bolts, and washers
five of each size cotter key used
  aboard

assorted clevis pins
assorted D shackles
assorted snap shackles
one standing rigging toggle
one genoa car
winch pawls
winch pawl springs
winch roller bearings

SAIL REPAIR KIT
scissors
sailmaker's wax
two palms
two seam rippers
hot knife
light thread for spinnaker
  repairs
six spools waxed polyester
needles (10 each #s 13, 15, 17,
  19)
Rip-stop tape
piece of stickyback
  Dacron/Terylene
yarn for telltales
seizing wire
three D rings
sailmaker's pliers
nylon bag to hold all of the above

SEALERS AND LUBRICANTS
two-part epoxy
two tubes clear silicone seal
two cans penetrating lubricant
can machine oil
silicone spray
special grease mixture
rolls of colored tape
two rolls of duct tape
felt-tip marker pens (black)

For yachts 45 feet and larger

TOOLS
Allen wrenches (long and short)
awls (small and large)
block plane
chisels (one cold, two regular)
drills (brace, hand drill, variable-
  speed reversible electric drill,
  two sets of metal bits)
files (mill bastard, three wood
  files, two rattails, one triangular)
hammers (ballpeen, baby sledge,
  claw and rubber mallet)

measuring gear (measuring tape,
  fold-up ruler, calipers)
mirror (one retrieving)
nail sets (five assorted)
oil stone
pipe cutter
pipe length (for battering
  ram)
pliers (two channel locks, two
  needle nose, four regular in
  assorted sizes)
putty knives

saws (cross-cut, hacksaw and 40
blades, jigsaw and 12 blades)
screwdrivers (17 assorted
regular, six assorted Phillips
head, two off-set, one set of
jeweler's)
tap and die set
tin snips
torch set
vise
vise grips
wire brushes
wire cutters
work gloves
wrenches (adjustable; pipe
wrench, strap wrench, complete
drive socket set, complete set
combination wrenches, popular-
sized open-end wrenches)
utility knife and six blades
wooden tool box to contain
the above

ELECTRICAL PARTS
compass light assembly
running light bulbs
spare bulb for each brand of light
aboard
three of each kind of fuse aboard
assorted wire crimps
wire stripper-crimpers
flashlight batteries and bulbs
assorted sizes of wire
black electrical tape
silicone grease
multimeter
solder
soldering gun or iron
spare anemometer cups
spare wind vane
spare knotmeter transducers
tackle box for the above

SEALERS AND LUBRICANTS
two-part epoxy
two tubes clear silicone
sealer
two cans penetrating lubricant
two non-aerosol cans machine oil
two cans silicone spray
special grease mixture
two rolls duct tape
two rolls of each colored tape
felt-tip marker pens (black)
Dacron bag to hold the above

SAIL REPAIR KIT
scissors
sailmaker's wax
two palms
two seam rippers
hot knife and spare tip
light thread for spinnaker repairs
eight spools waxed polyester
needles (one package each of
#s 13, 15, 17, 19)
two rolls Rip-stop spinnaker repair
tape
pieces stickyback Dacron
yarn (red, green, and blue for
telltales)
two weights seizing wire
three D or O rings
tubular webbing
sailmaker's pliers
assorted weight sailcloth
roll Dacron/Terylene tape
six awls
grommet set (stud, spur, mallet,
die, rings, liners)
Dacron bag to hold the above

RIGGING PARTS
Nico-press tool (size of halyards,
two preferable)
12 Nico-press sleeves for each
size wire aboard
assorted stainless steel thimbles
assorted snap shackles
assorted D shackles
several lengths different weight
wire
assorted rigging toggles
assorted clevis pins
assorted track cars
link plate set
spare main halyard
spare genoa halyard
good size turnbuckle
plastic fishing tackle box for above

ENGINE AND MECHANICAL SPARES
gallon of oil for hydraulic rigging
adjusters
length hydraulic hose, assorted
fittings
two cans transmission fluid
oil for engine oil change
set engine filters, gaskets
complete set engine belts

voltage regulator for each
alternator
canvas drop cloth with grommets
assorted hose clamps
drift punch
set of injectors
grease gun with special grease
two cans starting spray
keel bolt wrench
rudder-packing wrench
spare set steering cables
master links (12) for steering
chain and spinnaker pole chain

SPARES
clear plastic tackle box containing
12 of each size SS cotter pins
clear plastic box of nuts, bolts,
and washers (12 each size
including #s 6, 8, 12 and 1/4",
5/16", 3/8")
head repair kit: spare pump
parts, diaphragms, impellers
hand pump for bilge, for
changing oil

electric drill pump, hoses
sleeve bronze wool
12 sheets each wet/dry
sandpaper in 220, 400,
600 grits
three sheets each crocus cloth,
emery paper
spare packing for propeller and
rudder glands

WINCH PARTS
12 pawls
24 pawl springs
assorted roller bearings
six split rings
toothbrush
tweezers
dental pick
extra handle
clear plastic box to hold the above

OPTIONAL
banding tool, bands, and clips

APPENDIX B

The COLREGS—International Regulations for Preventing Collisions at Sea—are one of the primary tools to avoid nautical emergencies. Too many collisions, strandings, and pile-ups on the rocks are caused by ignorance and disregard of the COLREGS. Any prudent yachtsman should be thoroughly familiar with the following and seek counsel if questions exist as to their meanings, intentions, or applications.

The International Regulations for Preventing Collisions at Sea

PART A. GENERAL

Rule 1: Application
(a) These Rules shall apply to all vessels upon the high seas and in all waters connected therewith navigable by seagoing vessels.
(b) Nothing in these Rules shall interfere with the operation of special rules made by an appropriate authority for roadsteads, harbours, rivers, lakes or inland waterways connected with the high seas and navigable by seagoing vessels. Such special rules shall conform as closely as possible to these Rules.
(c) Nothing in these Rules shall interfere with the operation of any special rules made by the Government of any State with respect to additional station or signal lights or whistle signals for ships of war and vessels proceeding under convoy, or with respect to additional station or signal lights for fishing vessels engaged in fishing as a fleet. These additional station or signal lights or whistle signals shall, so far as possible, be such that they cannot be mistaken for any light or signal authorized elsewhere under these Rules.
(d) Traffic separation schemes may be adopted by the Organization for the purpose of these Rules.
(e) Whenever the Government concerned shall have determined that a vessel of special construction or purpose cannot comply fully with the provisions of any of these Rules with respect to the number, position, range or arc of visibility of lights or shapes, as well as to the disposition and characteristics of the vessel, such vessel shall comply with such other provisions in regard to the number, position, range or arc of visibility of lights or shapes, as well as to the disposition and characteristics of sound-signalling appliances, as her Government shall have determined to be the closest possible compliance with these Rules in respect to that vessel.

RULE 2: Responsibility
(a) Nothing in these Rules shall exonerate any vessel, or the owner, master or crew thereof, from the consequences of any

neglect to comply with these Rules or of the neglect of any precaution that may be required by the ordinary practice of seamen, or by the special circumstances of the case.

(b) In construing and complying with these Rules due regard shall be had to all dangers of navigation and collision and to any special circumstances, including the limitations of the vessels involved, which may make a departure from these Rules necessary to avoid immediate danger.

RULE 3: General definitions

For the purpose of these rules, except where the context otherwise requires:

(a) The word "vessel" includes every description of watercraft, including non-displacement craft and seaplanes, used or capable of being used as a means of transportation on water.

(b) The term "power-driven vessel" means any vessel propelled by machinery.

(c) The term "sailing vessel" means any vessel under sail provided that propelling machinery, if fitted, is not being used.

(d) The term "vessel engaged in fishing" means any vessel fishing with nets, lines, trawls or other fishing apparatus which restrict maneuverability, but does not include a vessel fishing with trolling lines or other fishing apparatus which do not restrict maneuverability.

(e) The word "seaplane" includes any aircraft designed to maneuver on the water.

(f) The term "vessel not under command" means a vessel which through some exceptional circumstance is unable to maneuver as required by these Rules and is therefore unable to keep out of the way of another vessel.

(g) The term "vessel restricted in her ability to maneuver" means a vessel which from the nature of her work is restricted in her ability to maneuver as required by these Rules and is therefore unable to keep out of the way of another vessel.

The following vessels shall be regarded as vessels restricted in their ability to maneuver:

(i) a vessel engaged in laying, servicing or picking up a navigation mark, submarine cable or pipeline;

(ii) a vessel engaged in dredging, surveying or underwater operations;

(iii) a vessel engaged in replenishment or transferring persons, provisions or cargo while underway;

(iv) a vessel engaged in the launching or recovery of aircraft;

(v) a vessel engaged in minesweeping operations;

(vi) a vessel engaged in a towing operation such as severely restricts the towing vessel and her tow in their ability to deviate from their course.

(h) The term "vessel constrained by her draught" means a power-driven vessel which because of her draught in relation to the available depth of water is severely restricted in her ability to deviate from the course she is following.

(i) The word "underway" means that a vessel is not at anchor, or made fast to the shore, or aground.

(j) The words "length" and "breadth" of a vessel mean her length overall and greatest breadth.

(k) Vessels shall be deemed to be in sight of one another only when one can be observed visually from the other.

(l) The term "restricted visibility" means any condition in which visibility is restricted by fog, mist, falling snow, heavy rainstorms, sandstorms or any other similar causes.

PART B. STEERING AND SAILING RULES

Section I. Conduct of vessels in any condition of visibility

RULE 4: Application
Rules in this Section apply in any condition of visibility.

RULE 5: Look-out
Every vessel shall at all times maintain a proper look-out by sight and hearing as well as by all available means appropriate in the prevailing circumstances and conditions so as to make a full appraisal of the situation and of the risk of collision.

RULE 6: Safe speed
Every vessel shall at all times proceed at a safe speed so that she can take proper and effective action to avoid collision and be stopped within a distance appropriate to the prevailing circumstances and conditions.
In determining a safe speed the following factors shall be among those taken into account:
(a) By all vessels:
(i) the state of visibility;
(ii) the traffic density including concentrations of fishing vessels or any other vessels;
(iii) the maneuverability of the vessel with special reference to stopping distance and turning ability in the prevailing conditions;
(iv) at night the presence of background light such as from shore lights or from back scatter of her own lights;
(v) the state of wind, sea and current, and the proximity of navigational hazards;
(vi) the draught in relation to the available depth of water.
(b) Additionally, by vessels with operational radar:
(i) the characteristics, efficiency, and limitations of the radar equipment;
(ii) any constraints imposed by the radar range scale in use;
(iii) the effect on radar detection of the sea state, weather and other sources of interference;
(iv) the possibility that small vessels, ice, and other floating objects may not be detected by radar at an adequate range;
(v) the number, location and movement of vessels detected by radar;
(vi) the more exact assessment of the visibility that may be possible when radar is used to determine the range of vessels or other objects in the vicinity.

RULE 7: Risk of collision
(a) Every vessel shall use all available means appropriate to the prevailing circumstances and conditions to determine if risk of collision exists. If there is any doubt such risk shall be deemed to exist.
(b) Proper use shall be made of radar equipment if fitted and operational, including long-range scanning to obtain early warning of risk of collision and radar plotting or equivalent systematic observation of detected objects.
(c) Assumptions shall not be made on the basis of scanty information, especially scanty radar information.
(d) In determining if risk of collision exists the following considerations shall be among those taken into account:
(i) such risk shall be deemed to exist if the compass bearing of an approaching vessel does not appreciably change;
(ii) such risk may sometimes exist even when an appreciable bearing change is evident, particularly when approaching a very large vessel or a tow or when approaching a vessel at close range.

RULE 8: Action to avoid collision

(a) Any action taken to avoid collision shall, if the circumstances of the case admit, be positive, made in ample time and with due regard to the observance of good seamanship.

(b) Any alteration of course and/or speed to avoid collision shall, if the circumstances of the case admit, be large enough to be readily apparent to another vessel observing visually or by radar; a succession of small alterations of course and/or speed should be avoided.

(c) If there is sufficient sea room, alteration of course alone may be the most effective action to avoid a close-quarters situation provided that it is made in good time, is substantial and does not result in another close-quarters situation.

(d) Action taken to avoid collision with another vessel shall be such as to result in passing at a safe distance. The effectiveness of the action shall be carefully checked until the other vessel is finally past and clear.

(e) If necessary to avoid collision or allow more time to assess the situation, a vessel shall slacken her speed or take all way off by stopping or reversing her means of propulsion.

RULE 9: Narrow channels

(a) A vessel proceeding along the course of a narrow channel or fairway shall keep as near to the outer limit of the channel or fairway which lies on her starboard side as is safe and practicable.

(b) A vessel of less than 20 meters in length or a sailing vessel shall not impede the passage of a vessel which can safely navigate only within a narrow channel or fairway.

(c) A vessel engaged in fishing shall not impede the passage of any other vessel navigating within a narrow channel or fairway.

(d) A vessel shall not cross a narrow channel or fairway if such crossing impedes the passage of a vessel that can safely navigate only within such channel or fairway. The latter vessel may use the sound signal prescribed in Rule 34 (d) if in doubt as to the intention of the crossing vessel.

(e) (i) In a narrow channel or fairway when overtaking can take place only if the vessel to be overtaken has to take action to permit safe passing, the vessel intending to overtake shall indicate her intention by sounding the appropriate signal prescribed in Rule 34 (c) (i). The vessel to be overtaken shall, if in agreement, sound the appropriate signal prescribed in Rule 34 (c) (ii) and take steps to permit safe passing. If in doubt she may sound the signals prescribed in Rule 34 (d).

(ii) This Rule does not relieve the overtaking vessel of her obligation under Rule 13.

(f) A vessel nearing a bend or an area of a narrow channel or fairway where other vessels may be obscured by an intervening obstruction shall navigate with particular alertness and caution and shall sound the appropriate signal prescribed in Rule 34 (e).

(g) Any vessel shall, if the circumstances of the case admit, avoid anchoring in a narrow channel.

RULE 10: Traffic separation schemes

(a) This Rule applies to traffic separation schemes adopted by the Organization:

(b) A vessel using a traffic separation scheme shall:

(i) proceed in the appropriate traffic lane in the general direction of traffic flow for that lane;

(ii) so far as practicable keep clear of a traffic separation line or separation zone;

(iii) normally join or leave a traffic

lane at the termination of the lane, but when joining or leaving from the side shall do so at as small an angle to the general direction of traffic flow as practicable.

(c) A vessel shall so far as practicable avoid crossing traffic lanes, but if obliged to do so shall cross as nearly as practicable at right angles to the general direction of traffic flow.

(d) Inshore traffic zones shall not normally be used by through traffic which can safely use the appropriate traffic lane within the adjacent traffic separation scheme.

(e) A vessel, other than a crossing vessel, shall not normally enter a separation zone or cross a separation line except:

(i) in cases of emergency to avoid immediate danger;

(ii) to engage in fishing within a separation zone.

(f) A vessel navigating in areas near the terminations of traffic separation schemes shall do so with particular caution.

(g) A vessel shall so far as practicable avoid anchoring in a traffic separation scheme or in areas near its terminations.

(h) A vessel not using a traffic separation scheme shall avoid it by as wide a margin as is practicable.

(i) A vessel engaged in fishing shall not impede the passage of any vessel following a traffic lane.

(j) A vessel of less than 20 meters in length or a sailing vessel shall not impede the safe passage of a power-driven vessel following a traffic lane.

Section II. Conduct of vessels in sight of one another

RULE 11: Application
Rules in this Section apply to vessels in sight of one another.

RULE 12: Sailing vessels
(a) When two sailing vessels are approaching one another, so as to involve risk of collision, one of them shall keep out of the way of the other as follows:

(i) when each has the wind on a different side, the vessel which has the wind on the port side shall keep out of the way of the other;

(ii) when both have the wind on the same side, the vessel which is to windward shall keep out of the way of the vessel which is to leeward;

(iii) if a vessel with the wind on the port side sees a vessel to windward and cannot determine with certainty whether the other vessel has the wind on the port or on the starboard side, she shall keep out of the way of the other.

(b) For the purposes of this Rule the windward side shall be deemed to be the side opposite to that on which the mainsail is carried or, in the case of a square-rigged vessel, the side opposite to that on which the largest fore-and-aft sail is carried.

RULE 13: Overtaking
(a) Notwithstanding anything contained in the Rules of this Section any vessel overtaking any other shall keep out of the way of the vessel being overtaken.

(b) A vessel shall be deemed to be overtaking when coming up with another vessel from a direction more than 22.5 degrees abaft her beam, that is, in such a position with reference to the vessel she is overtaking, that at night she would be able to see only the sternlight of that vessel but neither of her sidelights.

(c) When a vessel is in any doubt as to whether she is overtaking another, she shall assume that this is the case and act accordingly.

(d) Any subsequent alteration of the bearing between the two vessels shall not make the overtaking vessel a crossing vessel within the meaning of these

Rules or relieve her of the duty of keeping clear of the overtaken vessel until she is finally past and clear.

RULE 14: Head-on situation

(a) When two power-driven vessels are meeting on reciprocal or nearly reciprocal courses so as to involve risk of collision each shall alter her course to starboard so that each shall pass on the port side of the other.

(b) Such a situation shall be deemed to exist when a vessel sees the other ahead or nearly ahead and by night she could see the masthead lights of the other in a line or nearly in a line and/or both sidelights and by day she observes the corresponding aspect of the other vessel.

(c) When a vessel is in any doubt as to whether such a situation exists she shall assume that it does exist and act accordingly.

RULE 15: Crossing situation

When two power-driven vessels are crossing so as to involve risk of collision, the vessel which has the other on her own starboard side shall keep out of the way and shall, if the circumstances of the case admit, avoid crossing ahead of the other vessel.

RULE 16: Action by give-way vessel

Every vessel which is directed to keep out of the way of another vessel shall, so far as possible, take early and substantial action to keep well clear.

RULE 17: Action by stand-on vessel

(a) (i) Where one of two vessels is to keep out of the way the other shall keep her course and speed.

(ii) The latter vessel may however take action to avoid collision by her manoeuvre alone, as soon as it becomes apparent to her

that the vessel required to keep out of the way is not taking appropriate action in compliance with these Rules.

(b) When, from any cause, the vessel required to keep her course and speed finds herself so close that collision cannot be avoided by the action of the give-way vessel alone, she shall take such action as will best aid to avoid collision.

(c) A power-driven vessel which takes action in a crossing situation in accordance with sub-paragraph (a) (ii) of this Rule to avoid collision with another power-driven vessel shall, if the circumstances of the case admit, not alter course to port for a vessel on her own port side.

(d) This Rule does not relieve the give-way vessel of her obligation to keep out of the way.

RULE 18: Responsibilities between vessels

Except where Rules 9, 10 and 13 otherwise require:

(a) A power-driven vessel underway shall keep out of the way of:
    (i) a vessel not under command;
    (ii) a vessel restricted in her ability to maneuver;
    (iii) a vessel engaged in fishing;
    (iv) a sailing vessel.

(b) A sailing vessel underway shall keep out of the way of:
    (i) a vessel not under command;
    (ii) a vessel restricted in her ability to maneuver;
    (iii) a vessel engaged in fishing.

(c) A vessel engaged in fishing when underway shall, so far as possible, keep out of the way of:
    (i) a vessel not under command;
    (ii) a vessel restricted in her ability to maneuver.

(d) (i) Any vessel other than a vessel not under command or a vessel restricted in her ability to maneuver shall, if the circumstances of the case admit, avoid impeding the safe

passage of a vessel constrained by her draught, exhibiting the signals in Rule 28.
(ii) A vessel constrained by her draught shall navigate with particular caution having full regard to her special condition.
(e) A seaplane on the water shall, in general, keep well clear of all vessels and avoid impeding their navigation. In circumstances, however, where risk of collision exists, she shall comply with the Rules of this Part.

Section III. Conduct of vessels in restricted visibility

RULE 19: Conduct of vessels in restricted visibility
(a) This Rule applies to vessels not in sight of one another when navigating in or near an area of restricted visibility.
(b) Every vessel shall proceed at a safe speed adapted to the prevailing circumstances and conditions of restricted visibility. A power-driven vessel shall have her engines ready for immediate maneuver.
(c) Every vessel shall have due regard to the prevailing circumstances and conditions of restricted visibility when complying with the Rules of Section I of this Part.
(d) A vessel that detects by radar alone the presence of another vessel shall determine if a close-quarters situation is developing and/or risk or collision exists. If so, she shall take avoiding action in ample time, provided that when such action consists of an alteration of course, so far as possible the following shall be avoided:
(i) an alteration of course to port for a vessel forward of the beam, other than for a vessel being overtaken;
(ii) an alteration of course towards a vessel abeam or abaft the beam.
(e) Except where it has been determined that a risk of collision does not exist, every vessel which hears apparently forward of her beam the fog signal of another vessel, or which cannot avoid a close-quarters situation with another vessel forward of her beam, shall reduce her speed to the minimum at which she can be kept on her course. She shall if necessary take all her way off and in any event navigate with extreme caution until danger of collision is over.

PART C. LIGHTS AND SHAPES

RULE 20: Application
(a) Rules in this part shall be complied with in all weathers.
(b) The Rules concerning lights shall be complied with from sunset to sunrise, and during such times no other lights shall be exhibited, except such lights as cannot be mistaken for the lights specified in these Rules or do not impair their visibility or distinctive character, or interfere with the keeping of a proper look-out.
(c) The lights prescribed by these Rules shall, if carried, also be exhibited from sunrise to sunset in restricted visibility and may be exhibited in all other circumstances when it is deemed necessary.
(d) The Rules concerning shapes shall be complied with by day.
(e) The lights and shapes specified in these Rules shall comply with the provisions of Annex I to these Regulations.

RULE 21: Definitions
(a) "Masthead light" means a white light placed over the fore

and aft centerline of the vessel showing an unbroken light over an arc of the horizon of 225 degrees and so fixed as to show the light from right ahead to 22.5 degrees abaft the beam on either side of the vessel.

(b) "Sidelights" means a green light on the starboard side and a red light on the port side each showing an unbroken light over an arc of the horizon of 112.5 degrees and so fixed as to show the light from right ahead to 22.5 degrees abaft the beam on its respective side. In a vessel of less than 20 meters in length the sidelights may be combined in one lantern carried on the fore and aft centerline of the vessel.

(c) "Sternlight" means a white light placed as nearly as practicable at the stern showing an unbroken light over an arc of the horizon of 135 degrees and so fixed as to show the light 67.5 degrees from right aft on each side of the vessel.

(d) "Towing light" means a yellow light having the same characteristics as the "sternlight" defined in paragraph (c) of this Rule.

(e) "All round light" means a light showing an unbroken light over an arc of the horizon of 360 degrees.

(f) "Flashing light" means a light flashing at regular intervals at a frequency of 120 flashes or more per minute.

RULE 22: Visibility of lights

The lights prescribed in these Rules shall have an intensity as specified in Section 8 of Annex I to these Regulations so as to be visible at the following minimum ranges:

(a) In vessels of 50 meters or more in length:
- a masthead light, 6 miles;
- a sidelight, 3 miles;
- a stern light, 3 miles;
- a towing light, 3 miles;
- a white, red, green or yellow all-round light, 3 miles.

(b) In vessels of 12 meters or more in length but less than 50 meters in length:
- a masthead light, 5 miles; except that where the length of the vessel is less than 20 meters, 3 miles;
- a sidelight, 2 miles;
- a stern light, 2 miles;
- a towing light, 2 miles;
- a white, red, green or yellow all-round light, 2 miles.

(c) In vessels of less than 12 meters in length:
- a masthead light, 2 miles;
- a sidelight, 1 mile;
- a stern light, 2 miles;
- a towing light, 2 miles;
- a white, red, green or yellow all-round light, 2 miles.

RULE 23: Power-driven vessels underway

(a) A power-driven vessel underway shall exhibit:
(i) a masthead light forward;
(ii) a second masthead light abaft of and higher than the forward one; except that a vessel of less than 50 meters in length shall not be obliged to exhibit such light but may so;
(iii) sidelights;
(iv) a stern light.

(b) An air-cushion vessel when operating in the non-displacement mode shall, in addition to the lights prescribed in paragraph (a) of this Rule, exhibit an all-round flashing yellow light.

(c) A power-driven vessel of less than 7 meters in length and whose maximum speed does not exceed 7 knots may, in lieu of the lights prescribed in paragraph (a) of this Rule, exhibit an all-round white light. Such vessel shall, if practicable, also exhibit sidelights.

RULE 24: Towing and pushing

(a) A power-driven vessel when towing shall exhibit:
(i) instead of the light prescribed

in Rule 23 (a) (i), two masthead lights forward in a vertical line. When the length of the tow, measuring from the stern of the towing vessel to the after end of the tow exceeds 200 meters, three such lights in a vertical line;
(ii) sidelights;
(iii) a stern light;
(iv) a towing light in a vertical line above the stern light;
(v) when the length of the tow exceeds 200 meters, a diamond shape where it can best be seen.

(b) When a pushing vessel and a vessel being pushed ahead are rigidly connected in a composite unit they shall be regarded as a power-driven vessel and exhibit the lights prescribed in Rule 23.

(c) A power-driven vessel when pushing ahead or towing along-side, except in the case of a composite unit, shall exhibit:
(i) instead of the light prescribed in Rule 23 (a)(i), two masthead lights forward in a vertical line;
(ii) sidelights;
(iii) a stern light.

(d) A power-driven vessel to which paragraphs (a) and (c) of this Rule apply shall also comply with Rule 23 (a) (ii).

(e) A vessel or object being towed shall exhibit:
(i) sidelights;
(ii) a stern light;
(iii) when the length of the tow exceeds 200 meters, a diamond shape where it can best be seen.

(f) Provided that any number of vessels being towed alongside or pushed in a group shall be lighted as one vessel,
(i) a vessel being pushed ahead, not being part of a composite unit, shall exhibit at the forward end, sidelights;
(ii) a vessel being towed alongside shall exhibit a stern light and at the forward end, sidelights.

(g) Where from any sufficient cause it is impracticable for a vessel or object being towed to exhibit the lights prescribed in paragraph (e) of this Rule, all possible measures shall be taken to light the vessel or object towed or at least to indicate the presence of the unlighted vessel or object.

RULE 25: Sailing vessels underway and vessels under oars

(a) A sailing vessel underway shall exhibit:
(i) sidelights;
(ii) a stern light.

(b) In a sailing vessel of less than 12 meters in length the lights prescribed in paragraph (a) of this Rule may be combined in one lantern carried at or near the top of the mast where it can best be seen.

(c) A sailing vessel underway may, in addition to the lights prescribed in paragraph (a) of this Rule, exhibit at or near the top of the mast, where they can best be seen, two all-round lights in a vertical line, the upper being red and the lower green, but these lights shall not be exhibited in conjunction with the combined lantern permitted by pragraph (b) of this Rule.

(d) (i) A sailing vessel of less than 7 meters in length shall, if practicable, exhibit the lights prescribed in paragraph (a) or (b) of this Rule, but if she does not, she shall have ready at hand an electric torch or lighted lantern showing a white light which shall be exhibited in sufficient time to prevent collision.
(ii) A vessel under oars may exhibit the lights prescribed in this Rule for sailing vessels, but if she does not, she shall have ready at hand an electric torch or lighted lantern showing a white light which shall be exhibited in sufficient time to prevent collision.

(e) A vessel proceeding under sail when also being propelled by machinery shall exhibit forward where it can best be seen a conical shape, apex downwards.

RULE 26: Fishing vessels

(a) A vessel engaged in fishing, whether underway or at anchor, shall exhibit only the lights and shapes prescribed in this Rule.

(b) A vessel when engaged in trawling, by which is meant the dragging through the water of a dredge net or other apparatus used as a fishing appliance, shall exhibit:

(i) two all-round lights in a vertical line, the upper being green and the lower white, or a shape consisting of two cones with their apexes together in a vertical line one above the other; a vessel of less than 20 meters in length may instead of this shape exhibit a basket;

(ii) a masthead light abaft of and higher than the all-round green light; a vessel of less than 50 meters in length shall not be obliged to exhibit such a light but may do so;

(iii) when making way through the water, in addition to the lights prescribed in this paragraph, sidelights and a stern light.

(c) A vessel engaged in fishing, other than trawling, shall exhibit:

(i) two all-round lights in a vertical line, the upper one being red and the lower white, or a shape consisting of two cones with apexes together in a vertical line one above the other; a vessel of less than 20 meters in length may instead of this shape exhibit a basket;

(ii) when there is outlying gear extending more than 150 meters horizontally from the vessel, an all-round white light or a cone apex upwards in the direction of the gear;

(iii) when making way through the water, in addition to the lights prescribed in this paragraph, sidelights and a stern light.

(d) A vessel engaged in fishing in close proximity to other vessels engaged in fishing may exhibit the additional signals described in Annex II to these Regulations.

(e) A vessel when not engaged in fishing shall not exhibit the lights or shapes prescribed in this Rule, but only those prescribed for a vessel of her length.

RULE 27: Vessels not under command or restricted in their ability to maneuver

(a) A vessel not under command shall exhibit:

(i) two all-round red lights in a vertical line where they can best be seen;

(ii) two balls or similar shapes in a vertical line where they can best be seen;

(iii) when making way through the water, in addition to the lights prescribed in this paragraph, sidelights and a stern light.

(b) A vessel restricted in her ability to maneuver, except a vessel engaged in minesweeping operations, shall exhibit:

(i) three all-round lights in a vertical line where they can best be seen. The highest and lowest of these lights shall be red and the middle light shall be white;

(ii) three shapes in a vertical line where they can best be seen. The highest and lowest of these shapes shall be balls and the middle one a diamond;

(iii) when making way through the water, masthead lights, sidelights and a sternlight, in addition to the lights prescribed in sub-paragraph (i);

(iv) when at anchor, in addition to the lights or shapes prescribed in sub-paragraphs (i) and (ii), the lights, lights or shape prescribed in Rule 30.

(c) A vessel engaged in a towing operation such as renders her unable to deviate from her course shall, in addition to the lights or shapes prescribed in sub-paragraph (b) (i) and (ii) of this Rule, exhibit the lights or shape prescribed in Rule 24 (a).

(d) A vessel engaged in dredging or underwater operations, when restricted in her ability to maneuver, shall exhibit the lights and shapes prescribed in paragraph (b) of this Rule and shall in addition, when an obstruction exhibit:

(i) two all-round red lights or two balls in a vertical line to indicate the side on which the obstruction exists;

(ii) two all-round green lights or two diamonds in a vertical line to indicate the side on which another vessel may pass;

(iii) when making way through the water, in addition to the lights prescribed in this paragraph, masthead lights, sidelights and a stern light;

(iv) a vessel to which this paragraph applies when at anchor shall exhibit the lights or shapes prescribed in sub-paragraphs (i) and (ii) instead of the lights or shape prescribed in Rule 30.

(e) Whenever the size of a vessel engaged in diving operations makes it impracticable to exhibit the shapes prescribed in paragraph (d) of this Rule, a rigid replica of the International Code flag "A" not less than 1 meter in height shall be exhibited. Measures shall be taken to ensure all-round visibility.

(f) A vessel engaged in minesweeping operations shall, in addition to the lights prescribed for the power-driven vessel in Rule 23, exhibit three all-round green lights or three balls. One of these lights or shapes shall be exhibited at or near the foremast head and one at each end of the fore yard.

These lights or shapes indicate that it is dangerous for another vessel to approach closer than 1,000 meters astern or 500 meters on either side of the minesweeper.

(g) Vessels of less than 7 meters in length shall not be required to exhibit the lights prescribed in this Rule.

(h) The signals prescribed in this Rule are not signals of vessels in distress and requiring assistance. Such signals are contained in Annex IV to these Regulations.

RULE 28: Vessels constrained by their draught

A vessel constrained by her draught may, in addition to the lights prescribed for power-driven vessels in Rule 23, exhibit where they can best be seen three all-round red lights in a vertical line, or a cylinder.

RULE 29: Pilot vessels

(a) A vessel engaged on pilotage duty shall exhibit:

(i) at or near the masthead, two all-round lights in a vertical line, the upper being white and the lower red;

(ii) when underway, in addition, sidelights and a stern light;

(iii) when at anchor, in addition to the lights prescribed in sub-paragraph (i), the anchor light, lights or shape.

(b) A pilot vessel when not engaged on pilotage duty shall exhibit the lights or shapes prescribed for a similar vessel of her length.

RULE 30: Anchored vessels and vessels aground

(a) A vessel shall exhibit where it can best be seen:

(i) in the fore part, an all-round white light or one ball;

(ii) at or near the stern and at a lower level than the light pre-scribed in sub-paragraph (i), an all-round white light.

(b) A vessel of less than 50 meters in length may exhibit an all-round white light where it can best be seen instead of the lights prescribed in paragraph (a) of this Rule.

(c) A vessel at anchor may, and a vessel of 100 meters and more in length shall, also use the available working or equivalent lights to illuminate her decks.

(d) A vessel aground shall exhibit the lights prescribed in paragraph (a) or (b) of this Rule and in addition, where they can best be seen:

  (i) two all-round red lights in a vertical line;
  (ii) three balls in a vertical line.

(e) A vessel of less than 7 meters in length, when at anchor or aground, not in or near a narrow channel, fairway or anchorage, or where other vessels normally navigate, shall not be required to exhibit the lights or shapes prescribed in paragraphs (a), (b) or (d) of this Rule.

RULE 31: Seaplanes

Where it is impracticable for a seaplane to exhibit lights and shapes of the characteristics or in the positions prescribed in the Rules of this Part she shall exhibit lights and shapes as closely similar in characteristics and position as is possible.

PART D. SOUND AND LIGHT SIGNALS

RULE 32: Definitions

(a) The word "whistle" means any sound signaling appliance capable of producing the prescribed blasts and which complies with the specifications in Annex III to these Regulations.

(b) The term "short blast" means a blast of about one second's duration.

(c) The term "prolonged blast" means a blast of from four to six seconds duration.

RULE 33: Equipment for sound signals

(a) A vessel of 12 meters or more in length shall be provided with a whistle and a bell and a vessel of 100 meters or more in length shall, in addition, be provided with a gong, the tone and sound of which cannot be confused with that of the bell. The whistle, bell and gong shall comply with the specifications in Annex III to these Regulations. The bell or gong or both may be replaced by other equipment having the same respective sound characteristics, provided that manual sounding of

the required signals shall always be possible.

(b) A vessel of less than 12 meters in length shall not be obliged to carry the sound signaling appliances prescribed in paragraph (a) of this Rule but if she does not, she shall be provided with some other means of making an efficient sound signal.

RULE 34: Maneuvering and warning signals

(a) When vessels are in sight of one another, a power-driven vessel under-way, when maneuvering as authorized or required by these Rules, shall indicate that maneuver by the following signals on her whistle:

  - one short blast to mean "I am altering my course to starboard";
  - two short blasts to mean "I am altering my course to port";
  - three short blasts to mean "I am operating astern propulsion."

(b) Any vessel may supplement the whistle signals prescribed in paragraph (a) of this Rule by light signals, repeated as appropriate, whilst the maneuver is being carried out:

(i) these light signals shall have the following significance:
- one flash to mean "I am altering my course to starboard";
- two flashes to mean "I am altering my course to port";
- three flashes to mean "I am operating astern propulsion."

(ii) the duration of each flash shall be about one second, the interval between flashes shall be about one second, and the interval between successive signals shall be not less than ten seconds;

(iii) the light used for this signal shall, if fitted, be an all-round white light, visible at a minimum range of 5 miles, and shall comply with the provisions of Annex I.

(c) When in sight of one another in a narrow channel or fairway:

(i) a vessel intending to overtake another shall in compliance with Rule 9 (e) (i) indicate her intention by the following signals on her whistle:
- two prolonged blasts followed by one short blast to mean "I intend to overtake you on your starboard side";
- two prolonged blasts followed by two short blasts to mean "I intend to overtake you on your port side."

(ii) the vessel about to be overtaken when acting in accordance with Rule 9 (e) (i) shall indicate her agreement by the following signal on her whistle:
- one prolonged, one short, one prolonged and one short blast, in that order.

(d) When vessels in sight of one another are approaching each other and from any cause either vessel fails to understand the intentions or actions of the other, or is in doubt whether sufficient action is being taken by the other to avoid collision, the vessel in doubt shall immediately indicate

such doubt by giving at least five short and rapid blasts on the whistle. Such signal may be supplemented by a light signal of at least five short and rapid flashes.

(e) A vessel nearing a bend or an area of a channel or fairway where other vessels may be obscured by an intervening obstruction shall sound one prolonged blast. Such signal shall be answered with a prolonged blast by any approaching vessel that may be within hearing around the bend or behind the intervening obstruction.

(f) If whistles are fitted on a vessel at a distance apart of more than 100 meters, one whistle only shall be used for giving maneuvering and warning signals.

RULE 35: Sound signals in restricted visibility

In or near on area of restricted visibility, whether by day or night, the signals prescribed in this Rule shall be used as follows:

(a) A power-driven vessel making way through the water shall sound at intervals of not more than 2 minutes one prolonged blast.

(b) A power-driven vessel underway but stopped and making no way through the water shall sound at intervals of not more than 2 minutes two prolonged blasts in succession with an interval of about 2 seconds between them.

(c) A vessel not under command, a vessel restricted in her ability to maneuver, a vessel constrained by her draught, a sailing vessel, a vessel engaged in fishing and a vessel engaged in towing or pushing another vessel shall, instead of the signals prescribed in paragraphs (a) or (b) or this Rule, sound at intervals of not more than 2 minutes three blasts in succession, namely one prolonged followed by two short blasts.

(d) A vessel towed or if more than one vessel is towed the last vessel of the tow, if manned, shall at intervals of not more than 2 minutes sound four blasts in succession, namely one prolonged followed by three short blasts. When practicable, this signal shall be made immediately after the signal made by the towing vessel.

(e) When a pushing vessel and a vessel being pushed ahead are rigidly connected in a composite unit they shall be regarded as a power-driven vessel and shall give the signals prescribed in paragraphs (a) or (b) of this Rule.

(f) A vessel at anchor shall at intervals of not more than one minute ring the bell rapidly for about 5 seconds. In a vessel of 100 meters or more in length the bell shall be sounded in the forepart of the vessel and immediately after the ringing of the bell the gong shall be sounded rapidly for about 5 seconds in the after part of the vessel. A vessel at anchor may in addition sound three blasts in succession, namely one short, one prolonged and one short blast, to give warning of her position and of the possibility of collision to an approaching vessel.

(g) A vessel aground shall give the bell signal and if required the gong signal prescribed in paragraph (f) of this Rule and shall, in addition, give three separate and distinct strokes on the bell immediately before and after the rapid ringing of the bell. A vessel aground may in addition sound an appropriate whistle signal.

(h) A vessel of less than 12 meters in length shall not be obliged to give the above-mentioned signals but, if she does not, shall make some other efficient sound signal at intervals of not more than 2 minutes.

(i) A pilot vessel when engaged on pilotage duty may in addition to the signals prescribed in paragraphs (a), (b) or (f) of this Rule sound an identity signal consisting of four short blasts.

RULE 36: Signals to attract attention

If necessary to attract the attention of another vessel any vessel may make light or sound signals that cannot be mistaken for any signal authorized elsewhere in these Rules, or may direct the beam of her searchlight in the direction of the danger, in such a way as not to embarrass any vessel.

RULE 37: Distress signals

When a vessel is in distress and requires assistance she shall use or exhibit the signals prescribed in Annex IV to these regulations.

PART E. EXEMPTIONS

RULE 38: Exemptions

Any vessel (or class of vessels) provided that she complies with the requirements of the International Regulations for Preventing Collisions at Sea, 1960, the keel of which is laid or which is at a corresponding stage of construction before the entry into force of these Regulations may be exempted from compliance therewith as follows:

(a) The installation of lights with ranges prescribed in Rule 22, until four years after the date of entry into force of these Regulations.

(b) The installation of lights with color specifications as prescribed in Section 7 of Annex I to these Regulations, until four years after the date of entry into force of these Regulations.

(c) The repositioning of lights as a

result of conversion from Imperial to metric units and rounding off measurement figures, permanent exemption.

(d) (i) The repositioning of masthead lights on vessels of less than 150 meters in length, resulting from the prescriptions of Section 3 (a) of Annex I, permanent exemption.

(ii) The repositioning of masthead lights on vessels of 150 meters or more in length, resulting from the prescriptions of Section 3 (a) of Annex I to these Regulations, until nine years after the date of entry into force of these Regulations.

(e) The repositioning of masthead lights resulting from the prescriptions of Section 2 (b) of Annex I, until nine years after the date of entry into force of these Regulations.

(f) The repositioning of sidelights resulting from the prescriptions Sections 2 (g) and 3 (b) of Annex I, until nine years after the date of entry into force of these Regulations.

(g) The requirements for sound signal appliances prescribed in Annex III, until nine years after the date of entry into force of these Regulations.

ANNEX I: POSITIONING AND TECHNICAL DETAILS OF LIGHTS AND SHAPES

1. Definition

The term "height above the hull" means height above the uppermost continuous deck.

2. Vertical positioning and spacing of lights

(a) On a power-driven vessel of 20 meters or more in length the masthead lights shall be placed as follows:

(i) the forward masthead light, or if only one masthead light is carried, then that light, at a height above the hull of not less than 6 meters, and, if the breadth of the vessel exceeds 6 meters, then at a height above the hull not less than such breadth, so however that the light need not be placed at a greater height above the hull than 12 meters;

(ii) when two masthead lights are carried the after one shall be at least 4.5 meters vertically higher than the forward one.

(b) The vertical separation of masthead lights of power-driven vessels shall be such that in all normal conditions of trim the after light will be seen over and separate from the forward light at a distance of 1,000 meters from the stem when viewed from sea level.

(c) The masthead light of a power-driven vessel of 12 meters but less than 20 meters in length shall be placed at a height above the gunwale of not less than 2.5 meters.

(d) A power-driven vessel of less than 12 meters in length may carry the uppermost light at a height of less than 2.5 meters above the gunwale. When however a masthead light is carried in addition to sidelights and a stern light, then such masthead light shall be carried at least 1 meter higher than the sidelights.

(e) One of the two or three masthead lights prescribed for a power-driven vessel when engaged in towing or pushing another vessel shall be placed in the same position as the forward masthead light of a power-driven vessel.

(f) In all circumstances the masthead light or lights shall be so placed as to be above and clear of all other lights and obstructions.

(g) The sidelights of a power-driven vessel shall be placed at a height above the hull not greater than three-quarters of that of the forward masthead light. They shall not be so low as to be interfered with by deck lights.

(h) The sidelights, if in a combined lantern and carried on a power-driven vessel of less than 20 meters in length, shall be placed not less than 1 meter below the masthead light.

(i) When the Rules prescribe two or three lights to be carried in a vertical line, they shall be spaced as follows:

(i) on a vessel of 20 meters in length or more such lights shall be spaced not less than 2 meters apart, and the lowest of these lights shall, except where a towing light is required, not be less than 4 meters above the hull;

(ii) on a vessel of less than 20 meters in length such lights shall be spaced not less than 1 meter apart and the lowest of these lights shall, except where a towing light is required, not be less than 2 meters above the gunwale;

(iii) when three lights are carried they shall be equally spaced.

(j) The lower of the two all-round lights prescribed for a fishing vessel when engaged in fishing shall be at a height above the sidelights not less than twice the distance between the two vertical lights.

(k) The forward anchor light, when two are carried, shall not be less than 4.5 meters above the after one. On a vessel of 50 meters or more in length this forward anchor light shall not be less than 6 meters above the hull.

3. Horizontal positioning and spacing of lights

(a) When two masthead lights are prescribed for a power-driven vessel, the horizontal distance between them shall not be less than one-half of the length of the vessel but need not be more than 100 meters. The forward light shall be placed not more than one-quarter of the length of the vessel from the stem.

(b) On a vessel of 20 meters or more in length the sidelights shall not be placed in front of the forward masthead lights. They shall be placed at or near the side of the vessel.

4. Details of location of direction-indicating lights for fishing vessels, dredgers, and vessels engaged in underwater operations

(a) The light indicating the direction of the outlying gear from a vessel engaged in fishing as prescribed in Rule 26 (c) (ii) shall be placed at a horizontal distance of not less than 2 meters and not more than 6 meters away from the two all-round red and white lights. This light shall be placed not higher than the all-round white light prescribed in Rule 26 (c) (i) and not lower than the sidelights.

(b) The lights and shapes on a vessel engaged in dredging or underwater operations to indicate the obstructed side and/or the side on which it is safe to pass, as prescribed in Rule 27 (d) (i) and (ii), shall be placed at the maximum practical horizontal distance, but in no case less than 2 meters, from the lights or shapes prescribed in Rule 27 (b) (i) and (ii). In no case shall the upper of these lights or shapes be at a greater height than the lower of the three lights or shapes prescribed in Rule 27 (b) (i) and (ii).

5. Screens for sidelights

The sidelights shall be fitted with inboard screens painted matt black, and meeting the requirements of Section 9 of this Annex. With a combined lantern, using a single vertical filament and a very narrow division between the green and red sections, external screens need not be fitted.

6. Shapes

(a) Shapes shall be black and of the following sizes:
 (i) a ball shall have a diameter of not less than 0.6 meter;
 (ii) a cone shall have a base diameter of not less than 0.6 meter and a height equal to its diameter;
 (iii) a cylinder shall have a diameter of at least 0.6 meter and a height of twice its diameter;
 (iv) a diamond shape shall consist of two cones as defined in (ii) above having a common base.

(b) The vertical distance between shapes shall be at least 1.5 meters.

(c) In a vessel of less than 20 meters in length shapes of lesser dimensions but commensurate with the size of the vessel may be used and the distance apart may be correspondingly reduced.

7. Color specification of lights

The chromaticity of all navigation lights shall conform to the following standards, which lie within the boundaries of the area of the diagram specified for each color by the International Commission on Illumination (CIE).

The boundaries of the area for each color are given by indicating the corner co-ordinates, which are as follows:

Color		Co-ordinates					
White	x	0.525	0.525	0.452	0.310	0.310	0.443
	y	0.382	0.440	0.440	0.348	0.283	0.382
Green	x	0.028	0.009	0.300	0.203		
	y	0.385	0.723	0.511	0.356		
Red	x	0.680	0.660	0.735	0.721		
	y	0.320	0.320	0.265	0.259		
Yellow	x	0.612	0.618	0.575	0.575		
	y	0.382	0.382	0.425	0.406		

8. Intensity of lights

(a) The minimum luminous intensity of lights shall be calculated by using the formula:

$$I = 3.43 \times 10^6 \times T \times D^2 \times K^{-D}$$

where **I** is luminous intensity in candelas under service conditions,

T is threshold factor 2×10^7 lux,

D is range of visibility (luminous range) of the light in nautical miles,

K is atmospheric transmissivity. For prescribed lights the value of **K** shall be 0.8, corresponding to a meteorological visibility of approximately 13 nautical miles.

(b) A selection of figures derived from the formula is given in the following table:

Range of visibility (luminous range) of light in nautical miles	Luminous intensity of light in candelas for K=0.8
D	I
1	0.9
2	4.3
3	12
4	27
5	52
6	94

Note: The maximum luminous intensity of navigation lights should be limited to avoid undue glare.

9. Horizontal sectors

(a) (i) In the forward direction, sidelights as fitted on the vessel must show the minimum required intensities. The intensities must decrease to reach practical cut-off between 1 degree and 3 degrees outside the prescribed sectors.

(ii) For stern lights and masthead lights and at 22.5 degrees abaft the beam for sidelights, the minimum required intensities shall be maintained over the arc of the horizon up to 5 degrees within the limits of the sectors prescribed in Rule 21. From 5 degrees within the prescribed sectors the intensity may decrease by 50 per cent up to the prescribed limits; it shall decrease steadily to reach practical cut-off at not more than 5 degrees outside the prescribed limits.

(b) All-round lights shall be so located as not to be obscured by masts, topmasts or structures within angular sectors of more than 6 degrees, except anchor lights, which need not be placed at an impracticable height above the hull.

10. Vertical sectors

(a) The vertical sectors of electric lights, with the exception of lights on sailing vessels shall ensure that:

(i) at least the required minimum intensity is maintained at all angles from 5 degrees above to 5 degrees below the horizontal;

(ii) at least 60 percent of the required minimum intensity is maintained from 7.5 degrees above to 7.5 degrees below the horizontal.

(b) In the case of sailing vessels the vertical sectors of electric lights shall ensure that:

(i) at least the required minimum intensity is maintained at all angles from 5 degrees above to 5 degrees below the horizontal;

(ii) at least 50 percent of the required minimum intensity is maintained from 25 degrees above to 25 degrees below the horizontal.

(c) In the case of lights other than electric these specifications shall be met as closely as possible.

11. Intensity of non-electric lights

Non-electric lights shall so far as practicable comply with the minimum intensities, as specified in the Table given in Section 8 of this Annex.

12. Maneuvering light

Notwithstanding the provisions of paragraph 2 (f) of this Annex the maneuvering light described in Rule 34 (b) shall be placed in the same fore and aft vertical plane as the masthead light or lights and, where practicable, at a minimum height of 2 meters vertically above the forward masthead light, provided that it shall be carried not less than 2 meters vertically above or below the after masthead light. On a vessel where only one masthead light is carried the maneuvering light, if fitted, shall be carried where it can best be seen, not less than 2 meters vertically apart from the masthead light.

13. Approval
The construction of lanterns and shapes and the installation of lanterns on board the vessel shall be to the satisfaction of the appropriate authority of the State where the vessel is registered.

ANNEX II: ADDITIONAL SIGNALS FOR FISHING VESSELS FISHING IN CLOSE PROXIMITY

1. General
The lights mentioned herein shall, if exhibited in pursuance of Rule 26 (d), be placed where they can best be seen. They shall be at least 0.9 meter apart but at a lower level than lights prescribed in Rule 26 (b) (i) and (c) (i). The lights shall be visible all round the horizon at a distance of at least 1 mile but at a lesser distance than the lights prescribed by these Rules for fishing vessels.

2. Signals for trawlers
(a) Vessels when engaged in trawling, whether using demersal or pelagic gear, may exhibit:
  (i) when shooting their nets:
  two white lights in a vertical line;
  (ii) when hauling their nets:
  one white light over one red light in a vertical line;
  (iii) when the net has come fast upon an obstruction:
  two red lights in a vertical line.
(b) Each vessel engaged in pair trawling may exhibit:
  (i) by night, a searchlight directed forward and in the direction of the other vessel of the pair;
  (ii) when shooting or hauling their nets or when their nets have come fast upon an obstruction, the lights prescribed in 2 (a) above.

3. Signals for purse seiners
Vessels engaged in fishing with purse seine gear may exhibit two yellow lights in a vertical line. These lights shall flash alternately every second and with equal light and occultation duration. These lights may be exhibited only when the vessel is hampered by its fishing gear.

ANNEX III: TECHNICAL DETAILS OF SOUND SIGNAL APPLIANCES

1. Whistles

(a) Frequencies and range of audibility

The fundamental frequency of the signal shall lie within the range 70–700 Hz.

The range of audibility of the signal from a whistle shall be determined by those frequencies, which may include the fundamental and/or one or more higher frequencies, which lie within the ranges 180–700 Hz (+/- 1 percent) and which provide the sound pressure levels specified in paragraph 1 (c) below.

(b) Limits of fundamental frequencies

To ensure a wide variety of whistle characteristics, the fundamental frequency of a whistle shall be between the following limits:

(i) 70–200 Hz, for a vessel 200 meters or more in length;
(ii) 13–350 Hz, for a vessel 75 meters but less than 200 meters in length;
(iii) 250–700 Hz, for a vessel less than 75 meters in length.

(c) Sound signal intensity and range of audibility

A whistle fitted in a vessel shall provide, in the direction of maximum intensity of the whistle and at a distance of 1 meter from it, a sound pressure level in at least 1/3rd-octave band within the range of frequencies 180–700 Hz (+/- 1 percent) of not less than the appropriate figure given in the table below.

Length of vessel in meters	⅓rd-octave band level at 1 meter in dB referred to 2×10^{-5} N/m²	Audibility range in nautical miles
200 or more	143	2
75 but less than 200	138	1.5
20 but less than 75	130	1
Less than 20	120	0.5

The range of audibility in the table above is for information and is approximately the range at which a whistle may be heard on its forward axis with 90 percent probability in conditions of still air on board a vessel having average background noise level at the listening posts (taken to be 68 dB in the octave band centered on 250 Hz and 63 dB in the octave band centered on 500 Hz).

In practice the range at which a whistle may be heard is extremely variable and depends critically on weather conditions; the values given can be regarded as typical but under conditions of strong wind or high ambient noise level at the listening post the range may be much reduced.

(d) Directional properties

The sound pressure level of a directional whistle shall be not more than 4 dB below the sound pressure level on the axis at any direction in the horizontal plane within +/- 45 degrees of the axis. The sound pressure level at any other direction in the horizontal plane shall be not more than 10 dB below the sound pressure level on the axis, so that the range in any direction will be at least half the range on the forward axis. The sound pressure level shall be measured in that 1/3rd-octave band which determines the audibility range.

(e) Positioning of whistles
When a directional whistle is to be used as the only whistle on a vessel, it shall be installed with its maximum intensity directed straight ahead.

A whistle shall be placed as high as practicable on a vessel, in order to reduce interception of the emitted sound by obstructions and also to minimize hearing damage risk to personnel. The sound pressure level of the vessel's own signal at listening posts shall not exceed 110 dB (a) and so far as practicable should not exceed 100 dB (a).

(f) Fitting of more than one whistle
If whistles are fitted at a distance apart of more than 100 meters, it shall be so arranged that they are not sounded simultaneously.

(g) Combined whistle systems
If due to the presence of obstructions the sound field of a single whistle or of one of the whistles referred to in paragraph 1 (f) above is likely to have a zone of greatly reduced signal level, it is recommended that a combined whistle system be fitted so as to overcome this reduction. For the purposes of the Rules a combined whistle system is to be regarded as a single whistle. The whistles of a combined system shall be located at a distance apart of not more

than 100 meters and arranged to be sounded simultaneously. The frequency of any one whistle shall differ from those of the others by at least 10 Hz.

2. Bell or gong
(a) Intensity of signal
A bell or gong, or other device having similar sound characteristics shall produce a sound pressure level of not less than 110 dB at 1 meter.

(b) Construction
Bells and gongs shall be made of corrosion-resistant material and designed to give a clear tone. The diameter of the mouth of the bell shall be not less than 300 mm. for vessels of more than 20 meters in length, and shall be not less than 200 mm. for vessels of 12 to 20 meters in length. Where practicable, a power-driven bell striker is recommended to ensure constant force but manual operation shall be possible. The mass of the striker shall be not less than 3 percent of the mass of the bell.

3. Approval
The construction of sound signal appliances, their performance and their installation on board the vessel shall be to the satisfaction of the appropriate authority of the State where the vessel is registered.

ANNEX IV: DISTRESS SIGNALS

1. The following signals, used or exhibited either together or separately, indicate distress and need of assistance:

(a) a gun or other explosive signal fired at intervals of about a minute;

(b) a continuous sounding with any fog-signalling apparatus;

(c) rockets or shells, throwing red stars fired one at a time at short intervals;

(d) a signal made by radiotelegraphy or by any other signalling method consisting of the group ... - - - ... (SOS) in the Morse Code;

(e) a signal sent by radiotelephony consisting of the spoken word "Mayday";

(f) the International Code Signal of distress indicated by N.C.;

(g) a signal consisting of a square flag having above or below it a ball or anything resembling a ball;

(h) flames on the vessel (as from a burning tar barrel, oil barrel, etc.);

(i) a rocket parachute flare or a hand flare showing a red light;

(j) a smoke signal giving off orange-coloured smoke;

(k) slowly and repeatedly raising and lowering arms outstretched to each side;

(l) the radiotelegraph alarm signal;

(m) the radiotelephone alarm signal;

(n) signals transmitted by emergency position-indicating radio beacons.

2. The use or exhibition of any of the foregoing signals except for the purpose of indicating distress and need of assistance and the use of other signals which may be confused with any of the above signals is prohibited.

3. Attention is drawn to the relevant sections of the International Code of Signals, the Merchant Ship Search and Rescue Manual and the following signals:

(a) a piece of orange-colored canvas with either a black square and circle or other appropriate symbol (for identification from the air);

(b) a dye marker.

GLOSSARY

A

ABAFT: Toward the rear (stern) of the boat. Behind.

ABEAM: At right angles to the keel of the boat, but not on the boat.

ABOARD: On/within the boat.

ABOVE DECK: On the deck (not over it—see ALOFT).

ABREAST: Side by side; by the side of.

ADRIFT: Loose, not on moorings or a towline.

AFT: Toward the stern of the boat.

AGROUND: Touching or fast to the bottom.

AHEAD: In a forward direction.

AIDS TO NAVIGATION: Artificial objects to supplement natural landmarks indicating safe and unsafe waters.

ALEE: Away from the direction of wind. Opposite of windward.

ALOFT: Above the deck of the boat.

AMIDSHIPS: In or toward the center of the boat.

ANCHORAGE: A place suitable for anchoring in relation to the wind, seas, and bottom.

ASTERN: In back of the boat, opposite of ahead.

ATHWARTSHIPS: At right angles to the centerline of the boat; rowboat seats are generally athwartships.

AWEIGH: The position of the anchor as it is raised clear of the bottom.

B

BATTEN DOWN: Secure hatches and loose objects within the hull and on deck.

BEAM: The greatest width of the boat.

BEARING: The direction of an object expressed either as a true bearing as shown on the chart, or as a bearing relative to the heading of the boat.

BELOW: Beneath the deck.

BIGHT: The part of the rope or line, between the end and the standing part, on which a knot is formed.

BILGE: The interior of the hull below the floorboards.

BITTER END: The last part of a rope or chain. The inboard end of the anchor rode.

BOAT: A fairly indefinite term. A waterborne vehicle smaller than a ship. One definition is a small craft carried aboard a ship.

BOAT HOOK: A short shaft with a fitting at one end shaped to facilitate use in putting a line over a piling, recovering an object dropped overboard, or in pushing or fending off.

BOOT TOP: A painted line that indicates the designed waterline.

BOW: The forward part of a boat.

BOW LINE: A docking line leading from the bow.

BOWLINE: A knot used to form a temporary loop in the end of a line.

BRIDGE: The location from which a vessel is steered and its speed controlled. "Control Station" is really a more appropriate term for small craft.

BRIDLE: A line or wire secured at both ends in order to distribute a strain between two points.

BRIGHTWORK: Varnished woodwork and/or polished metal.

BULKHEAD: A vertical partition separating compartments.

BUOY: An anchored float used for marking a position on the water or a hazard or a shoal, and for mooring.

BURDENED VESSEL: That vessel which, according to the applicable Navigation Rules, must give way to the privileged vessel. The term has been superseded by the term "give-way."

C

CABIN: A compartment for passengers or crew.

CAPSIZE: To turn over.

CAST OFF: To let go.

CATAMARAN: A twin-hulled boat, with hulls side by side.

CHAFING GEAR: Tubing or cloth wrapping used to protect a line from chafing on a rough surface.

CHART: A map for use by navigators.

CHINE: The intersection of the bottom and sides of a flat or V-bottomed boat.

CHOCK: A fitting through which anchor or mooring lines are led. Usually U-shaped to reduce chafe.

CLEAT: A fitting to which lines are made fast. The classic cleat to which lines are belayed is approximately anvil-shaped.

CLOVE HITCH: A knot for temporarily fastening a line to a spar or piling.

COAMING: A vertical piece around the edge of a cockpit, hatch, etc., to prevent water on deck from running below.

COCKPIT: An opening in the deck from which the boat is handled.

COIL: To lay a line down in circular turns.

COURSE: The direction in which a boat is steered.

CUDDY: A small shelter cabin in a boat.

CURRENT: The horizontal movement of water.

D

DEAD AHEAD: Directly ahead.

DEAD ASTERN: Directly aft.

DECK: A permanent covering over a compartment, hull, or any part thereof.

DINGHY: A small open boat. A dinghy is often used as a tender for a larger craft.

DISPLACEMENT: The weight of water displaced by a floating vessel, thus, a boat's weight.

DISPLACEMENT HULL: A type of hull that plows through the water, displacing a weight of water equal to its own weight, even when more power is added.

DOCK: A protected water area in which vessels are moored. The term is often used to denote a pier or a wharf.

DOLPHIN: A group of piles driven close together and bound with wire cables into a single structure.

DRAFT: The depth of water a boat draws.

E

EBB: A receding current.

F

FATHOM: Six feet.

FENDER: A cushion, placed between boats, or between a boat and a pier, to prevent damage.

FIGURE EIGHT KNOT: A knot in the form of a figure eight, placed in the end of a line to prevent the line from passing through a grommet or a block.

FLARE: The outward curve of a vessel's sides near the bow. A distress signal.

FLOOD: An incoming current.

FLOORBOARDS: The surface of the cockpit on which the crew stand.

FLUKE: The palm of an anchor.

FOLLOWING SEA: An overtaking sea that comes from astern.

FORE-AND-AFT: In a line parallel to the keel.

FOREPEAK: A compartment in the bow of a small boat.

FORWARD: Toward the bow of the boat.

FOULED: Any piece of equipment that is jammed or entangled, or dirtied.

FREEBOARD: The minimum vertical distance from the surface of the water to the gunwale.

G

GALLEY: The kitchen area of a boat.

GANGWAY: The area of a ship's side where people board and disembark.

GEAR: A general term for ropes, blocks, tackle, and other equipment.

GIVE-WAY VESSEL: A term used to describe the vessel that must yield in meeting, crossing, or overtaking situations.

GRAB RAILS: Hand-hold fittings mounted on cabin tops and sides for personal safety when moving around the boat.

GROUND TACKLE: A collective term for the anchor and its associated gear.

GUNWALE: The upper edge of a boat's sides.

H

HARD CHINE: An abrupt intersection between the hull side and the hull bottom of a boat so constructed.

HATCH: An opening in a boat's deck fitted with a watertight cover.

HEAD: A marine toilet. Also the upper corner of a triangular sail.

HEADING: The direction in which a vessel's bow points at any given time.

HEADWAY: The forward motion of a boat. Opposite of sternway.

HELM: The wheel or tiller controlling the rudder.

HELMSPERSON: The person who steers the boat.

HITCH: A knot used to secure a rope to another object or to another rope, or to form a loop or a noose in a rope.

HOLD: A compartment below deck in a large vessel, used solely for carrying cargo.

HULL: The main body of a vessel.

I

INBOARD: Toward the center of a boat; inside; a motor fitted inside a boat.

INTRACOASTAL WATERWAY ICW: Bays, rivers, and canals along the coasts (such as the Atlantic and Gulf of Mexico coasts of the US), connected so that vessels may travel without going out to sea.

J

JACOBS LADDER: A rope ladder, lowered from the deck, as when pilots or passengers come aboard.

JETTY: A structure, usually masonry, projecting out from the shore; a jetty may protect a harbor entrance.

K

KEDGE: A second anchor used to haul the boat off when grounded, or move it when sail or power is not possible.

KEEL: The centerline of a boat running fore and aft; the backbone of a vessel.

KNOT: A measure of speed equal to one nautical mile (6,076 feet) per hour.

KNOT: A fastening made by interweaving rope to form a stopper, bind an object, form a loop or noose, tie a small rope to an object, or tie the ends of two small ropes together.

L

LATITUDE: The distance north or south of the equator measured in degrees.

LAZARETTE: A storage space in a boat's stern area.

LEE: The side sheltered from the wind.

LEEWARD: The direction away from the wind.

LEEWAY: The sideways movement of the boat caused by either wind or current.

LINE: Rope and cordage used aboard a vessel.

LOG: A record of courses or operation. A device to measure speed.

LONGITUDE: The distance in degrees east or west of the meridian at Greenwich, England.

LUBBER'S LINE: A mark or permanent line on a compass indicating the direction forward parallel to the keel when properly installed.

M

MARLINSPIKE: A tool for opening the strands of a rope while splicing.

MIDSHIP: Approximately in the location equally distant from the bow and stern.

MOORING: An arrangement for securing a boat to a mooring buoy or a pier.

N

NAUTICAL MILE: One minute of latitude; approximately 6,076 feet— about $1/8$ longer than the statute mile of 5,280 feet.

NAVIGATION: The art and science of conducting a boat safely from one point to another.

NAVIGATION RULES: The regulations governing the movement of vessels in relation to each other, generally called steering and sailing rules.

O

OUTBOARD: Toward or beyond the boat's sides. A detachable engine mounted on a boat's stern.

OVERBOARD: Over the side or out of the boat.

P

PIER: A loading platform extending at an angle from the shore.

PILE: A wood, metal, or concrete pole driven into the bottom. Craft may be made fast to a pile; it may be used to support a pier (see PILING) or a float.

PILING: Support, protection for wharves, piers, etc.; constructed of piles (see PILE).

PILOTING: Navigation by use of visible references, the depth of the water, etc.

PLANING: A boat is said to be planing when it is essentially moving over the top of the water rather than through the water.

PLANING HULL: A type of hull shaped to glide easily across the water at high speed.

PORT: The left side of a boat looking forward. A harbor.

PRIVILEGED VESSEL: A vessel which, according to the applicable Navigation Rule, has right-of-way (this term has been superseded by the term "stand-on").

Q

QUARTER: The sides of a boat aft of amidships.

QUARTERING SEA: Sea coming on a boat's quarter.

R

RODE: The anchor line and/or chain.

ROPE: In general, cordage as it is purchased at the store. When it comes aboard a vessel and is put to use it becomes line.

RUDDER: A vertical plate or board for steering a boat.

RUN: Allow a line to feed freely.

RUNNING LIGHTS: Lights required to be shown on boats underway between sundown and sunup.

S

SATELLITE NAVIGATION: A form of position-finding using radio transmissions from satellites with sophisticated on-board automatic equipment.

SCOPE: Technically, the ratio of length of anchor rode in use to the vertical distance from the bow of the vessel to the bottom of the water.

Usually six to seven to one for calm weather and more scope in storm conditions.

SCREW: A boat's propeller.

SCUPPERS: Drain holes on deck, in the toe rail, or in bulwarks or (with drain pipes) in the deck itself.

SEA COCK: A through hull valve, a shut off on a plumbing or drain pipe between the vessel's interior and the sea.

SEAMANSHIP: All the arts and skills of boat handling, ranging from maintenence and repairs to piloting, sail handling, marlinespike work, and rigging.

SEA ROOM: A safe distance from the shore or other hazards.

SEAWORTHY: A boat or a boat's gear able to meet the usual sea conditions.

SECURE: To make fast.

SET: Direction toward which the current is flowing.

SHIP: A larger vessel usually thought of as being used for ocean travel. A vessel able to carry a "boat" on board.

SLACK: Not fastened; loose. Also, to loosen.

SOLE: Cabin or saloon floor. Timber extensions on the bottom of the rudder. Also the molded fiberglass deck of a cockpit.

SOUNDING: A measurement of the depth of water.

SPRING LINE: A pivot line used in docking, undocking, or to prevent the boat from moving forward or astern while made fast to a dock.

SQUALL: A sudden, violent wind, often accompanied by rain.

SQUARE KNOT: A knot used to join two lines of similar size. Also called a reef knot.

STANDING PART: That part of a line which is made fast. The main part of a line as distinguished from the bight and the end.

STAND-ON VESSEL: That vessel that has right-of-way during a meeting, crossing, or overtaking situation.

STARBOARD: The right side of a boat when looking forward.

STEM: The forwardmost part of the bow.

STERN: The after part of the boat.

STERN LINE: A docking line leading from the stern.

STOW: To put an item in its proper place.

SWAMP: To fill with water, but not settle to the bottom.

T

TIDE: The periodic rise and fall of water level in the oceans.

TILLER: A bar or handle for turning a boat's rudder or an outboard motor.

TOPSIDES: The sides of a vessel between the waterline and the deck; sometimes referring to onto or above the deck.

TRANSOM: The stern cross-section of a square-sterned boat.

TRIM: Fore-and-aft balance of a boat.

U

UNDERWAY: Vessel in motion, i.e., when not moored, at anchor, or aground.

V

V BOTTOM: A hull with the bottom section in the shape of a "V."

W

WAKE: Moving waves, track or path that a boat leaves behind it, when moving across the waters.

WATERLINE: A line painted on a hull which shows the point to which a boat sinks when it is properly trimmed (see BOOT TOP).

WAY: Movement of a vessel through the water such as headway, sternway, or leeway.

WINDWARD: Toward the direction from which the wind is coming.

Y

YACHT: A pleasure vessel, a pleasure boat; in American usage the idea of size and luxury is conveyed, either sail or power.

YAW: To swing or steer off course, as when running with a quartering sea.

INDEX